Praise for *Edge of Grace*

"*Edge of Grace* is an extraordinary medicine story. One that can have a powerful effect. I love how it reveals the reality behind the illusions of the patriarchal world and plucks the chord of knowing that the invisible caregivers are actually the ones holding the world together with their embodied prayers. Thank you for doing this. The benefits extend far beyond your family."

—Charles Eisenstein, Speaker, and Author, *The More Beautiful World Our Hearts Know is Possible, The Coronation, Climate: A New Story*

"There is magic in Prajna's voice—the breathtaking honest telling of a dramatic human story. The moving, uplifting, cleansing, surging power that makes you feel you'll never be the same again!"

—Sarah Tavner, *BBC Documentary Producer*

"*Edge of Grace* is both heartbreaking and heart opening. When decisions about our bodies are made by others and our voice is stifled, deep pain ensues. Prajna's memoir is a potent, inspirational feminine voice. With self-honesty and tenderness, she reshapes deep pain, using it as a catalyst for our evolution. Her words are a significant offering for the silenced feminine."

—Jac O'Keeffe, Co-Founder of the Association for Spiritual Integrity, Author of *Born to be Free, How to be a Spiritual Rebel*

"A beautiful, powerful story of one woman's search for spiritual awakening in the midst of enormous challenges, and how those challenges—particularly the traumatic birth of her twin daughters and the experience of raising children with disabilities—are a pivotal part of that journey. With great honesty, clarity, and engaging storytelling, Prajna takes readers on her inner and outer quest to live a life of spirit, heart, and truth that does not flinch from the difficulties of everyday life, but rather finds pearls amidst the pain and struggle. Her extraordinary warrior resourcefulness is an inspiration."

—Maxima Kahn, author of *Fierce Aria*, founder *BrilliantPlayground.com*

"Prajna offers us a moving story of one woman's profound commitment to mothering, awakening, and love. Her fierce dedication to follow her own feminine wisdom and truth is so inspiring. Her story shines with courage, beauty, authenticity and redemption."

—Lisa Schrader, Founder of *AwakeningShakti.com*

"This is the story of a Spiritual BadAss! It's impressive when the gurus and yogis of the world can attain peace by sitting in lotus position in a cave somewhere… But when you can attain true peace and equanimity with the Heroine challenges Prajna faces– THAT's a Spiritual BadAss!"

—Sonika Tinker & Christian Pedersen, Founders of *loveworksforyou.com*

"A story overflowing with authenticity, vulnerability and the light of a wisdom rooted in real life, in the heart and body opened by pain to become a source of compassion for all. You will not be able to put it down."

—Christine Mulvey, Author of *Mine to Carry*

"A remarkable mother and teacher of the Sacred Feminine. In *Edge of Grace,* Prajna shines light, embraces grace, and connects us to Mother Earth. Each chapter embodies the radiance she carries."

—Chloe Goodchild, author and founder of *The Naked Voice*

"Prajna has authored an extraordinary work of heartbreaking beauty through devastating hardship that reveals the traumatic protocols of industrialized childbirth. She compassionately invites fierce and tender discernment for restoring the sovereignty of motherhood and reimagining a future without unnecessary medical intervention."

—Monica Rodgers, Founder: *The Revelation Project & Podcast*

"Prajna's story is a striking illustration of the beauty and fragility of life and the courage and dedication of a mother's love. Her honesty and bravery are truly inspiring, an example to follow for navigating challenging times."

—Nicole Beasley Ph.D. *Clinical Psychologist, Mom*

"Edge of Grace draws you in and doesn't let go. A real-life page-turner. Emotional, difficult, joyous, all in one. Like life but turned up several notches…. to the ultimate happy ending — Acceptance for All of Life As It Is!"

—Anatta Campbell Author of *The Ordinary Buddha*

"Prajna's riveting account of her path through life's great challenges simultaneously broke and healed my heart. It reminds me of the quote by Muriel Rukeyser, 'What would happen if one woman told the truth about her life? The world would split open.' Prajna's telling of her truth is such a blessing to each reader, and the world."

—Amber Aldrich, *Mother*

"I devoured *Edge of Grace* in two days. I found Prajna's story profoundly inspiring, beautifully written, and a total page-turner. I was totally captivated by this book."

—Eleanor Tara, Founder, *Vedic Astrologer and Healing Musician*

To Jessica
May our journey
inform yours with fierce
love. Prajna + her little women

Edge
of
Grace

Fierce Awakenings to Love

Prajna O'Hara Ginty

FLOWING RIVER PRESS

Published 2014
Printed in the United State of America
Print ISBN: 978-0-9908760-07
E-ISBN: 978-0-9908760-1-4
Library of Congress Control Number: 2014917643

For information, address:
Flowing River Press
407 California Ave
Santa Cruz, CA 95060
prajna@prajnaohara.com

Flowing River Press is an affiliate of Flowing River School and Sangha Inc.

Authors Note: The events, stories, and experiences described here are rendered as the author remembers them or as they are told to her to the best of her ability. Some names and identifying characters have been changed to protect the privacy and sensitivity of certain individuals. Traumatic events are disclosed, please take care to pause and resource yourself.

For Autumn, Abby, and Libby

for being my girls

"Truly, my life is one long hearkening
unto myself and unto others, unto Love.
And if I say that I hearken, it is really
Love who hearkens inside me."

— *Etty Hillesum*

"Patriarchy does not have a gender.
Harms our earth mother and all people.
We can change this."

— *Wise Elder*

Table Of Contents

Prologue

I live with longings. Before I discover who I truly am, I exhaust all the ways I know of being in the world. As with any spiritual quest that one believes culminates in a refuge of solace and safety, I have to descend the mountain peak of nirvana, and reclaim my feminine soul. I have to uncover early stories that shaped me and assured me that men come first. I have to shed secrets and undo decades of cultural conditioning and institutional loyalties, so I can ultimately realize and embody fierce love.

My first secret was at age seven. I am staring through the stained-glass windows of St. John's Catholic Church, unable to be an altar boy, sad that I am a girl. When the family purse runs dry, I plead with the priests to cook in exchange for a sanctioned religious education. While there, I habitually sneak to the lavatory, clandestinely seizing the smallest vestment. In front of a full-length mirror, I perform self-crafted ceremonies while fervently reciting the rosary to our merciful holy mother, praying for ascension to heavenly realms, hopeful that she is listening.

As my junior year of high school draws to a close, the football coach cajoles me into his car, promising to safely drive me home. Instead, he takes me to the football field, violates me, and threatens, "If you ever speak a word, pretty little Catholic girl, I'll find you." Left silenced; disassociated, drowning in a pool of shame. He resumes his post—unchecked. Me—unhomed. Over time, this shame intertwines with longing—an insatiable hunger for connection and an unrelenting urge to flee.

Later, I learn that shame is a trauma-induced affliction, a distortion that grows rapidly and exponentially, like a tsunami, when left untended. It becomes the jagged edge that steers my life, cutting and inscribing me with unconscious behaviors, that cause me to shape-shift into mistaken identities and deny my feminine soul. One version of shame passionately tries to prove itself, puffing up like an exotic peacock fixated on external validation, pouring into endless tasks of self-improvement and certified achievements. Another version of shame I live with is a disturbing sense of being peripheral to my own life. The body that I think belongs to me is functioning, but I lose contact with something instinctive, holy, deep in my bones. I ache with longing as if a familiar, precious possession is being inexplicably withheld from me.

After this assault, my feet uproot from the ground of Mother. Trust eludes me. I sabotage success and teeter extremes. Fight, flight, freeze, and appease responses are primed, whether in danger or not. I mechanically perform like a bamboozled addict, yielding to assumed knights in shining armor—*rescue me.* I make last-ditch efforts as a spiritual junkie for absolution from crimes I did not commit. Until I meet Eunice, my first spiritual guide and therapist, who sees me and became a compassionate mentor. Immediately, a seed is planted, and a remarkable journey of healing, learning, and self-love begins.

My backstory forms the foundation for the more urgent story I am compelled to tell you, one I cannot bury like countless women before. One I hope will give women permission to voice her story, restore sovereignty to our bodies, and transform the culture of birth. This narrative unfolds after extensive recovery of my true self and awakening to a spiritual calling—dharma. My journey is deeply intertwined with early instinct injuries that impact our collective female body. My journey reaches a shocking reality when I am initiated into motherhood. At first, an ecstatic life-affirming experience that honors the intelligence of both baby and me as mother, in alignment with our instinctive knowing, wholly connected to nature. Soon, followed and overshadowed by the tragic interventions of obstetric birth protocols that disrupt and shake our world.

This is the edge I walk, one with grace, tenderness, and anguish. This fuels my passion for understanding the history of women and restoring the wisdom of Mothers to birth safely and ecstatically. Through my story, I seek to open eyes and hearts to profound possibilities for celebrating our most vulnerable moments within birthing, living, and dying. Walking this edge is an ever-awakening journey of fierce love and deep respect for the divine feminine force that births us and our vital connection to Mother Earth.

Her story is my story.

1
The Edge

March 1999. It is shortly after midnight; the early winter sky is pitch black. All the lights in our two-story condominium are off. The only sound I hear is the burly, maroon recliner rocker squeaking—swaying back and forth, back and forth.

Something is calling me. I have to satisfy this nagging impulse, have to find out what is calling me—consuming me from the inside out. What is insisting I get up, what is pulling me out of our little house on Surfside Avenue?

I've been rocking inconsolable baby Libby for more hours than I can count. Since she woke from a semi-coma, her only respite has come when I hold her tight, through movement, or through acupuncture needles. Otherwise, she is screaming and unable to digest liquid food or manage sounds. Together, we darken, but my screams remain unheard. Abby and Autumn are tucked safely in bed and sound asleep upstairs. My craving for sleep is so strong that, if my eyelids close, they will never open again, not in a million years. My right ankle is sweltering like an ember hot off the flames, but I don't dare stop rocking.

Then, it happens: my eyes seal shut, the rocking stops, the night stands still— I am gone, wasted, knocked out, spent, whipped to the gills, done in. Over the past few months, after our trusted doctor moved his acupuncture clinic and our nurse quit due to a family emergency, I've been drifting into a familiar fugue state, neither awake nor asleep. Even though I am in a state of constant fatigue, I push through the daily robotic mechanics of cooking, feeding, and hygiene routines. When night falls, I can't sleep. There is a cumulative effect of being on call, on constant alert, like a vigilant soldier in the trenches anticipating the jolt of the next explosive. This hypervigilance has been going on for nearly three years. Now dangerous thoughts haunt me regularly, the ultimate taboo of all cultures and religions, more so for a mother of three—absolutely for a woman in recovery with spiritual training and realization.

I cannot do this.

The inner voice and all of its spiritual platitudes and slogans—Breathe. Meditate. Pray. One day at a time—are on pause.

A high-pitched shriek pierces my mind like the scream of a banshee, signaling something terrible is about to happen. Like the tales my Irish grandmother spooked us with about the spirits of our ancestors, the cry comes over me like a trance, igniting the repetitive rocking motion and a stabbing pain in my ankle. "Get out!" it says. "You have to get out. Walk. Move. Get out!"

The voices rivet me to an unassailable place completely outside of the spiritual context I have become well-versed in, ruthlessly coaxing my dense body into the night.

Forcing myself out of the chair, my arms automatically take over rocking the baffling creature nestled tightly in the sling that binds my torso. Without the continuous rocking motion, Libby will scream and wake the babies and Hank, their father. Her load of sixteen pounds is minuscule, yet her rigid limbs weigh on me as much as my own corpse-like body.

I stumble to the front door a few feet in front of me. As soon as I open it, ocean air and the barking of sea lions invigorate my gait, reminding me of the morbid sense of isolation I live in, despite the picturesque surroundings of Santa Cruz. I regret that I rarely go out during the day anymore to enjoy the ocean zephyrs, the sunsets, the redwoods, and the blooming plants.

Over the past few months, I've only walked after twilight. I don't want anyone to see my tears, my sorrows, my failings. Few people know my secrets that, in rare moments, I covet to uncover. No, I'm the self-reliant, competent Scorpio yogini with a Capricorn rising. I'm the woman who broke free of a tumultuous Irish-Catholic patriarchal family, conquered self-destructive addictions, put herself through university, and built a successful alternative therapy business.

At age five my grandma O'Hara gave me a tin oven that I immediately put to use, pleasing my brothers with miniature vanilla cakes, hoping they would bring my father home. I was the little girl who crossed herself every time she heard a siren blaring in the streets, prayed for the children with disabilities who rode in the little yellow bus to school and bagged extra lunch food for Rosy and Michelle.

I worked alongside my mother from an early age, unconsciously internalizing the myth of female inferiority, so easily adopted. At age twelve I helped my mother pay the bills by working on her kitchen crew at summer camps. I didn't understand the roots of my mother's inferiority complex. Later, I saw she was unfairly blamed for a multitude of problems: too many children, my father's absence, my brother's delinquent behaviors, unpaid bills, or the inability to clothe us in suits or dresses for Sunday mass. As her designated helper, I heard all about it, especially when she discovered she was pregnant with child number eight.

"I went to confession again. I told Father Clancy that I couldn't take care of any more babies. Harry isn't paying the bills. I'm on my own."

"No matter, my child, the good Lord will provide," Father said. "Now be a good girl and say your Hail Mary's and Our Fathers."

I could feel her fuming, her ensnared entrapment, enmeshed inside of myself as if she were me, and me her. In retrospect, I see the Church was a resource she hoped would offer her guidance, birth control, assistance, and permission to divorce the man who was abusing her and me. She desperately pursued validation from the patriarchal system and found it not only absent but horribly destructive. Like so many women who became mothers in the 1940s and 1950s, she was subject to manipulation, containment, and suppression rampant throughout society.

When I stripped off my apron, I was eager to abandon the role of mother's helper altogether. I enjoyed helping my mom, but I feared being like her, confined to the kitchen with children gripped to my legs. My mom would give a stranger her coat, a quality I admired, but her generosity toward herself was forced underground. I imagine her rage felt dark, as if devouring the stagnation of a life unlived.

I felt disloyal leaving my mother and siblings but I ached for freedom. I knew help would not come from my home. On the rare occasions, I asked or cried for help, it was my mother's voice that implanted itself into my psyche, saying, "You're fine, you don't need anything. You're the strong one." She said it like a prayer. *Please don't need me.* I internalized: *It's not okay to need; don't ask.*

I never imagined I'd be here decades later, fraught, alone with three young children, twins I was unable to protect at birth. Now all the customary frilly outfits that relatives gift to our twins go straight to the Goodwill donation basket, as they will not be worn. There will be no commemorative milestones for the girls, and no need for such dresses. Instead of being a family amidst a thriving spiritual community with two healthy hands in which children are the long, slender fingers, some of the fingers are bruised and broken.

I pass the bench marked West Cliff Drive, cross the road without looking left or right, and climb over the fence with signs that read, "Steep Edge. Do Not Cross. Unsafe." I make no attempt to see past the darkness enshrouding me. With each stride, it is closing in—drowning out my thoughts, enforcing its own agenda. My legs take on a life of their own, traversing the narrow path with determination.

At this precipitous edge, all feelings of being a protective mother and 'this too shall pass' are gone. Like the waves crashing on steep boulders below, the life presented to me is insurmountable. Noise conceals said and unsaid words, grief over the life I am never going to have—the utterly uncomplicated life of a spiritual honeymoon laced with bliss, peace, and serenity; or a close-knit family with healthy children, an enchanting toddler, capable partner, and caring friends.

The life I have is not the life I can live.

My feet cling to the rough edge. The ocean waves crash fiercely against the rocks and send chills up my tremoring legs. My heartbeat is grinding against my throat. I quiver at the narrow edge of the cliff, baby around my middle. The question—*why?*—bellows from beneath the knot in my gut.

Eyes closed, I feel myself leaning, my weary body releasing toward the abyss.

Without explanation, the ocean wind howls, "You're staying." Instead of falling forward, the wind suddenly surges, throwing us backward, away from this slippery edge. The electrified air summons me like Hera, the goddess of childbirth. Her matter-of-fact tone speaks fiercely—yet kindly—directly to my worn-out body: "Turn around. Go home. Get some rest."

The salty gust steers us back down the path like a good shepherd herding her sheep. I'm dazed, unsure of what just happened or what is happening now. I am carried, effortlessly, unable to resist. A strong current invigorates my gait. It is moving us, as though we are being delivered from an obscure dream. When I open the door to our house, the aroma of the sea comes with us. I feel released from a death walk. A decision has been made.

I drop into the chair. I recline all the way back in the big burly rocker and bow to a deep, uninterrupted sleep that lasts four hours. It is the longest continuous sleep I have had in two-and-a-half years. When I wake, Libby continues to sleep with an intriguing glow of light upon her face, as if she is part of a secret conspiracy.

That's when I began to see that many of the truths a mother starts out believing morph into something wholly other.

2
Soul Reading

In the summer of 1976, I bought a used, broken-down red Toyota Corolla for 200 bucks from a friend. My brother Joe helped me replace the battery, seal a few leaks, and check the brakes. We fastened a wooden block in place for a gas pedal and tied the passenger door closed with a thick rope. Without insurance or a reference point for safety, I thought, if the engine revs, *drive it, go*. I loaded the car up with a milk crate of albums and a few handfuls of clothes and escaped six hours to the distant end of New York State. Secrets came with me.

Months earlier, through a series of fortunate events that involved lessons on how to complete college applications, I was accepted to a small college located in a quiet village amidst the rolling hills of Schoharie County. I told myself, *I am good enough*. I could stop crawling on my knees and learn to love myself. I could become something other than a wife or a mother.

On my first day, I was washing up in the campus dorm bathroom when I catch the eyes of a young woman with pitch black hair three sinks over. Our eyes meet in the mirror, hers chestnut, mine hazel. We steadily hold each other's gaze for a timeless moment. Soon we become roommates. One cloudy afternoon, a few weeks into classes that I scarcely attend, Alice shakes me awake. "Nan, your behavior is not normal. I know someone who can help you."

I rub the fog from my eyes. "Huh?"

I wasn't accustomed to anyone taking note of my secret escapades. She was tracking the men, both young and old, who escorted me to my room in a blackout night after night. I didn't know how to stop. I could disappear into my swimming lane, stroke nonstop for two hours, and no one would track me.

At sundown, my episodes repeat. Alice sees the humiliation that hangs over me. She tells me about RW, an oracle that speaks through a woman named Sheila. I know very little about how Alice met Sheila, only that she is part of her mother's spiritual community. Alice dropped out of college due to a heroin addiction. The reading with RW gave her instructions that would change the course of her life. Alice wants the same for me. I don't consider meeting with an oracle to be strange. *I'm ready to do better.*

The big moment with RW is set for November 3, 1976, giving me precisely three weeks to sober up and consider what I am doing.

"Grand Central Station. Last stop. Everybody out."

I marvel at the bustling streets—hurried people waving down cabs, buying or selling coffee, donuts, newspapers, or art. I follow Alice's directions and navigate my way through vibrant crowds. At age nineteen, I am brimming with anticipation to meet RW, pumped at a chance for a new beginning.

Alice is a huge fan of RW, the Oracle spirit Sheila channels. I will receive a soul reading with instructions for life. *Instructions for life—a road map.*

I turn right at Sixth Avenue to the residential area. *Imagine having instructions for life?* I trust Alice, a true friend, not afraid to shake me awake. "Not normal. RW can help." Number 396 is amidst a cluster of Brownstones four stories high, laced with dark green climbing ivy. I clank the bell three times for Apartment D, like Dorothy in The Wizard of Oz.

I am greeted by Sheila, a slender woman with flowing white attire.

"You must be Nan. Come in," she invites me with a gentle smile.

"Is RW here?" I peek inside.

"Yes, of course."

Sheila has long yellow hair and shiny blue eyes. She is wearing a gold-plated chain necklace with a teardrop rose crystal. I lower my eyes, notice the glittering gold nail polish on her bare feet, and sheepishly wonder where to hide my grubby hiking boots.

"I'm glad you are here. You can leave your boots by the door." *She heard my question.*

Sheila leads me through a hickory wood door to a room adorned in white shades and the faint scent of an early morning campfire. We sit down. She lights a candle and turns on the tape recorder, ready to contact RW.

Sheila closes her eyes. She is still like a relic of Mother Mary. Moments pass in silence until she vibrates slightly, reciting incantations. Overwhelmed by the transformation before me, I fall speechless and grapple with stage fright. Curious, I muster the courage to ask my first question. My hands jitter as I try to speak.

I'm lost in memories of dangerous people and secrets I hold when Alice's words become my own. *I can change.*

"What is your question?" RW pitches again, disrupting my preoccupation.

"Do I have a soul purpose?" I ask, assuming I do not, not clear on what the question means.

"Yes, everyone has a soul purpose."

RW's response intrigues and mystifies me. With eerie accuracy, she recounts the story of my early life, unveiling the dynamics within my family and my devotion to male authority figures. A surge of sorrow washes over me as she tells traumatic episodes, including the assault by the burly football coach when I was fourteen. The weight of the past presses upon me as tears stream down my face.

"This is not your fault." My throat is clogged—my body continues to shake.

"Nan. You're safe," RW announces, calling me back to myself. I wipe my face with my sleeve and reposition my body on the chair. I feel strange like thick slime is draining out of my pores. RW continues to tell me how I've unconsciously absorbed the shame of others and wrongfully blamed, punished, and numbed myself with drugs and alcohol as if it were my duty.

Later I will gather that hypervigilance, self-sabotaging, numbing, avoidance, anxiety, sexual promiscuity, blackouts, and other unbecoming behavior patterns are trauma responses that can be resolved—mended—healed.

I fall silent and sit still. A soft feeling is bubbling up inside of me like a gentle stream of goodness. *I long for this.* If I could name it, I would say innocence. A warm fluid moves through my body like a solvent. *Is she washing me with liquid light? I'm hungry for this.* I longed to hear this in my childhood. My breathing is slow, deep, and soft. *RW is resurrecting my soul—my innocence.*

RW continues with additional particulars about my life and my soul work.

"It will be good for you to cut your hair," RW spurts as if she almost forgot.

"What? Cut off my hair?" I am doubtful, running my fingers through my long, dark hair that touches my belly.

"Yes. Cut some off. It will change the way you feel about yourself."

I swallow, blushing slightly.

"And put curtains on your windows," RW says, lightheartedly, as if presenting a riddle.

"What do you mean, put curtains on my windows?" I venture, leaning forward.

"You have beautiful eyes. They are filled with light. Let them shine. Be a light," she says with the coolness of a sage. I am puzzled and delighted all at once.

RW's closing words accentuate a course to cultivate a life of learning to live in balance, awaken the power of the divine feminine, and realize that soul-spirit, the essence of love is inherent in all beings. "You will learn the healing wisdom of our female ancestors that teach us that our bodies and the earth are not separate, both are calling for care… This is challenging work, as it is a masculine image of power that dominates our culture as a supreme being. Others will join you in this work, including your children. To begin with, Eunice will be your guide."

Within a minute, as if on cue, the one-hour tape recorder clicks off. I sit with my mouth ajar, my eyes agog on Sheila. *My children?*

Sheila hands me a tissue with a cassette marked in red ink, "November 3, 1976," and walks me to the door to gather my boots.

Sheila smiles from the top of the stairs. "I wish you well, Nan."

I'm exhilarated by the reading. I skip to Grand Central Station. *RW is helping me.* I want to mend and I want to feel liquid light soothing my inner flight. *Is this what love feels like?* Contrary to my early religious dogma, everyone is equally divine. *In the time to come, I will realize it is love that guides our purpose—dharma—the great work of our lives.*

I'm eager to begin my work with Eunice.

In late November, the maple trees are bare, frost chills the air. I submit to any activity that will help rinse the sticky spiderwebs from my brain. Awkwardly, I quit smoking by joining a running-to-awareness club and swim laps. I was surprised when the swim team elected me to be their captain. Thankfully, I no longer arrive at our dorm room in a heap without a memory of how I got there.

It is a twenty-minute drive to Eunice's house in Bronxville, an affluent village north of midtown Manhattan. We travel through the blustery roads of Yonkers suburbs, around curves, and up gentle hills to arrive at a gated property surrounded by clusters of maple trees with bright apricot leaves. I pass through an iron gate that opens to a long, slim walkway and leads to a two-story brick carriage home with mauve trim. I stop to take in the burgundy glow of the shrubs that surround the house. A woman stands at the entrance, glances warmly at me, and waits at the open doorway. Her face is round, with high cheekbones, shrouded by snowy white hair tied in a bun. Her mouth is set in an expression of wise mirth.

"Welcome, Nan, come in. We will hold our session in the blue room at the end of the hallway," she says, glancing at her wristwatch, not giving way to chit-chat. "I'm Eunice. I've been waiting for you. We have exactly one hour and much to do. Come. Leave your shoes at the door."

I like her. She's ready to tackle the issue at hand, with no drivel. She reminds me of my grandmother, a former schoolteacher devoted to active prayer.

She leads me into a soothing room with soft blues. The rich smell of cedar wood graces the air between four sapphire walls; two cozy swivel rocking chairs sit beneath an oval-shaped window with indigo curtains. She wears a cerulean blouse that matches her clear sky eyes.

"Have a seat, Nan. I listened to the tape you sent of your reading with RW. Let's get started."

I sit across from her. My eyes drift to hers. I'm consoled by her gaze like she is touching me inside with a light feather, each brush softening the buzz in my body. In a moment, I might melt, dissolve in the flame of her presence.

After what feels like a prolonged embrace, she shifts her eyes to a large quartz crystal on the glass coffee table directly under the window, lights a rose votive sitting next to it, and begins spouting invocations. She doesn't cross herself, but closes her eyes, bows her head, and says, "May the will of the highest be done in me and through me…" She begins, "What are you grateful for?"

Eunice is tracking me closely. I feel her eyes penetrating my chest cavity as if she is prying open a dormant secret.

I stop. Or rather I am stopped by a former habit. I bow my head, cross myself, and pause for a moment. Then I say, "The hand-carved box that contains her rosary." I rest my hands on my lap. "My grandmother was in communion with, or connected to, something, maybe God … Spirit…. I long for that."

Eunice pulses ahead with glistening gestures, pausing long enough to capture my impressions. She wants to know when I lost touch with the feeling of gratitude. She wants to flush out memories that blur my vision and bury my aliveness—my light.

"I don't remember," I say it strongly as if I am protecting someone other than myself. "I can't say." Suddenly my voice arrested.

She scribbles on a piece of paper that looks like a prescription pad.

"You're not prescribing tranquilizers, are you?" I blurt out in an uncalled-for tone of horror.

"No, dear. This is your homework." Her cheeks crinkle in a smile.

"I want you to record your dreams every night and write them down in a journal. If it is difficult to write, place a tape recorder by your bed, and record them into the machine. Play it back and write everything you remember. Write about something you are grateful for in every year of your life."

"I'm not sure I can do that."

"Just begin," she says with the confidence of a crone.

I swallow, realizing she will hold me to this.

"This is your work," she declares, extinguishing the candle.

"Listen to the recording of your reading with RW. It will give you courage." She smiles, clasping my hands in hers like a prayer.

I lean closer, bowing to an unfamiliar tenderness, cherishing her motherly touch, and whisper "Thank you, Eunice."

"Now go and call me when you have a page for every year."

With shoes on, we bid farewell. During the long taxi ride and for many days to come, I will reflect on our first session, eagerly anticipating our next.

Our work together is to peel back the layers and discover the pearls.

3
Unmuting

O n the three-hour journey from Eunice to my college dorm, I ask myself; what am I *grateful for?* I think hard, trying to specify a timeline from now to before; the frequency of violations, the relationship with my family, the times I hid, the times I blacked out, the times I tried to run away, the times I showed up in the right or the wrong places. I am worried I won't remember enough or the right things—what was valuable, what was not, and if Eunice would judge me. Until now I hadn't kept a journal. I am not one to sit still, contemplate, center myself, put a pen to paper, and write about myself. I am functional, hearing my name, attending school, working jobs, and performing tasks as if I wear many faces who acquiesce to the bidding of others.

In first grade, I created a picture book titled *What I Like to Do*, by 'Nancy with the Laughing Face,' as I was called. I sported an apron adorned with pink and orange daisies, illustrated myself on each page with a beaming smile, wielding a broom, vacuum cleaner, or iron. I recall whistling with an upturned face, retrieving clothes from the ringer washer atop a milk crate with my mother nearby. At thirteen, my eyes gleamed with joy as I joined my mother's kitchen crew at summer camps and received my first paycheck. My chest swelled with pride, as together, mama and me, became the breadwinners.

In the early days of my youth when my father was home, I watched him closely. The ground level of our home consisted of four adjoining areas. The front room was elegantly decorated with creamy wall-to-wall carpeting, whimsical wallpaper, and family portraits, rarely occupied. I am perched at the edge of the entryway to the next room, where my father sits in a brown La-Z-Boy recliner adjacent to a shallow coffee table. There are no books or magazines on the table, only a crowded ashtray and an opened pack of Lucky Strike cigarettes. The television was blaring with the World Series. I saw his receding hairline behind the local newspaper he held. I wanted to ask how the Yankees were doing, but I didn't.

After a few minutes, the paper slips from his grasp, and a pained expression contorts his face. Gripping his left leg below the knee, he winced and groaned, tightening his grip. Determined to rise from the chair he let out a colorful curse, "Damn Gout!" With one hand supporting his leg, he propelled his lean body forward and struggled to his feet. I suppressed a giggle, as I watched him hobble forward with his Lucky Strikes in tow, dragging his leg along.

Momentarily he is out of sight, retrieving his customary grey suit jacket from the coat closet. He reappears, steadying himself against the wall, unaware of my watchful gaze. He looks the same, handsome and sad. His mood relatively subdued, it is still early afternoon. He is not drunk yet.

He will return home after the bars have closed. An internal alarm signals his arrival, louder than his shouts to my mother, "Camille, where is my dinner?" Vulgarities pierce the walls until he passes through the makeshift bedroom, I shared with my two younger sisters. Our three beds joined as bunks to the right of a narrow passageway that led to our one and only bathroom. I wanted a peaceful slumber like my sisters. I would play dead, hoping to prevent the nearness of his beer breath and prickly whiskers. My memory blanks here. *Nothing is happening.* A part of me goes dark—hides. Another part is hypervigilant—on guard. I listened, watched, and felt until I didn't. Mistrust, self-doubt, and hypervigilance would plague me into adulthood.

One night, I heard Camille's laughter echoing from downstairs. She found my two older sisters, smoking and smooching with boys behind our house. She belts out a playful tune, "Smoke, smoke, smoke that cigarette. Puff, puff, puff, and if you puff yourself to death, tell Saint Peter at the golden gate, you just hate to make him wait, but you got to have another cigarette."

My mother, the non-smoker in our family had rare drinking episodes. "One beer—hello, Camille. Two beers—wow, Camille. Three beers—no Camille," we joked. She was in the comedic phase of beer three, flexing her arms and flashing her shiny blue eyes, "Nancy, wake up Barb and Tracy. I'll fight all five of you at once." She is so out of character. Hysterically amused, we'd press our legs together, trying not to wet ourselves, yet appreciating her newfound Karate skills.

"Go, Camille!" I cheered as she bounced us around, gladdened by her resolve.

"Father Clancy can go to hell and take his holy sacraments with him."

Unmuted, Camille was claiming her life. She filed for divorce and to have the house deed put in her name. Next, she left us for what felt like an eternity. Later, I learned she had to find full-time employment, open a bank account, and clear her mind to establish a plan to launch my father out. Worry consumed me when my oldest sister announced she was getting married and moved out. "Why would you do that?" I asked with tear-filled eyes.

My next sister blared Elton John, locked in her room. My two older brothers recklessly took to the streets. At night, I pilfered my father's pockets scraping change to feed my siblings. Eventually, my mother returned after she found work at Buffalo University. She would excel as chief commissary cook for two decades before she retired with honors for exemplary service. My father would continue to drink.

What am I grateful for?

I sit by a cool stream with my back against a huge boulder and write. Thoughts land on the page without permission. The more I write, the more they come. I weep for pain—for triumphs. It doesn't matter. I want to return to the sanctuary of the blue room and be cradled in the soft gaze of Eunice's eyes. I want to claim what RW called *soul purpose*. And I long to love and be loved.

I'm thankful to Alice, for caring enough to fiercely shake me awake. For high school completion and the generous guidance of Michael, Scott, Tom, Molly, Max, and Joe, who engineered my way to college.

I'm thankful to my mother, brave enough to stand up to my father. Grateful to my boss who taught me the ropes of Orville's Ice Cream Parlor and showered me with lavish bonuses. And those sacred moments with Cherokee elders, smoking tobacco, are etched in my heart.

Amidst the shadows of Irish tragedy, I appreciate the flickers of comedy. When the church bells rang and my parents believed in their vows before pain eclipsed their hearts. When they walked arm in arm, leaving my older sisters in charge. Pam, the homecoming queen, and Maggie, ready to revel and rebel. The extravagant parties that amplified Bruce Springsteen and Queen, with kegs of beer flowing alongside moonlit howls, silenced only by our grumpy neighbors who called the police. One unforgettable night—my father stumbled home early, inebriated. He summoned Pam, Maggie, Barbara, and me for what he called "a whooping." He told us to, "Line up." But as he took off his belt, his pants fell to his ankles. Left standing in boxer shorts and knee-high socks, we erupted with uncontrollable laughter, wetting ourselves as we scattered to our rooms.

As I run my fingers through my mid-length haircut, I delve into the damp pages. It was 1969. The *Deer Hunter* was just released. My father invited me to the movie— a chance for a sober outing, just me and my dad, free from incidents involving stitches, raising bail, or yanking him off my mother or brother. Midway through a brutal scene in Vietnam, my father belched in his popcorn, sobbed, and crawled up the aisle, cursing out loud. Terrified, I remained glued to my seat. Until I found him in a familiar scene, sitting on a barstool, alone and sad.

Later, reading my journal, I realized that my father didn't harm or abandon anyone intentionally. He abandoned himself to survive the memories of WWII that haunted him day and night. Like so many veterans, his dreams shattered under the weight of war inhumanities. A fusion of anger, hurt, sadness, and embarrassment began to drain out of my body.

But my longing to love and be loved by him remained. Years later, he would visit me in Boston while I was in graduate school. We attended Thanksgiving liturgical mass at the Paulist Center, my place of ministerial internship. While we sang "The Our Father," he held my hand tight, and in that moment, I swear, he transcended his body with redemption. He stood tall and sang with exquisite joy, tears streaming down his face. After he embraced many strangers, we skipped together down Commonwealth Avenue to my apartment. Though he never told me, "I love you," I knew his love ran deep. Like many men, his heart was crushed under the brutal rules of patriarchy that order them to suppress tenderness, suck it up, and soldier on.

––––––––––––––

I slobber through more pages, highlighting occasions when an inner voice halted me in my tracks. The ringing phone, a knock at the door, an impulse to help, to rescue, to protect, or to stay home. Over the course of my sessions with Eunice, she helped me to reclaim my instincts and assured me that my intuition is good, to be honed, and coupled with self-care. She tells me, "Memory or understanding of an event is not the same as healing from it. With a reassuring nod, Eunice smiles, "Our work has begun. Your subconscious is cooperating."

4
Stop Signs

I will meet with Eunice regularly for the next five years until I move to Boston in 1981. I graduated with a BA in psychology and dance therapy. My therapy expands to include biodynamics, yoga, dance, and additional tools for self-care. I work to develop a vocational transition program for teenage girls in correctional facilities to enrich their confidence, build skills, and derail further institutionalization. I live on campus and feel safe in my room until the night watchman makes his rounds and comes knocking. It is late, his knocking wakes me up. "What do you want?" I ask.

He jingles a bundle of keys and announces his name while he pounds. "Security, routine safety check. I need to check your room." Fear grips me, *He's stronger than me, possibly armed, yet married.* Reluctantly I unbolt the door and step back.

"Let me in." He demands, pushing his way in.

In my knee-length nightgown, I tremble, voice sunk. I've witnessed his lewd jokes and felt his eyes on me or the one other woman at our staff meetings. He shoves in—uninvited. Petrified, I wonder, *what to do when the 'security police' barges into your room, locks the door and assaults you?* Numbness engulfs me. When he finally leaves, my breath and body convulse under my covers. *Nothing happened. No one will believe you. I will leave—run.*

Toyota motor vehicles are known for their reliability and performance. Mine is red, committed to safety. I launched my escape to Cambridge, Massachusetts. Why Cambridge? Three years of working as head cook at World Fellowship Center (WFC) has woven solid friendships. Rachel, a vibrant guest at the center, told me, "You're always welcome." When I gave my two weeks' notice at the correctional facility, I contemplate revealing the truth of the assault to my male superiors, only to envision their dismissive laughter and further erosion of my spirit. Instead, I swallow my emotions, lift my chin, and reserve my farewell to the girls in my program.

My little brother Max questions my decision, puzzled that I am closing the door to professional advancement. I am the sister he idolizes, the one who rose above adversity. I reply, "It's time to move on. I want to explore what the Boston area has to offer."

On the eight-hour drive to Cambridge, I only stopped to pee. The vivid hues of orange and red in the forest along the highway transport me back to the summers I spent in New Hampshire's white mountains. Autumn signals the end of daily open-water swimming, hiking expeditions, and the comraderies of growing and cooking food with friends from around the world. One summer, I surprised myself by asserting a boundary.

The directors at WFC never doubted my culinary prowess, regardless of the guest count. Two consecutive "best cook" awards attested to my skills, yet it was during my third summer that an incident unfolded. The kitchen became my haven and timing my specialty. However, the director's anxious behavior about meal readiness irked me, lifting lids, clicking spoons, and rubbing his hands, while pacing the kitchen floor, "Is everything under control?" One morning, while flipping countless pancakes over a hot grill, his words ignited a fuse. I removed my apron, and thrust my spatula at him, "Here you do it. I'm done!" I stomped out, went to my room, and wailed. *What gives him the right to stampede our work space?*

Moments later, his wife came to my room. I assumed dismissal, but instead, she expressed admiration, "How did you do that? I've been trying to do that for thirty years!" We connect in sisterly solidarity. I realize that confident, well-educated, powerful women also struggle to protect their spaces from men. *Why?*

I think about this as I navigate the road sealed in my red Corolla, traversing the painted lines and signs that convey rules: "Do not cross," "Stay in your lane," "Signal before passing," "Yield to pedestrians," and "STOP." I want to shield my body with huge red signs shaped like octagons, a hope for protection from the bad behavior of men.

Welcomed by my friend Rachel to her home in Cambridge, she settles me in a room near her son's reggae and pot-filled space. After a brief nap, I awaken drenched in sweat, allured by vivid dream instructions. "Go to the church, there you will find someone you can trust." Surprised I jot it down. *Church?* I haven't been since high school. But the dream's pull is fierce. I rush to Rachel and inquire about nearby churches. She reminds me of her Jewish heritage, but I explain it's not about a specific denomination. "I need spiritual nourishment." She mentions The Paulist Center. The next morning, I make the call.

"Hello, this is Father Jim, may I help you?"

Admitting anguish, "I'm in a dark place and desperately need to talk…"

"My office is open all morning. I'm available."

I followed the directions he gave me and rang the bell at the side entrance of Boston Commons. I anticipate a traditional priest donned in black with a white collar. The door opens to a tall, well-built middle-aged man dressed in a polo and blue jeans. He could easily pass as a fill-in for Christopher Reeve ready to play Superman. I don't ask about his missing vestment. Father Jim leads me through a corridor lined with religious décor, a framed portrait of Thomas Hecker, the founder of the Paulist Center in 1858, along with other Roman Catholic men.

Father Jim invited me to sit in one of two cushioned chairs flanking a coffee table. His amber eyes absorb my attention. I sense loneliness, an ache, a hunger within him. We spoke for two hours about my dream and longing for a spiritual vocation. He advised me to explore several options, including missionary work and the local theological consortium. Soon, I accept matriculation at Boston University School of Theology, enticed by its diverse faiths, interdisciplinary approach, courses in women's studies, and Jungian Psychology. Father Jim offers to be my mentor for a field placement and we agree to meet weekly for the next two years.

My time in Boston inspired my passion for civil rights and feminist movements marching ahead. As a student immersed in the theological consortium, I learn from esteemed scholars like Mary Daily and Carol Gilligan and join the Women's Ordination Conference. A scholarship takes me to study in Israel and live on a kibbutz. Carol Bohn guides my thesis to research and raise awareness about sexual abuse and violations toward women. Teaching yoga to incarcerated women, and producing a liturgical drama *In Silence Secrets Turn to Lies, Secrets Shared Become Sacred Truths,* I witness the catharsis of countless untold stories. This sacred drama invites participants to write their names in a sacred book at the altar. I'm stunned by the number of names that fill the pages with unearned shame. An initiation toward healing and sovereignty unfolds.

Ironically, in the spring of 1984, when my colleagues and I were approaching graduation, I am blindsided by the very violations I am actively working to resolve—the misuse of power. In retrospect, I see that Father Jim was preying upon me and four other women, waiting for the ideal moment to pounce. *How could I not see this coming? Idiot. Idiot. Idiot.* The times he acted strange and poured me extra wine before morning mass; the day he closed his office door and pressed into my body with his stiff dick. The day I broke free before he had his way with me.

My voice stolen, I returned home, engulfed by searing pain and an enduring headache. Gashed. It takes immense courage to confide in Jane, a liturgical minister. Together we uncover five additional victims, all young women, one married. We meet with the senior priest to report the scandalous transgressions of Father Jim. Recounting violations is a daunting task, as women fear blame, shame, judgment, and banishment. The heaviness in the room is suffocating. Bodies shake and squirm with loud exhalations as if expelling demons with chilling wishes to die. My eyes burn and will not ash until every woman's voice is heard and believed. And she is offered resources for healing. I berate myself for misplacing my trust. The ministry I felt empowered by and called to, escapes me. Everything I worked for is devoured by doubt.

Father Jim receives a mere slap on the wrist and a transfer to Berkeley. A feeble response—devoid of justice. *Where is the STOP SIGN?*

I flee Boston to join a small cluster of Carmelite nuns at a Monastic Hermitage near the coast of Maine. Amidst anxious solitude, I immerse myself in mystical literature, *The Cloud of Unknowing*, and *Therese of Lisieux*, and yearn for rest. During coastal walks, I'm tempted to submerge myself beneath crashing waves, yet I resist their icy allure, determined to keep my head above water and absorb the quiet kindness of the black-clad sisters.

During my short visit, postulancy captivates me—a time to contemplate the vows of chastity, obedience, and worldly relinquishment. Shedding material attachments seems easy; notions of sex choke my entire body like a venomous snake. I want to build a barricade around my body like the thick skin of a rhinoceros, and let nobody in. Obedience, hell no. I have sharp horns. I answer to no one. I want to ask the nuns: *When is it safe to come out? Reclaim soul purpose?* I wander, spending weeks lost in hushed longing.

The aftermath of violation is isolation, disassociation, and degradation. I judge myself and my body as flawed. My instincts—misguided, not sharp. Yet, in quiet moments the clear voice of Eunice caresses my soul. "Our job is to peel back the layers to reveal the pearls."

I recall Eunice's unwavering dedication, coaching me through biodynamic sessions, beads of sweat dripping down my back and the exhilaration of release that came from punching pillows or slamming tennis rackets. If I felt numb, she told me, "Run hard in the forest where no one will bother you." I savored pounding my feet on the earth and shouting out obscenities as I ran through an excluded forest. I felt powerful.

One morning, shaken awake by a recurring nightmare, I embarked on a cathartic run. Alone in the wilderness, I ran hard, tears mingled with sweat while I screamed, "STOP! No! Don't touch me! Leave me alone!" Suddenly figures appeared on either side of my body, gripping me firmly under the arms.

"We're taking you back. You're not supposed to be out here."

"WAIT. This is my therapy. I'm releasing bottled-up emotions. I'm healing."

"Sure, you are."

Urgently, they led me to a towering gate—a psychiatric hospital, one I must have escaped from. They loosened their grip when the gate attendant said all patients were accounted for. I was granted permission to make one phone call. I called Eunice, who confirmed my story. When Eunice arrived, I could tell she was suppressing a giggle. Reunited, our laughter interlaced with a plan for alternative running fields. Eunice never hesitated to express her reflections that question the incessant unearned advantage of men, "Why do men insist on patrolling women's bodies? They're in our homes, swimming pools, schools, churches, and forests, telling us 'You need to have a lie down, dear.'"

Eunice has never given me a reason to mistrust her or fear judgment. I'm unsure why I don't phone her about Father Jim. *Will I disappoint her?* Perhaps I don't want to look at what still lingers in my unconscious. My desire is to return to embodied practices like dance and yoga. I happenchance upon Kripalu Center for Yoga and Health in the Berkshire mountains. The details of how I get there are foggy. My initial plan is to spend a month in a residential teacher training program. I find it easy and convenient to disappear into the purity culture of this large community. I'm thrilled to join the staff as a bodyworker and teacher.

In this structured haven, my identity is defined. The days unfold with precise schedules. Buffet-style meals are laid out before us, in a large dining hall, separating the male and female residents. The rules are clear; silence reigns unless related to our Seva yoga, the selfless service we undertake without personal expectations or rewards. My first Seva is household maintenance. I covet the task of vacuuming, the opportunity to create straight lines that breathe tranquility into every room, reminiscent of Madeline and her boarding school companions. I recall numerous urges to run victory laps, for the indescribable satisfaction I feel exiting an exquisitely vacuumed space without leaving a trace of footprints. Vacancy, emptiness, lines, boundaries—control.

5
Get On With It

It is 1986, close to three years that I've resided at Kripalu. My heart leaps for joy when I see Eunice's name on the guest roster, I'm on household duty. I take special care in preparing her room, adorning it with flowers, candles, and writing supplies. Her unannounced weekend visit initiates a new dynamic within our relationship outside of therapy sessions. We hike together, enjoy a picnic, and find levity amidst recent struggles, as friends would do. She reminds me, "Transformation and comfort do not live on the same street." Her optimism, plants yet another seed to nurture when she says, "There is no such thing as a mistake—only learning."

At the end of the weekend, as we walk to her car another side of her personality emerges. Like a Zen policewoman, she pulls me to the curb. Referring to the ashram and the guru (Yogi Amrit Desai), she looks fiercely into my eyes, and says, "He is not your teacher. This is not your path. Get on with it!" Then she drives off in her polished black Subaru, leaving me stunned.

I stagger, considering Eunice's lack of appreciation for the rigorous purifying practices we engage in—day and night. Her words flag me, "It is better to fail, stumble, and learn along the way than to follow someone else's path." While I enjoy selfless service, social borders, silence, clean living, and routine yoga, I wonder, *am I hiding in someone else's path? Am I playing it safe?* I tell myself, I'm here for professional development and community, not the guru. But when I'm honest, I know, deep down, that I will not heal relational trauma without genuine interactions with people.

Three days after Eunice's departure, her daughter calls with devastating news. "Eunice just died. We thought you should know."

The phone drops from my hand, and a chilling sensation cuts through my body like gallons of ice water. Gradually, it began to dawn on me what Eunice meant by, "Get on with it!" She wants me to remember the tools and guidance she gave me. "Don't forget your soul purpose." I cradle my head and tremble. *Remember, everyone has a spiritual purpose.* She doesn't want me to forget the importance of crawling through the mud and the muck of challenge to grow fierce in love. *Emulating male authority is a cul-de-sac. Where is the exit?*

Eunice emphasized living the life I am meant to live—being authentic. Not succumbing to the dictates of cultural, religious, patriarchal conditioning, or borrowed shame. "There will be signposts along the way that will point you back to yourself—to self-love."

At the time, I didn't grasp all of her teachings. I may have kept myself distracted on a yogic path that didn't foster grappling with inner doubt. *How will I know when I am truly safe to love and receive love in return?* Years will pass before I let myself savor pleasure, watch sunsets, and feel at ease to soak naked in hot tubs, or simply read a book on a warm coastal beach. Trauma triggers extreme behaviors—deprivation or overindulgence—with no ground for balance. Eunice's words echo through my being, "When your subconscious suppresses dark unwitnessed memories, your behaviors are unconsciously driven in unnatural ways."

I leave Kripalu in two weeks for California. My friend Angie a former nun who I met in Boston gifts me a one-way ticket. Life at the ashram was sparse, $35 a month, a closet half the size of the end of my bunk, and two small drawers. I had zero cash and all of my belongings fit into a backpack. When I arrive at Angie's home, she tells me, "Your timing is perfect; I'm taking my daughters on a camping trip."

I soon discover a generously stocked pantry in which I have unlimited access. "Help yourself to whatever you want."

Whatever I want! I am the thinnest I have ever been. Once I enter the pantry, the size of a small kitchen, I dig in—I gobble. I lick out the inside of one Oreo cookie after another and stuff myself with Little Debbie's and salty chips. The pendulum swings wildly, from years of deprivation to unbridled indulgence.

I stuff without restraint, surpassing the ache in my gut, past wooziness, and nausea, until I find myself sprawled out on the pantry floor unable to see straight—an unconsciousness mess.

After several days of torment, extreme misery haunts me. In the ashram, I had a solid identity, an unyielding routine that sculpted the day. I vacuumed rooms in straight lines, led yoga classes, gave massages, and coasted along—comfortable; mindless while pretending to be mindful. Eunice's visit disrupted my trance—and catapulted me out of the ashram. Now she's dead. Bewildered, lost amidst cracker crumbs, aching to the bone—hungry and sad, *who will guide my soul?*

After weeks of unrestricted gluttony, heaviness, and self-loathing, I get stern with myself: *This is absurd!*

It doesn't occur to me that there are no rules. No one is preventing me from going out and meeting people, from speaking. I consider this possibility, but grief engulfs me, imploding within. Despite our limited interactions, I miss the camaraderie of group practice and the rigor of a rock-solid routine. Like a sailor gone overboard, I need a life preserver and directions for how to be a human. *I miss Eunice. The friend that called me back to myself.* This ache is all-consuming, numbing, suppressing my instincts, voice, needs, and wants—self-harming behaviors that I do not want to repeat. Later I will see that Eunice's death compounds unresolved trauma. I fled the ashram, I shattered. I am not able to be carefully kept. I have sharp edges. I am messy. *Eventually, I will learn that what I ache for is me.*

It's not unusual for me to arrive at a new place with little regard for how it might go; to cast a line and see if anyone will bite and reel me in. On impulse, I crawl out of the pantry, swim a few laps, tidy myself, and venture into town. A poster catches my eyes in the window of a health food store. In vibrant colors, it announces a 'potluck gathering' hosted by a spiritual community.

People in spiritual communities tend to be gentle and generous, much like Angie, Jane, Alice, Rachel, and others who greeted me with warmth. I attend.

The door is open to a well-crafted two-story house nestled on the hillside; shoes haphazardly scattering the entryway. The air is alive with conversations. I hesitate and fuss with my hair before entering until I spot a table teeming with mouthwatering dishes.

I am grazing at the dessert table when Cathy introduces herself. She stands as tall as my neck with long black wispy hair, wearing a flowing beige dress. As if she senses my predicament, she mentions a computer company she works for that is seeking to hire individuals on a spiritual path. "That's me! I'm spiritual." I blurt out, aware that I don't know the first thing about computers. But I desperately need a job. I land it and Cathy becomes my office mate. That's when she tells me about Satsang.

Cathy's invitation to Satsang piques my curiosity. "Yes!" My hunger for spirituality, like food, is insatiable. I wake with the burning question, *Who Am I?* We drive Highway 280, heading to San Francisco, and arrive at a nondescript building just before the majestic Golden Gate Bridge. Along the journey, I learn that Cathy is an astute student of *Ramana Maharshi[1]* and other sages including *Anandamayi Ma[2]*. I'm captivated by her stories.

She tells me of when she had an extensive visit with the renowned Sage *Nisargadatta Maharaj[3]* in India. His Satsang took place in the upper level of a barn above his family home. As she sat with Nisargadatta daily, she untangled misconceptions about spirituality. Other Westerners would climb up the ladder to his Satsang space and disparage his claim to self-knowledge by criticizing his smoking of bidis and sitting upon animal skins. Unfazed, he would blow more smoke into the room and say, "If you seek an image of enlightenment, go down the road, you will find it there."

Cathy remained steadfast, discerning the distinction between a liberating teaching that set you free and mental constructs surrounding enlightenment as a static, rigid, flawless state of perfection. Historically, enlightenment is depicted as a serene male figure seated in lotus posture, blissfully happy, and transcendent of the complexities of human existence. I chuckle as Cathy says,

---

[1] Ramana Maharshi was much revered sage and teacher from India in the first part of the twentieth century.
[2] Anandamayi Ma was a twentieth-century Indian saint from Bengal.
[3] Nisargadatta Maharaj was also a revered sage and teacher from India in the first part of the twentieth century.

"Behind every Buddha, there is, of course, a woman cooking and cleaning!" I find her perspective refreshing.

Later, I will wrestle consciously with transcendent dogmas that suppress the natural rhythms of our human experience, disregard inherent cycles of life—in the body of a woman—in nature, or any individual pursuing spirituality beyond prescriptive ideation.

On the way to the meeting hall, warm smiles and whispers of "namaste" greet us. The room is softly lit, lined with rows of meditation cushions. I'm drawn to the cadence of a woman chanting, it is a recording of Anandamayi Ma, the 'Bliss Permeated Mother.' I'm pulled inside by *Who am I?* as I settle on a cushion near the front. Soon the chant ends and we sit in silent meditation.

With my eyes closed, I receive silence like an old friend. A sense of goodness comforts me. About fifteen minutes pass when the main teacher (Sage Nome) quietly enters the room, wearing flowing saffron clothing similar to the Hare Krishnas, his head is shaven. Nome takes his place on a large, flat white cushion in a full lotus posture and begins to discourse on the teachings of Ramana Maharishi. The atmosphere is serene, akin to a tropical seashore with the sweet fragrance of incense in the air. I listen, feel, and drop inside.

The words "You are the Self" touch a ravenous space inside, a vacancy; a nonverbal, nonintellectual recognition awakens an abandoned place in myself. A truth opens, my body feels spacious, alive, gently energized, like luminous generosity. I'm held, warmed, known. I remember that what I am, and what life is, are one and the same. This feels evident, inborn—intrinsic, not something my rational mind understands. Knowing wakes up; *You are the Self.* This knowing stirs deep in my bones, my blood, my soul, shedding a former cloak of irrelevance. I remember. The questions *Who am I? What is my purpose?* surge with meaning. In this moment, I feel fed—nourished. My soul is homing me and will satiate longing in the years to come.

Remarkably, my struggles with overeating begin to leave me and I don't starve myself. Over time, the unyielding impulse to numb myself, to wall myself in with remorseful cyclical habits of binging on food or denying my hunger, along with violently ill feelings weaken their grip. The pendulum swing from one extreme to another is less dramatic. I catch myself; I remember to breathe and that I can feel good. Self-harming behaviors are transmuting to self-care and compassion, as they did years before when I fought hard to recover myself with Eunice. More often than not, I laugh at my silly thoughts. Somehow, I let them float by like bubbles on a vast sea, like they belong to someone else. Judging, and shaming thoughts continue to creep in, but stick less and less. As the days continue, I feel myself responding to life more like I did when I was much younger, when I cared about connecting to others. *I am kinder to myself but I also keep to myself, not always sure of my value.*

The way I represented myself to the world, as a person defined by a sequence of experiences, also fades. The potency of those experiences is dissolving (at least for now). I resonate with the words of Nisargadatta, who becomes a favorite sage, "*I am* is that state where there is a total absence of any concept of presence or absence. You are also in that state but don't know it."[4] You don't know it intellectually. *I'm curious.*

As I continue to practice at SAT, in seated meditation, over time I feel saturated with liquid light—still, quiet, as I felt with RW, and wondered, *is this love?* I learn this to be a state referred to as *Nirvikalpa Samadhi*[5]. There is awareness of what is going on around me, but I'm concentrated inside—absorbed in peace. This space is void of need, want, or recognition. When the meditation period ends, my functionality engine turns on to give focused attention to my work projects. During this 'samadhi,' there is not a sense of beginning or ending, no inner or outer boundary. What I am feels untouched, unwounded, whole, as if a precious jewel inside is being restored, revived—preserved by inherent knowing. *Is this feminine—motherly love?* I intuit this feeling as inborn, with me since the day my soul entered through the birth canal as the fifth child of my mother Camille, and perhaps prior to that time. I am this, *where could this (I) go?*

> "She is without beginning and without end.
> She is the whole and also the parts.
> The whole and the parts together make up real connection."[6]

---

[4] Maharaj, Nisargadatta. I Am That. Published 1973.
[5] Nirvikalpa Samadhi: A state of non-duality, absorption in Spirit without self-consciousness or mental activity. A state in which the practitioner realizes that he/she is one with God/Goddess.
[6] Fitzgerald J. (2007), The Essential Sri Anandamayi Ma, Life and Teaching of a 20th Century Indian Saint.

In the depths of this intimacy with myself, I smile through tears, gently releasing, warming like an inner sun. *Can I claim this—remain with this? Happiness without a border.* I question the value of traditional renunciation. *Doesn't Spirit include all of who we are?* I'm not always aware of my unconscious entrainment toward male leadership and their dictums.

While in this state of fluid absorption, my body naturally contorts itself, which draws corrective attention from the sages and revives self-consciousness. Russ advises me to sit up straight, cautioning me against misleading impressions for visitors. Unbeknownst to me, I undulate like a snake when I should be still like a statue. *Am I truly misleading anyone by embodying fluidity like water— occupying space, and following my own inner rhythm?* These interruptions trigger doubt and signal the rise of instincts that perhaps require reckoning. Once again, I attribute my dharma to external sources with a need to conform and present myself favorably. *How does this transference occur, allowing men to confidently proclaim spiritual knowledge while my natural instincts are flattened? And, here I am, wondering, who gets to flourish?*

Years pass at SAT. I witness the group's preoccupation with attracting affluent members. Initially, I complied with blind faith, even providing unpaid therapeutic massages to the leaders that visited my home. Naively, I feel special in their eyes and unwittingly contribute to the organization's growth and temple construction. I am even convinced to go after some of my stellar clients for donations. *Embarrassing, I know.*

No one ever holds a gun to my head. I simply believe I'm serving a higher purpose for the benefit of humanity. Yet I'm beginning to see my enduring loyalty to religious patriarchy—God portrayed as male. It is deceptive, almost invisible to me, until I invite my closest friend and business colleague Debbie to a Satsang.

Debbie who shared the corporate frenzy of Silicon Valley's dot-com era with me often asks, "Why don't you party with us?"

"I don't want to break my focus."

I don't judge Debbie, nor do I share my former blackouts. I know she won't resonate with the purity culture of SAT—an environment of white-clad bodies, silence, and namaste greetings. Curious, I invite her, "Do you want to come to Satang with me?"

Debbie meets me at the new SAT temple in Santa Cruz, where an overzealous middle-aged white man dressed in white greets her. I sense her reluctance as we pass iconic Hindu statues and framed photos of male sages. We continue up a short flight of carpeted stairs to join those already seated in silent meditation. She keeps her eyes open. As usual, Sage Nome begins his discourse, his eyes penetrating the audience, pausing occasionally to accentuate his transmission with mudras (hand gestures). With all eyes watching Debbie abruptly walks out.

Later, I ask, "Why did you leave?"

"You're in a cult. These people do not think for themselves. Who are they surrendering to?"

Holy Mother! Her use of the word "cult" shocks me. I don't investigate its meaning immediately. A cult is defined as "a system of veneration and devotion directed toward a particular figure or object; a group of people having religious beliefs or practices regarded by others as strange or sinister."

Debbie's keen observations, as an unorthodox unyielding woman, not afraid to question and challenge the dominant male voice, prompts me to question my own blind spots. *Am I getting lost in the trappings of spirituality; bypassing instinctive knowing? Have I become a sheep?* I return to SAT with a commitment to scrutinize the organization and practice critical thinking. My quiet samadhi ignites into a fierce game of ping-pong with the teachers. I ping, they pong until I openly address the subservient elephant in the room (all of us). *Why 'enlightened' men? Why are we—the women—arranging flowers, pouring water, and not rescuing our own voices?*

The cloak of male supremacy that centers a long lineage of spirituality written by men is disrupted. *Doesn't my experience as a woman count?* Pong. Soon I am unpopular and receive a letter demanding that I "cease and desist."

The letter shakes me. I do not feel an urge to drink, yet I wonder if Alcoholics Anonymous will shed light on my frenzy. *Could I be addicted to the male voice?* I find the nearest AA meeting, sit down, admit I am an addict, and find a female sponsor. It dawns on me that I may unconsciously fear the steps required to heal the relational trauma I experienced with men in power—men I admired and trusted. *How do I navigate relationships where disagreements do not lead to abuse or exile? How does a woman embody sovereignty?*

I attend 365 meetings in 365 days, conduct an extensive inventory of myself, and rework the steps with my sponsor. Through AA, I realize that sobriety is not the opposite of addiction; connection is. *It's learning how not to abandon inner knowing.* My sponsor deems God is honesty. When I'm honest, I feel connected, nourished, at peace. I understand that inner peace doesn't rely on proximity to 'enlightened' men. *How do I ground this certainty with roots in my authentic expression?*

I will continue to grapple with oppressive patriarchal teachings and structures. Nevertheless, a year passed, and I take deep breaths, ready to rebirth the stirrings in my soul. An AA slogan comes to mind, "Take what you like and leave the rest." I leap to my desk and pen a letter to the teacher who dismissed me. "Can I stop desisting?" I tell myself; I will gaze inward. I return with an implied agreement to behave. I'm invited to volunteer in the service of the publication of ancient Sanskrit and Tamil texts in English. I accept, with hope that these teachings will feed my soul.

It was the early 1990s, spiritual teachings weren't easily accessible, and female spiritual leaders remained unknown. I deliberately seek a divine force like Kali within me as my inner guru. I imagine she welcomes undulations, and messiness that honor the natural rhythms of our bodies and foster sisterhood.

The teachings at SAT do not adhere to specific traditions like Hinduism, Buddhism, or Christianity. I thoroughly enjoy the Gnostic texts such as *The Gospel of Mary* and *Thomas* that emphasize the inherent divinity within all beings. Luckily, these texts infuse a growing confidence to step away from centuries-old doctrines, and toward feminine wisdom.

6
Top of The Mountain

I'm thirty-five when Hank and I clumsily become a couple. Hank had been pursuing me for close to the entire ten years I have been an active member of SAT (or cult, if you like). He arrived at a potluck supper put on by our household, where he sheepishly invited me for a walk. We stroll to the end of a dusty trail by my house where a single donkey is grazing. No sooner have I fed Eeyore a bright orange carrot when Hank says, "I thought you and I could have a relationship." *Is that a question, a statement, or a probe?* Part of me knew this was coming, the part that outruns men. I'm not equipped to examine this part closely, not here, not now. I haven't been in a relationship since I fled from a marriage proposal in my early twenties while submerged in work or water—unaware of why I dodge intimacy. I met David in late spring just before our summer commitment to work at WFC. We got to know each other through extensive conversations in the kitchen. No one had ever found me interesting in the way he had. We spent our free days hiking through the White Mountains, never noticing the steep climbs as we were lost in each other, foraging wild berries, or taking in the exquisite beauty all around us. He even crafted a pair of handmade leather hiking boots for me, so we could continue to share our passion for nature—together. Initially, I accepted his marriage proposal but when it came time to meet his parents and tie the knot, I fled.

It's not that I don't like men, to the contrary, I do not have a gender preference and engage in varied platonic friendships. I think it is fair to say that neither Hank nor I are well-versed in up-close exposure or commitment. He is a nice enough guy with a charismatic singing voice. *Why not?* We have this one ginormous thing in common, the pursuit of non-dual truth. I'm at the top of the mountain (so to speak). But I would rather sidestep relationships, even though a part of me gets that intimacy won't develop in a void. We quietly comingle within the SAT culture, which doesn't lend itself to transparency or closeness. He chants, I sit nearby in silence, awkwardly wondering to myself, *how do you do relationships sober?*

When I find out I am pregnant with our first baby, my impulse is not to mention a word to Hank, to muzzle myself like a dog. I know he will not jump with joyful anticipation like I am. In the eight years I've known him, his attention to his spiritual practice is single-pointed. He never misses an opportunity to disappear into his closet to meditate, as if having a conversation with me about our pregnancy would diminish his dedication to enlightenment or incur disappointment from the male leaders that he venerates.

In an ambiguous, taciturn way, he conveys his view that the role of a parent does not fit in with spiritual progression—'enlightenment.' He wants to pursue his own process of awakening and perhaps imagines that a baby will not keep quiet through hours of meditation.

As a woman, I may be expected to accept his views and adjust to an accommodating role in our relationship, like a dress on a secondhand clothing rack. My early religious training in Catholicism centered on the men who officiated mass and performed sacraments. Sisters (nuns) taught religious education and took a vow of abstinence from sexual relationships that would lead to building a family. I have yet to see women who become mothers maintain a central role in a spiritual community. My friend Cathy, who traveled through India in her youth, received validation for her spiritual dedication until she and her husband decided to have children. Their contributions were no longer valued. Soon they left the organization with conflicted feelings. Among my female friends who are spiritual teachers, every one of them feels they have had to make a choice between having children or teaching. They do not see a way to bridge spiritual devotion with raising children as a valued dharma. I draw back, listen intently inside, and announce to myself, *I AM and I AM with baby.* I imagine that birthing a baby is the most ecstatic sacred experience a woman might have. I imagine birth opens spirituality to include all human experiences and emotions, like anguish and heartbreak. The courage to love and give birth must be included—*who are we without the mother?*

Little by little, I will learn how the institutionalization of male dominance overshadows the choices of women, placing the life of the householder on the periphery of spiritual significance and care. The more I discover, the hungrier I feel to unpack our past and research the actual facts of women's history to learn how our consciousness evolves to mature, heal, and live in natural beautiful ways.

———

The publication I dedicate myself to is *The Ribhu Gita*—a lengthy dialogue between Ribhu and a disciple named Nidhaga on the nature of Reality. When Ramana Maharshi was asked "What scripture do you recommend reading for *sadhana[7]?*" he said, "Read *The Ribhu Gita* over and over again."

With no time to dally, the project gives me a sense of routine and purpose, tickled with our baby taking up more space in my womb. Little do I know that these teachings will not help me to understand myself as a woman. *Could it be that Ribhu and Nidhaga are men?*

———

In 1994 when I told Hank about our pregnancy, I was aware that outside of SAT ashram life—we do not have an independent life. Our discussion ends with Hank seeking guidance and validation from his spiritual guru. The history of inequality and injustices toward women sits in me like rocks but I'm learning to unbury myself.

For the first time in my life, I recognize the extent of the danger that has surrounded me my entire life. In centering men, women are not safe. *Is it safe to have a baby?*

Do I believe that bread crumbs from the table of patriarchy can feed me with something I do not already possess inside? Probably—unconsciously. My instinct to trust my lived experience is overshadowed by power dynamics I stumble to navigate. Again, I yearn to circle with wise women like Eunice around a cook fire, hear stories, and share about the good fortune of birthing life. Later, I will realize that telling the truth is different than finding the truth.

---

[7] Sadhana: literally means spiritual practice. A means of following your heart rather than the conditioned mind or egoic nature and fulfilling your soul's purpose or the deep call of your life.

I fell prey to funding positions of privilege without considering that I was depriving myself of power and meaningful connections. *Was I complacent in perpetuating a damaged system?*

Hank returns from the meeting with his spiritual teacher. His guru tells him he can renounce our child into my care. The sun sinks. I know I will not sleep. I toss and turn, considering women's history, our exclusion from spirituality is savagely alive. I wrinkle like a glacial rock. My body ice cold, trembling under the sheets, my mind flogging me with *I told you so. Relationships are dangerous; you'll never get it right; run—that's what you do best.* My eyes wander, not really seeing anything. After many nights of thrashing in bed, something jolts awake inside my body and plagues me with a certain, edgy feeling, one that I won't shed for some years to come.

"Get on with it! He is not your teacher." These were the final words I heard from Eunice. As if she said them yesterday.

7
She is Here — Ecstatic Birth

E arly Sunday afternoon, November 13, 1994, on the forty-minute drive from Satsang to our home, I crave pumpkin pie. Unfortunately, Hank and I have not grown any closer. He crosses his arms when I bring up the topic of baby. I rub my back and wave to our soon-to-be-born baby without rebelling against his spiritual ideation to renounce this precious child. I have to reserve my energy and keep my shoulders wide—my breath in my belly. I'm so huge I move like a tortoise. The all-too-common responses—"we'll see," "maybe," "I don't know"—weigh on me when I try to provoke interest. I guard myself from flares of insults with fantasies of the girl to come. I continue to work through this pregnancy. I'm covering the bills while he completes a degree at San Jose State University that will advance him from a tech writer to a computer programmer. *Odd, I know.*

Hank is strumming his guitar in the living room. I waddle into the kitchen, eager to whip together pumpkin filling for pies. Luckily, I bought two pre-made shells at the market, given I've never been successful at making homemade pie shells. I want to eat the filling raw, but I slide the pies in the oven, pretending Hank is singing for our child soon to come. The moment I close the oven door, an intense contraction thrusts through my pelvis. I grip the table and plant my feet firmly on the ground. I know I am in labor because my mom called for our traditional Sunday check-in, we're timing the minutes between each contraction. She wishes she were here, aware of the distance between Hank and I. Surprisingly, the time between contractions decreases rapidly. I'm not concerned, we have a carefully designed birth plan with a midwife team. Everything is in place for a natural home birth. We're keeping our birth space small and intimate, just us and our friends Julie and Karl (who also want a natural birth). Now, it's time to call the midwife.

Hank stiffens as if to stifle a gasp when I ask him to call Carolyn, our midwife. It will take her an hour to drive over Highway 17. Nevertheless, I relax and feel immense joy flooding through my body. Suddenly I find myself able to advocate for our birth with sharp clarity. I know what I need and repeat a flock of requests to Hank: "I need ice, no, a heating pad, crackers!" He wipes sweat from his forehead, treading to keep up with my fluctuating requests: "I need food. I'm shivering. My back burns." As soon as he settles me in the bathtub, I holler: "Are they here yet? Get ready—this baby is coming!" I don't think Hank imagined he could be the sole attendant to Autumn's birth. He jogs around the house gathering water, blankets, pillows, soothing music, and the food that I think I want to eat. He doesn't say more than "coming," but when Julie and Karl pop in through the front door an hour later, he embraces them like they are long-lost friends, finally found.

I find the prospect of Hank catching our baby on our living room floor rather comical—to face, head-on, something he hoped to avoid. *Now she is here.* I chuckle between contractions—*no way to bypass this reality.* I have no idea what Hank is thinking, he doesn't tell me. I've enjoyed every moment of this life chugging along nicely inside. With or without him, I savor every moment. As I breathe through each contraction, on the other side is a euphoric sensation. *I'm confident my body knows what do.* I yell and sweat in one moment and cry or laugh in the next. The range of feelings is exquisite—new life. Our friend's arrival gives Hank a chance to catch his breath and process the scene. Thirty minutes later, our midwife Carolyn and her assistant burst through the front door with baskets on each arm, only ten minutes before baby Autumn crowns her head. By this time, there isn't much left to do but breathe through an occasional robust push.

Carolyn coaches me through the final whirl of breathing, while Hank, Karl, and Julie hold my body as if they fashioned a stool with Velcro. They hold me firmly for indelible minutes until my body produces an epic, orgasmic push. All the cells in my body breathe in unison with our baby, collectively singing our praises. In some strange way, I am caught by a powerful line of mothers, who are at my back accentuating this sacred rite of passage. Autumn's head crowns, and with a gentle push she slips into Carolyn's hands. "Ahh," we chant in unison. Her head is shaped like a cone, elongated with vernix covering her shoulders, hands, and feet. Her eyes are wide open as if to anticipate an intimate audience. She peers around the room, taking a moment to look at each one of us. Her gaze pauses on Hank, unblinking, eyes shining as light as the hair on her head, without a sound. All of us remain perfectly still while she takes him in.

Hank is transformed on the spot, as if all tension left his body, proud of our creation. *At this moment, I imagine he forgot about renouncing her altogether.* Later, he will tell me, "I've never seen anything more beautiful, more perfect." I imagine he begins to consider himself as the father he is to our child. In the days to follow, he will be more present in our home life and will demonstrate a growing attachment to this delightful baby. *How could he not?* She is a direct reflection of him. She has his fair skin, blue eyes, light hair, and quiet nature. When he first heard about the pregnancy, he doubted he could be a father and advance spiritually simultaneously. Now, I sense his struggle, borne from his male privilege, to choose renunciation vanishing. He is the lead musician for the temple. I'm sure he doubts his ability to keep up with the pressure of producing and practicing new songs. He has not spoken about this, and perhaps I've held back from asking, anticipating the casual pass or rejection on tender topics.

But by the time Carolyn asks him to cut the umbilical cord, all of those concerns wash away. He steadily takes the scissors and smiles while he snips the cord, the way he had been shown in our birthing classes, with precision and grace; the same way he strums his guitar.

It is time for Autumn to latch onto my breast for her first suckle outside of my womb that carried her full term. Hank places her in my arms; she instinctively finds her way, as she did through the birth canal. The memory of Autumn's birth will etch itself deep in my soul memory. I will forever cherish the rightness, the ease, the beauty, the intelligence in my body, and the trust that powerfully—ecstatically birthed her through me. I will hold this experience dearer when later I learn that the euphoric, uninterrupted progression of our natural birth is not common for many women.

Autumn is a champion at nursing from the start. As I nurse her, I feel infinite gratitude for the miracle of milk flowing through my body to grow her and nourish our emotional bond. I feel hope reverberating from my womb to the womb of Mother Earth, fostering a connection that extends beyond time. In my work as a massage therapist, I've met mothers who schedule the delivery of their babies in a hospital. They tell me, "I'm afraid. Hospitals are safe." I don't judge this, I'm mildly aware of the flooding of medical interventions and movies that depict birth as a frightful experience, even a medical emergency. I tremble when I learn that some Hollywood celebrities schedule a C-section and a tummy tuck in one visit.

My midwife tells me that the ancient practice of women assisting other women to birth babies is lost to many women. It has become difficult for her to remain in practice, as obtaining insurance is prohibitive and most families cannot afford private pay expenses. I don't have a reason to consider this at the time but later I will. *Why would the medical complex instill fear into women about birth, and numb the powerful intelligence in our bodies, potentially severing our connection to baby and Mother Earth?*

Every time I nurse, I'm entranced. It's wild—instinctive, like a primordial connection to an ancestral line of women who birthed babies—an ecstatic initiation into motherhood. I want this experience for all mothers, to feel confident in an ancient practice that, with proper support and care, profoundly enriches life. We have infinite moments soaked in bliss, unable to imagine that this could go any other way.

8
Cast Out

B ut things do become different. When Autumn is six months old, Hank has a falling out with his teachers. He expressed his discontent in a letter to the guru who initially fueled his male entitlement. Like others who left or were asked to leave when their commitment shifted from the organization, Hank feels devalued—demoted. He's not happy when others perform the roles he fulfilled. Without consent, he adds my signature to his complaint. We are immediately axed from the community, for doubting 'enlightened' teachers demands for devotion. It doesn't matter that I did not write the letter with him, or that I am nourished by *The Ribhu Gita* project that consumes me. The Gita influences both baby and me in quiet, subtle ways, it guides me clear of the superficial gossip and narcissism that pervades the ashram. Shock, disbelief, and unfairness overwhelm me, followed by a hallowing void within.

My spiritual loss is accompanied by betrayal. I am excluded from a vital decision that warrants conversation, mutuality, and consent. *Is he not able to respect my choice of spiritual discipline? Am I invisible to him?* I feel violated at a soul level. Not being part of his decision to put my name on the letter adds to a growing stack of memories that are surfacing. Communication on topics that I genuinely care about is compromised. I'm not sure my thoughts and feelings register with him and if we are a team. I realize that the foundation of our relationship is built on our involvement with SAT and lacks the depth of true friendship that fosters brave conversations. I long for authentic connection. And I want Autumn to have her father in her life. Running isn't an option. I will not leave, and I want to understand why I stay in unfulfilling relationships with emotionally unavailable men and the communities they control. I nod to our precious daughter, who loves her daddy and I seek to be wise.

Later, on the day we are ejected from SAT, I sit on the sofa with Autumn on my lap—a prayer spontaneously rises within me: *If serving this teaching is not my dharma, my purpose—what is?*

I cherish this delightful child attached to me day and night. I initiate Mommy and Me yoga classes where we meet playmates to celebrate the joys of motherhood together. It doesn't take long for my spiritual practice to take a surprising turn, an exciting turn: this community of mothers and babies promptly replaces SAT, offering meaningful ordinary connections. During meditation, I question spirituality altogether. The blinders to life outside spiritual allegiances fade. I see the spark of divinity within me, my baby, and everyone I meet. *Isn't being a mother to Autumn enough? Am I devaluing motherhood?*

It's June 1996. After missing my moon for two months, I ride my bicycle six blocks to the drugstore to purchase the home pregnancy kit rated 99% accurate. I already know what the result will be for two reasons: first, my body rhythm is regular, and second, Hank and I are not like the couples you hear about in Tantric workshops or Cosmopolitan magazine. I can count our passion episodes on one hand and three fingers.

I edge my way to the store bathroom, close the door, double-lock it, pee on the stick, close my eyes, and wait three minutes. When I open my eyes, the stick is flashing—baby green. It's time to tell Hank.

On Sunday afternoon the sea is calm and the sun is beginning its descent. A soft cool breeze gingers the entryway of the open door. Hank and Autumn are building a bridge over an imaginary lake that spans the center of our living room carpet. I finish arranging the dinner table for three while wishing my mom a happy seventy-sixth birthday over the telephone.

"You better tell Hank," She urges before hanging up.

I decide to let dinner wait a bit longer and enter the game. I slither around the circumference of the lake.

"Close it, Daddy."

"It's a floating bridge, Pumpkin; it's not needed."

"Mommy, a bridge, water," spouts Autumn.

"I see the big bridge reaching across the lake."

"Hey, is it time to eat?" queries Hank.

I pause, anxiously wondering how to form a bridge. I plunge as if entering a race. "I have news for you. We're having a baby!"

"Baby. Me baby," Autumn chimes in with her singsong voice, lightening a tongue-tied moment.

Hank mutters, on his way to the kitchen, "Oh, really?"

"Yes, really." I sharpen, eyeing his face for an emotional read.

"Oh, really?"

Strike or ball? I wonder. Like a pitcher, I wind up again and aim for the strike zone. In one breath, I divulge, "I took two tests; it is absolutely certain!"

"That's interesting," he comments as if speaking to no one at all. Then he walks toward the kitchen while rubbing his nose, "What did you make for dinner?"

"Minestrone soup," I mumble, picking up a wooden block. I toss it in a woven basket like a foul ball, aiming to alleviate the pressure building in my body.

"Market. Mommy. Bozo. Clown," Autumn cheers as she pops up and totters to her booster seat.

Hank lifts Autumn to her chair, sits down next to her, and samples the piping hot soup.

"It's hot. Want to have some cereal while it's cooling, Pumpkin?"

I look at Hank with incredulous eyes. "What? No. We're not bringing out cereal!"

That is one of the many directions from my mother not easily shed in my adult life. Substitute boxed cereal for homemade cooking? Never. Irked, I remember to breathe, then I try to ignore Hank's gesture and the fury it triggers in me. I blew on Autumn's soup and lectured about the nutritional value of homemade soup. "Remember the vegetables from the farmer's market, when we saw Bozo the clown and picked herbs from our garden?" I stop; my voice is shaky. Suddenly I'm overtaken with an urge for a hot fudge ice cream with bananas and nuts. Hank proceeds to eat Cheerios with milk as if he were the only person in the room. Like gravy congealing over a low flame, the invisible wall between our worlds thickens. Like many conversations before, this one is canceled. *Ugh!* I want to sprint out and scream, but baby Autumn is here. She needs one of us to be present. After I put Autumn to sleep, my eyes twitch. I want the release of tears, to know that I do not have to harden. Hank has retreated to his closet, probably to meditate. I sneak out for a brisk walk by the sea. I do this often to calm my nerves and connect to nature. It relaxes me for a while.

A few weeks later, on a Friday morning, I rise at dawn and take a walk along the coast. Autumn and Hank are just waking when I return, smelling of briny ocean air. I feel hearty and healthy in all ways except one. I spend most days on the verge of throwing up. I try not to complain, meeting each wave of nausea with joyful acceptance that the life inside is chugging along just fine.

After breakfast, Hank shoots out the front door to beat the traffic over Highway 17 to his job in San Jose. He seems to be fully focused on his career and playing his guitar. This might be his way of recovering from leaving the SAT. He collects everything he can find on a particular spiritual teacher or musician and spends days or weeks privately consuming. When he is finished, he gathers it all into a box, takes it to Logos, the local bookshop, and sells it without a word about it. I remember once seeing books about the Beach Boys. I asked him if I could have a look. He told me he already sold them back to the bookshop. Oh, I said, squeezing the ache in my belly. The ache to be valued as an equal— a friend.

Autumn and I take a warm lavender bath together in the upstairs bathroom. I've grown larger. Autumn's hands look smaller as she places them atop my extended belly.

"Baby, Mommy?"

"Yes, honey, the baby is inside growing a little bit each day," I say, as I lather up a washcloth and clean the sand out from between her toes, singing, "This little piggy went to market; this little piggy went wee-wee-wee ..."

"Ticka," Autumn splashes and giggles.

"The tickle queen," I say, plucking her out of the tub and placing her on the mat. "Carolyn the midwife will be here soon. We have to dry off and get dressed." I grasp the towel bar to steady myself on the way out of the tub.

Autumn turns her face to look at mine, the long lashes and round cheeks still wet from the bath. "Baby?"

The due date is still five months away. I am suddenly conscious that Autumn will only be two—still a baby when the new baby is born, and perhaps she is aware of the same.

Hank is home for our initial meeting with Carolyn but tells me he doesn't feel it is necessary for him to attend every bi-monthly visit. Autumn is latched onto my breast, absorbed in her own wonder when the doorbell rings. She stays on my lap throughout the examination until I have to lie down on the carpet to measure my girth. I am two months into the second trimester, a period marked by rapid growth. The amount of food I am eating is typical, yet I have already reached the width I was during my first pregnancy at seven months. "This is unusual."

Carolyn suggests an ultrasound at Dominican Hospital as soon as possible to rule out any complications due to extensive distention.

When Carolyn leaves, Kym Ann, her assistant, stays.

"Do you think you are going to have another girl like Autumn?" she asks, squeezing Autumn around the waist. "Maybe a girl. I haven't given it much thought."

I lower my eyes and return to an inner occupation. "Hank is still digesting the idea of another baby altogether. Even if I knew the sex, I imagine he doesn't want to talk about names. I can barely get him to talk about the book he is reading. He doesn't invite me into his private world. The door is shut."

Kym Ann listens quietly. She scheduled a sonogram for the following Tuesday. I asked her to come with me, Hank doesn't want to miss work.

The next Tuesday, Autumn, Kym Ann, and I make our way to the ultrasound department. The lab technician's name is Tracy, a sprite five-foot-two, wearing khaki pants and white sneakers as if she'd be equally at home on the tennis courts. After greeting us with a vigorous handshake and a flashing smile for Autumn, she leads us into a small, cubical-shaped room containing just two chairs and several hooks along the wall. She hands me a white gown to change into and directs me to come, alone, when I am ready to the radiology room.

"Your sister and the baby can wait in the room to the left. This won't take long. We'll snap a few pictures, look at the results, and you'll be on your way." She breezes away before I can tell her that Kym Ann is my midwife's assistant. I feel comforted knowing Kym Ann is nearby. There is a feeling in my gut that compels me to keep her close by like a sister helping me to birth well.

In the short time we wait for Tracy to return, the memory of the sudden expulsion from SAT when Autumn was six months old hits me like a lightning bolt, body tremors turn to an icy, eerie pulsation. A tenacious feeling not easy to dodge, like an inner gale foreshadowing a storm—danger. Without time to process, I'm pulled out of this when Tracy breezes through the door like a singing telegram.

"I have good news for you. Come close." I lick my lips, remembering where I am, sitting here in oversized stretch jeans that cover my width with a cotton smock. Autumn is snug on my right knee, bouncing and babbling a tune from Mother Goose. Kym Ann is to my left, perusing Life magazine.

Tracy pulls her chair closer to mine. Well-versed in the familiar behaviors of nervous mothers-to-be, including those who are required to have a sonogram taken mid-pregnancy, she takes my hands and whispers, "Are you ready?"

Her kind smile lightens my worry. I will never forget the easeful delight of birthing Autumn—the unequivocal ecstasy and confidence.

I tell myself: *everything is going to be fine. We'll have another natural home birth, like Autumn, with friends all around us.* Then Tracy exclaims, "You're having twins—girls."

My fingers fall from my mouth. A surge of panic and elation soar through my system. "What?" My attention caves inward. A hollowing sense similar to the abandon that I felt when Eunice died, when the *Ribhu Gita* project was swept out from under my feet, stripping away spiritual purpose is here now. Yet this time it's different; it's not empty. It is as if the same unsolicited prayer that rose in the pantry, "Who am I?" and on that stormy morning when I was axed from SAT community is here, now in the sonogram image—staring me in the face, mirroring a enigma. The longing for Spirit that has echoed through my body over and over since I was seven, and prophesized by RW, "Your children will join you." The longing I felt in my girlhood to weave my life with Spirit— to blaze a spiritual path that values the voice, body, and life of a woman— *motherhood*. It's extraordinary, exhilarating, and scary all at once. *What is happening?*

"Holy shit" are the exact words that come out of my mouth. *Is this some kind of initiation?* My inner reflection shifts to the conundrum with Hank. *How do I tell Hank?* Perhaps casually, as he heads out the door for work so as not to endure the stalemate that will likely follow. "Oh, by the way. We aren't having one baby; we're having TWO babies. Have a good day, honey!"

On the way home from the hospital with Kym Ann and Autumn, I'm speechless and preoccupied. Twins! My friend Leni is a twin. Other than Leni, the twins on *The Patty Duke Show* (the 60s sitcom) are my only reference point. Two of everything. Two more breakfast settings. Two more tricycles. Two more girls chasing each other barefoot on the beach, "Look what I found!" Autumn will have live-in playmates. These images delight something inside, while at the same time, I am not able to ignore a strange feeling that lingers in my gut—*a premonition?* What is going on behind the images of two four-month-old fetuses in the manila envelope tucked in my diaper bag? I can't tag it. *Is it my age? Loneliness in my relationship? How dharma might change?* I don't understand, only that I ache for connection.

Regardless of Hank's reluctance to acknowledge or participate in planning for these babies, I've hired Carolyn to be our midwife again. When I tell Carolyn about the sonogram and that I am pregnant with twins, she wants to track us closely. She reminds me to meet with an OBGYN at our local hospital. She schedules a sonogram with her professional technician toward the end of the second semester.

We set up regular prenatal care appointments as we plan for another home birth. When I ask her if she thinks we can have another home birth given I'll be thirty-nine at the time of delivery, she doesn't hesitate. She tells me, "Your body knows how to deliver babies. I'm sure you'll do well." In following predetermined directives maintained by obstetric medical authorities, she adds, "We will also create a hospital backup plan." I agree to plan B, which means I will speak with an OBGYN at our local hospital to arrange medical care if needed. But neither of us imagines that will happen. "Your body knows how to make babies. I barely made it in time to catch baby Autumn. And your pies are fabulous."

It is close to Autumn's naptime. She sings loudly from her car seat in the back as if she is switching stations on the radio. I usually lie down with her and fall asleep. I know I won't sleep today. I feel like I've had a double cappuccino with ten lumps of sugar. Activated. Telling Hank about one baby was like climbing Mt. Everest. Telling him about twins will be like climbing it in winter—naked!

Later that day, I stroll along a dirt path that trails beside a creek near our house, with Autumn like an appendage in the sling worn over my chest. I know of nothing more mesmerizing than watching this baby suckle herself to sleep.

When she was a newborn, I brought her to work with me. She slept in her baby carrier while I gave massages or kept the books. When she became more active, I sold my twelve-year-old business in Silicon Valley to stay home and track her every move. Health and wellness businesses thrived, and my client base was well-established. I easily received a lucrative sum for my business. This is one way the self-reliant character my mother instilled in me gains credibility. I hope to endure as a creative breadwinner. With Autumn at my side, I sell baby slings and teach Mommy and Me yoga classes. One night a week I work as a massage therapist at a local spa, while she is in good hands. One of the benefits of working at this spa is I get to use the hot tub, sauna, and cold plunge facilities, which will become an integral part of my self-care in the years to come.

Even though Hank and I barely connect emotionally, we manage to co-exist, finding cordiality—albeit shallow—as we parent Autumn in our family of three. Life seems simple and uncomplicated, perhaps better than many, given that we can afford to live in Santa Cruz. Weird and thorny though this is, it is the first time in almost twenty years that I am living outside of a cultish organization where I opted for celibacy and silence, ignorant of the need to build self-advocacy and relationship skills. Now, I'm unmarried, with a toddler and twins on the way, without a bona fide guide. I feel naïve as it dawns on me that Hank, like my father and the male teachers I followed, was never interested in my responses. They already confidently knew the answers; I just needed to adjust and comply.

In the shallows of my memory, I recall fragments of a lecture by Carol Gilligan, a psychologist at Harvard University, who wrote about the powerful messages young girls receive from those around them to be compliant, quiet, and to suppress open expression of feelings, especially if they are non-compliant.

"The way people talk about their lives is of significance, that the language they use and the connection they make reveal the world that they see and in which they act."[8]

I sat in the back of the crowded lecture hall, intimidated, littered with theological discourse from my graduate studies that suggests the logic of the male voice dictates the final act. In her research, Gilligan noticed the recurrent problems in interpreting women's development and connected these problems to the repeated exclusion of women from the progression of critical thinking to define their rights and shelter their choices. *I feel these imprints.* I tiptoe around the heaviest emotions. I want to rescue the soothing currents of my soul that were intact when I sat with Eunice. Her sagacious eyes revealing, guiding me to shed judgments, fantasies, and introjects that block my voice and keep me small. *I wonder what her life was like when she became a mother?*

These recollections are soothing me now as I sit by this bubbling brook in this grassy meadow with baby Autumn napping on my lap. I take long, deep, savoring breaths, drawn to her adorableness. I rub the ache in my neck from my irresistible habit of harvesting her serenity. Then, for seemingly no reason at all, tears pour down my face, splatter on Autumn's eyelids, and trickle across her face. Tears layered with gratitude, hope, and a reoccurring sinister swirling

---

[8] Carol Gilligan, *In A Different Voice: Psychological Theory and Women's Development* (Harvard University Press, 1993, 2016). Introduction.

of dread that plucks at my soma: *The felt sense of connection to my babies and the fracture from their father. The yielding to systems that endorse bad behavior for men. The ghostly slugs of toxicity. After all that I've learned, why do I shrink?*

My sleeping baby reminds me of the innocence we are born with. When I breathe deeply, one moment at a time, I feel that nothing in life is wasted. Every experience has a part to play in the larger unfolding of our lives. I've crawled on my knees through ugly and painful experiences only to muscle up and work harder as if this would make me impervious to heartbreak and trauma. Eunice showed me trust, a way to open, mend wounds, and stand on my legs. I have more layers to heal but don't I need a willing partner? *I want to understand the archetypes of women's psychology, shadow, and soul work.*

I imagine myself rooted like a robust tree, Autumn one of my branches. I know it is my responsibility to tend the weeds and nourish our soil to keep us strong. I delight in knowing that I am free to be Autumn's mommy and that dharma and motherhood intermingle as one path, maturing together. *How could it be different?* I am here with her on my lap.

I invite Kym Ann for dinner to help me navigate this long-standing emotional barricade. "I won't be able to fall asleep until I tell Hank and make another effort to connect," I say, rubbing my face with my hands.

"The suspense is killing me," she admits.

"I could eat this entire jar," I say, licking the spoon, reckoning I'm both frustrated and hungry. Pissed that I find communicating with Hank nearly impossible.

Kym Ann pours both of us a cup of mint tea. We sit at the kitchen table for a bit before Autumn wakes up. She counsels. I heap and crunch slice after slice. I binge.

Hank arrives home from work at the usual time, 5:10 p.m. Autumn brings Kym Ann a cloth book from a wicker basket on the floor when Hank walks in the front door, black briefcase in his hand.

"Hello, Pumpkin." He lifts Autumn up into his arms and gives her a big hug. She wraps her arms around his neck, "Daddy."

He nods his head to Kym Ann and me; we are on all fours, lowering our bellies downward, raising butts and lifting heads, inhaling for cow pose. I can't hold the inhale, I raise my back, lower my head, and exhale loudly like an angry cat, fiery sensations swirling.

"What are you guys up to?"

"Prenatal yoga. Kym Ann is here for dinner, it's almost ready." I say, aware that I'm taming my angry cat pose with man-pleasing, a habit that frequently saved my ass in my younger days. My eyes dart to the envelope that is sitting on the wooden coffee table in front of the couch. My fingers fumble as I pick it up. Heat flushes to my head, accompanied by familiar nausea. I fiddle with the envelope as I remind Hank of the recent examination with Carolyn and her suggestion to get a sonogram.

"Hmmm. We'll have to see," is his measured response, revealing less than a sliver of emotion. Now, his posture appears the same; uninformative, absent of emotion. He reaches for the envelope.

Kym Ann lifts Autumn onto her lap and begins reading *Hop on Pop* by Dr. Seuss. Autumn is happily jumping her body up and down.

"I want to show you," I tell him, clutching the envelope to my chest. "Would you like to sit down?" I deliberately breathe width to my thinning voice.

He sits at the other side of the table and adjusts his glasses. "What is it?"

I tip my head toward Kym Ann. She nods in my direction as if I'm holding the last present on Christmas waiting to be opened.

I pull out the photographs and nimbly place them on the table.

"Hank, we're having twins—two babies."

The only sound that can be heard is a drop of water from the faucet in the kitchen.

"This is baby A and this is baby B. Two babies. We're having twins," I pepper, trying to smooth the ruffled edges in my voice.

Hank methodically picks up the first photo, examines it for a minute, and places it back down on the table without uttering a sound. Then he picks up the second picture, looks at it closely, and sets it down. Full stop.

Blank yet matter-of-fact, he says, "Oh, I see. This is side A and this is side B."

I swallow, my voice dissolves. I pull it up again, clear my throat, exhale a cough, and push on. "No. This is baby A and this is baby B. There are two babies. Twins. Double. Two."

He picks up both photos and holds them up to the light, shifting his eyes back and forth from one to the other and back again. He sets them back on the table. "Yes. I see. Side A and side B of the same baby."

I look at Kym Ann and narrow my eyes as if to say *Am I the only one seeing double? What the fuck?*

Like a mid-morning summer breeze, Kym Ann pipes in, "Hank, they are two different images of two distinct babies, not a back side and a front side. You are having two babies. Twins."

I pour glasses of ice water to chill the air and give the news a chance to land with Hank. I'm sure it doesn't. He walks upstairs, without a pardon.

9
Plan B

O ctober 18, 1996. Autumn is my favorite season, the cool air is glistening with festive red, yellow, and orange leaves that remind me to harvest this precious time with my toddler. My twins are due in three months. I am twenty-six weeks into our pregnancy when a strong tightening across my abdomen wakes me up. My heart is fluttering. The pain is sharp but bearable; I don't want to arouse Autumn, she is nestled beside me, fast asleep. I attempt to get out of bed. Her ruby lips open, colored with my milk, and shaped in perfect symmetry, like a smooth octagon. An angelic glow of bliss illuminates her delicate face.

I slowly roll over, gasp for breath, and muffle the sound with a pillow. After taking a long inhalation, I wipe the sweat from my forehead. I apply gentle pressure with both hands to the cramping in my lower abdomen. A smile crosses my lips as I feel the thrust of subtle movements from the two lives chugging along inside. I push myself up to a sitting position, swing my legs over the edge of the bed, and anchor my feet to the ground. My pelvis aches from the weight of the twins. I make a feeble attempt to push myself out of bed; my body craves sleep. My feet ache and no longer fit into my size-nine slippers, they look like puffed-up clouds before a rainstorm.

Weakening, I fall back onto the violet sheet and notice a few spots of bright red blood where I was sleeping. I turn toward the open screen door of the balcony window and stare blankly out at a gray and orange misty sky. Fishy seaweed aroma infuses the ocean air. Nauseated, I turn away, but the melodious barking of a family of sea lions shakes my trance. I gaze at the long golden eyelashes of my twenty-one-month-old toddler. She has her father's big blue eyes and resembles Hank in many ways, light complexion and quiet disposition. I'm happy that I didn't wake her, but I'm unsure of what to do. I'm concerned.

———————

The blood spots have dried. I edge my way past a tall wooden dresser that is slightly wider than me, making my way through a dark, narrow hallway to a second bedroom that is a temporary makeshift office and playroom. The intensity of the sensation passes. My body is limp. I do not see fresh blood. Hank and I haven't considered preparing this room for the twins. What the heck, they aren't due until January and we barely speak.

Halfway down the hallway I hastily turn back to pull on oversized underpants. I want to protect the beige tufted carpet from a possible blood stain, but I buckle over, struggling to breathe through the next wave of discomfort. Hank has already left the closet where he secludes for morning meditation and is driving to his office in San Jose. I don't bother to call him. It would take more than one hour to drive back home during Saturday morning beach traffic. Instead, I reach for the receiver of our push-button phone and press number 3 to speed dial Kym Ann. She lives in the same neighborhood, on the other side of Garfield Park.

I learn that Carolyn, our midwife, is in Half Moon Bay attending to the birth of another child. As a good midwife, she is aware that true delivery dates are rarely exact and is careful not to book clients within close proximity. She is not able to leave this birth.

I brace my body, sink into a cushioned rocker recliner, and drop the telephone receiver into a pile of wooden toys, warily reviewing plan B, the hospital backup agreement I made with Carolyn. I don't want to go there.

Getting off the phone with Carolyn, I feel baffled, curious, and uncertain.

She tells me our medical backup (plan B) is not optional. Soon, I will discover that women's sovereignty is not supported in modern pregnancy.

———————

Memories and questions implode in my body. Memories that remind me of Eunice and questions that I wish I could ask, receive answers to, and integrate into my current dilemma. *What road do I take?* Somehow, I know that the spiritual path I've been trained to follow has come to a dead end. The women who went before were not allowed to leave a trail.

Before I met Eunice, my early experience in Catholicism planted a deep-seated belief that the female gender by definition is inferior, silenced—devalued. I remember blushing the first time I heard the word "Goddess," as if it was a violation of an almighty code. My mind couldn't easily register the idea of feminine spirituality and dreaded the idea of a confined role as a mother. Eunice urged us to leave the house of the fathers and the hubris of the male system-builders.

Unworthiness is a trance I'm familiar with as if an unconscious psychic force insists that I prove myself—*I am capable.* This force was on board a few weeks prior to this sudden onset of contractions. I was the parent who walked into the course at Dominican Hospital for parents pregnant with two or more babies— alone, carrying my baby in a sling. Although I am uncomfortable with Western medicine, I agree with this part of plan B. I sat in the back of the class, bothered, while an assured nurse spouted out a list of common complications. The list was long—miscarriages, preemies, C-sections, the babies' inability to latch on, low birth weight, and bottle-feeding—and raised the temperature in the room, which activated my internalized self-reliant, overcompensating, afraid self. *Not me, not me,* I puffed to myself, sitting partnerless, as cool as a cucumber, in the back row. *None of that will happen to me. I am the proud mother of a home birth with zero complications. Thank you very much. We're good. Look at us. My baby is nursing just fine.* I walked out early as if the song "We Are the Champions" was playing over the loudspeaker just for Autumn and me.

In reality, I went to this childbirth class for twins to learn how to have a successful labor and delivery, and what to do if concerns arise. Soon I felt the confidence I reaped from Autumn's natural, ecstatic home birth drain out of me. The instructor spent most of the time covering complications as if these were the common course. Anxiety and doubt covered the room like a weighted blanket. *Why lead us to worry?* I knew from my work as a yoga instructor that higher levels of anxiety increase stress hormones. In labor, stress hormones chase away oxytocin, the hormone that helps labor progress naturally without intervention. I wanted to breathe oxygen into my brain. I knew the symptoms of trauma, which range from muddled thinking, agitation, numbness, exhaustion, and dissociation to blackout. Feeling afraid did not feel like a good way to approach birth. I reviewed Dr. Bradley's *Method for Natural Childbirth*, the book I read when I was pregnant with Autumn. It emphasizes birth as a natural process and helps me relax.

The significance of our women's circles with Eunice will take time to crystalize in my life. *Life cannot take place where women are not involved. We are uniquely different—we have wombs.* Eunice spoke of the need for women to join together, clarify our values, and trust our instincts, *as was the case for Autumn's ecstatic home birth.* I decided to stay with my yoga practice of deep breathing, eating well, and doing my best to remember what I know deep in my bones.

Back in my bedroom, as the first light of day is shining through the manila venetian blinds, the contractions feel light. Kym Ann arrives, double-steps up the stairs, a glass jar of red raspberry leaf tea in one hand, a bamboo basket overflowing with bundles of herbs, books, and bottles of water in the other. She kneels down next to me, pulling her full-length skirt above her knees.

"Are you hot?" she smiles, as she sticks a digital thermometer under my armpit.

"It's 99. 3," she reads aloud, setting the thermometer in her bag and tying her ruby-streaked brunette dreadlocks behind her. She smells of jasmine and rosemary mint. Her gentle blue eyes, olive skin, and rosy cheeks come into view.

"My back is burning."

Kym Ann flips on the ceiling fan, dabs my face and armpits with a cold washcloth from the bathroom, then offers me an ice-cold bottle of water from her ready-to-go bag. She is prepared to travel. By now, both of us have had a brief phone conversation with Carolyn and reluctantly decided that Kym Ann would drive me to Dominican Hospital to check for dilation of my cervix. Everything about my pregnancy has been normal, but we go to the hospital as planned. There is a good chance that I am having Braxton-Hicks contractions,[9] which is the body's way of preparing for true labor. They do not always indicate that labor has begun or is going to start. The tightening in my abdomen comes and goes, my body is tired. I'm hopeful that I will be asked to finish out this pregnancy with bed rest.

It's half past eight Friday morning when Kym Ann drives us in her blue Nissan through town up Highway 1 to the main entrance of Dominican Hospital. We walk through a glass door that automatically slides open to a neatly organized lobby with signs that direct the flow of traffic. Urgency splinters the air. A surge of adrenaline washes through my body. I want to turn around and go home but I also want to respect Plan B.

Kym Ann is holding me firmly under the arm, hauling me to the reception desk, where an aging woman with grey hair tied in a bun greets us with a sleepy smile through an open window. She rushes us through the inevitable signing of papers and insurance checks as if there is a long line behind us, but there isn't.

Kym Ann had called Hank at work. He returned home to make arrangements for Autumn to stay with his parents until we returned from the hospital. When Autumn heard that her mommy needed to go to the hospital without her, she ran around the living room, dumped over a basket of laundry, and tossed her tattered stuffed Piglet and slippers into the kitchen, screaming, "I want my Mommy!" I imagine Hank holding her in his arms, assuring her she would see me soon. When she wiggles free to bang her fists on the front door, calling for Mommy, Hank soothes her with the bribe of a vanilla cherry ice cream from the Polar Bear Parlor.

Registration is complete and a nurse walks me to an examination room; Kym Ann is close behind. Doctor Hopkins a jovial woman close to my age with a gentle demeanor, arrives in a white lab coat. The examination begins at a slow

---

[9] Braxton Hicks Contractions: Contractions that feel like a tight band around your abdomen and are normal during pregnancy. These contractions can occur with increasing frequency as you get closer to your due date, and occur more often if you have previously given birth. Braxton Hicks contractions do not open the cervix and do not mean you are likely to have a premature baby. They often occur when you have intercourse, lift heavy items, or urinate. You can have one per day or several, but they do not come at regular intervals.

pace with a light exchange about the anticipation of giving birth to twins, tempered with the sober details covered during a prenatal exam. The duration and frequency of my contractions are sporadic and mild. My water hasn't broken. I easily maintain an ebullient conversation. She begins another cervical exam without telling me why. The mood in the room shifts quickly, growing uneasy. My champion voice perks up, "My first baby was born at home, and you know what?"

Dr. Hopkins peeks her eyes above the glasses that have fallen to her nose, "What?" "She was born in just under two hours. Our midwife barely made it through the door in time to catch her. Dad almost had to catch her. It was a wild time!" I babble on about how I made pumpkin pies, put them in the oven to bake, the timer went off, and labor began. "Autumn was soon easily born and we all ate pie!"

Somewhere in the midst, of boosting my confidence about birth, the walls tighten. Dr. Hopkins is speaking rapidly to someone on the phone. I'm puzzled—stunned, actually, when I make out that she is arranging to take me up an elevator to meet a helicopter. She hangs up the phone, looks at me as if she just got wind of a terrorist in the building, and shudders; "If your babies are going to be born now, we cannot handle the high-risk factors." Without my consent, she announces, "We are sending you on a helicopter to Stanford Hospital, where they have the best neonatal intensive care unit in the country. You will be there in twenty minutes."

"Huh? What? Can you repeat, more slowly please?" I plead. I'm worried—uncertain about what is happening. She doesn't consider that I might not want to go, or that this could be Braxton-Hicks. "Not now. We have to go. The technician on the helicopter will explain." She hurries me down a hall in a wheelchair as if an alarm is sounding and everyone is evacuating the building. But I don't hear it. The pace accelerates. Dazed, I fade into the memory of Autumn's perfect birth—craving a fat piece of pumpkin pie covered in whipped cream, and a long nap.

Now I am half-dressed, secured to a gurney, winding through a brightly lit corridor, and whisked into an elevator more spacious than my kitchen. I'm wheeled onto an expansive rooftop, my hair is blown about by a swift wind, my twenty-six-week-old fetuses' snug in my ripening womb, with strangers loading us onto an emergency air transit helicopter. Kym Ann skids off; she is not allowed to travel with me. She will call Carolyn and Hank and meet me at Stanford Hospital. I'm alone with blurry thoughts to process a dramatic turn of events. I can't. I'm scared—a part of me numbing—disappearing, not believing that I am locked in a helicopter.

I do not meet the pilot; he is not visible. A medical technician is at my side, placing earmuffs over my head to protect my ears from the rapidly revolving overhead rotors that are swiftly lifting us up, up, and away from my people. I turn my head to the left, and look straight into his eyes, "What is happening?" He looks away, my voice muffled. I want him to pinch me and tell me, "This is a routine evacuation practice performed by the hospital, and you have been chosen for the surprise helicopter drill."

Just six weeks prior, Carolyn had taken me to a first-rate sonographer, Dr. Joseph Frank, in Los Gatos for a certified ultrasound. She takes all of her home-birthing mothers to him as an essential part of her prenatal care. He uses state-of-the-art instrumentation to produce and evaluate a clear graphical representation of the uterus. His words are fresh in my mind: "There, you see it; two of everything—the inner sac, the outer sac, and the dividing membrane. You're doing great. They're traveling first-class." Much later, I learned this formation (d-/di) carries little if any complications. More hopeful now that I recall his words, I focus on deep inhalations and exhalations, into my body, into my babies.

I drift, reminiscing about Autumn and abalone earrings. We are at the Monterey Bay Aquarium; she is slung across my torso. Happy not to push a stroller, we nose up to the glass, eye-to-eye with enormous colorful fish, some double her size. When Autumn sees enough fish, she reaches up with her tiny hand to ding one of the abalone earrings dangling from my earlobe as if it were a bell. This is her way of communicating, *I am hungry*. Not that I need her to ring a bell. We are naturally attached to each other as if we knew each other before she was planted in my womb thirty-two months ago. She will wean when she is ready. I miss her now and she misses me. I can tell, as drops of milk are appearing on my hospital gown. I remember her circling the periphery of my vision, gathering seashells on the beach we were visiting, feeling the contoured edges in her little hands, gathering colored shapes, and toddling back to sit by my side, one time exclaiming, "Mommy, look! A seashell like your earring." I reach for my abalone earrings, but they aren't here. My earlobes are naked, adding to a numbing aloneness.

10
Incalculable Consequences

I t is Friday mid-afternoon, October 18, 1996. Our entrance into Stanford is blurry. The helicopter lands; although my legs are fine, I'm strapped to a gurney. They roll me to the far side of a double room on the obstetrics floor and transfer me to a single bed. I scan a shut window, I want to open it, release the stagnant air, and escape with my babies. A swarm of medical professionals encroaches upon my body like bees, simultaneously they check my vital signs and my cervix and hook me up to a monitor at the foot of my bed that beeps regularly. As soon as I am left alone, contractions cease, my breath eases, and a soft glow lightens the room. I breathe. Minutes later they strike again— probing, prodding, measuring. Each time they return, my pulse quickens, and seemingly so do contractions. My eyes are misty but I don't cry. I crumble under the distress of frequent invasive examinations that persist throughout the weekend. Desperate, I ask, sometimes under my breath, other times as a bold plea: "Where is my midwife?" hoping for a response from the alternating attendant in blue scrubs.

Kym Ann has yet to arrive, an urge compels me to find her and bolt but I'm captured behind a closed door. *Would I feel safe with someone by my side to help me process, ask questions, and consider information?* My brain is ablaze, working hard to comprehend. I imagine that every bed is a commodity, that certain procedures pay better than others, and that my state insurance doesn't have optimal benefits. Apparently, our first doctor does not have time for eye contact, or Q&A. His shift will end soon. It is the weekend. He is guessing that my babies are two-and-a-half pounds, "large enough for a vaginal birth," but their state-of-the-art technology is down until Monday. I want to say, *Look at me, I'm here now.* I fist my hands, ready to punch, but I am strapped with no power to stop what is happening. When no one is intervening, I sleep.

Now I barely feel the pulse or slight kick of my babies, something I have come to count on and delight in. I want to feel this now. More than anything, I want to go home. *Has this abrupt change caused me to stop feeling—to disassociate?* I close my eyes, I enter a carefree world, ecstatically birthing the life of Autumn. She taught me to trust, *together we can do this.* Without intervention, *we feel what to do.* I listened and felt, a small quiet voice, an epic impulse, birthing new life. Now this instinct is crowded out, smothered by machines. The abrupt beeping, looming power dynamics, and the dense tension in a room the size of a cubicle smothers the connection I had come to trust about the lives nestled inside. I want to feel. I am forgetting—losing my grasp. Engulfed by an external mode of operation, my body clamors for sleep, rest, and quiet. For life. A wee voice prays to go home. I'm backed into a corner, muddled without an exit.

I vividly remember Carolyn arriving at the doorway, shock on her face, pushing to enter the room—to see me—to check the babies. Quickly she is turned away. "She is registered into our medical care. Midwives are prohibited on our grounds," she is told. I am told. We are told. I don't tag it at the time; it will take years of therapy to understand the trembling that engulfs me, a long-standing wound in the body of women, from high-ranking men that guard, explain, and dictate what is appropriate for her body as if she is an object of experimentation.

The attendant's pragmatic expression, pale white skin, and uncompromising charcoal eyes framed in wire-rim glasses run repeatedly through my mind as the pastel walls darken.

Under any other circumstance, I would not suppress my burning impulse to leap out of this dreadful bed like a deer fleeing a predator. This is not a possibility, as now there are three of us and every cell in my body is begging for sleep. I never consider that the doctors on duty are set to a different agenda, a regulated course of action that propels industrial childbirth. I am admitted, and once they register me, like it or not, I am their patient, subject to their laws—arrested. There's no plan for me to return home until a birth procedure takes place—yet the data is inconclusive: the baby's heart monitor is within normal range and my water is intact. My cervical exam registered three centimeters and to my knowledge that has not changed. A clear picture of the state or size of the babies has not happened. *What is happening?* This is what

I know. My babies are not in distress; I'm doing my best to remain calm. Our midwife Carolyn, who has been tracking my body closely for over three years is not permitted in this room. What I do not know or imagine are the incalculable ordeals that follow.

Kym Ann arrives on Friday afternoon but is not allowed to be by my side for several hours. When she finally comes in, she is unable to register the scene. She tries to smile, but her face is forlorn—subdued. My situation has radically shifted from a healthy pregnancy to what looks like a mama bear seized for a research experiment to accelerate birth production. She is not allowed to perform a cervical exam. Later I learn that labor can begin at 1 centimeter dilation, yet the time of giving birth varies greatly between women. Scenarios change, one woman may go from a closed cervix to giving birth in a matter of hours, while another is 1-2 centimeters dilated for days or weeks. My timed labor with Autumn was just less than two hours from when my water broke and climaxed with empowerment. Now I am numb, too tired to be angry, and I don't want to stress the babies.

When Hank arrives sometime in the night, his already light skin has faded to a pale, expressionless daze. He, like me, does not know what to say. Both of us are in the dark, perplexed to not be given hard data—accurate information within a prestigious hospital that holds great power. We tumble through dread. The emotional distance between us doesn't help.

There are two benefits to the semi-private room I am in. The lights are kept relatively low, and the bed next to me is vacant; either the person was transferred, released, or permanently asleep. I am the main attraction for the weekend staff. After Hank is able to settle Autumn with his parents on the other side of the hill, he and Kym Ann take turns visiting me. Both maintain a somewhat bemused yet supportive, quiet presence at my side. Intuitively, all of us understand that quiet and rest are the best we can count on other than hope for responsible action from an elusive staff. We press on with a calm, collected approach and finally convince the weekend staff to leave me alone. Whenever they do, sleep consumes me. We are told again that their state-of-the-art technology will be available first thing Monday morning to reveal vital information assumed to detain us. I wonder to myself and out loud: *Why don't they bring in the machine now, or send me home?*

By Sunday night, interventions are slight; my body is quiet—still. All three of us, Kym, Hank, and I picture us heading home soon.

On Monday morning, October 21, 1996, the hospital pace picks up; steam gathers like a locomotive pressed to reach a scheduled destination. I must have slept through the shift change from the weekend to the weekday staff. Dr. Arnold Kramer is the chief labor and delivery surgeon. He is at the end of my bed and curtly introduces himself, sizing me up before I can take in more than a scruffy dark beard. He is scribbling notes on his clipboard as I rub my eyes. My body is still—quiet. I push myself up, considering that he might be the sonogram technician ready to get a clear picture of the size and condition of my babies. I imagine that once he sees everything is fine, we'll be discharged home to bed rest. "Are you going to take a sonogram?"

"No." He answers with a coarse voice that does not invite comfort. He is not looking up from his clipboard. *I feel like an inconvenience.*

Apprehensive, I tip back like a defeated warrior and struggle to push myself up again. Before I ask another question, I fall back, shocked. Without permission, he has already advanced to a cervical exam. He looks at his watch and says with a big booming voice, "We're going to the OR. You have dilated to the point of no return."

My jaw drops open, throat gums, stricken, I fret, unsure if my voice sounds aloud. *"How can this be? I did not have any contractions throughout the night!"* I see the back side of his white lab coat saunter out the door. I manage to pull the sheet over my trembling body, face burning, panting like a child hiding from a monster. I want to outrun this nightmare. And I don't want to shake my babies. I agonize, too numb to fight, unsure of what is real. I remember to remember my babies, all of us trapped beneath wads of wires like chains. My arms stiffen around my womb. *Breathe calm. Breathe softly. Breathe calm. Stay here. Breathe. Slow, deep breath. We're okay. I'm staying. I'm here. I won't let anything bad happen to you.* But I have a stone in my throat. I've been here before. Unprotected. Unsafe. Without a voice. Without an ally.

Soon, a tall man appears wearing an identical white lab coat. I don't know if it is my powerlessness, his sheer size, or that his pockets are bulging with too many syringes. I quiver, my eyes shut.

When I open my eyes, I learn this tall man is an anesthesiologist. He sits in the chair next to my bed, huge white hands rearranging papers on his clipboard. An attendant with a clean-cut mustache in blue scrubs is patting my head with a cold washcloth. Confident men in white jackets fixating on my body offer zero comfort. In a jovial manner, and with more enthusiasm than I can handle, the anesthesiologist tells me that he will be attending the birth. Then he self-assuredly stresses that setting me up for an epidural will be adequate preparation. *Preparation for what?* There is a plan in place, but I am not privy to it. I am not in control or convinced that men in white coats understand my female body better than I do. At the same time, what I know and trust in my body has slipped away. *Where are my people?*

My mouth is dry. I purse my lips to sip water but my arms droop to my abdomen like a weighted blanket. "It can't be." My head snaps back, expelling an audible yet cut-off breath to release myself from a dream about someone else's life.

I swallow hard to focus. My lips press together and part toward the anesthesiologist, who is sitting quietly. He appears to be less of a hazard and friendlier than Doctor Kramer. Muttering "please" repeatedly under my breath, I let him know this is a drastic mistake:

"I am in the care of Carolyn Anderson, my midwife. We have been preparing for a natural home birth." Clenching and unclenching my fists, I edge in with my proud peacock voice.

"Each time I'm left alone to rest, contractions cease, and my body is relaxed." *My instincts know something beneath the pressures crashing my body.*

"I live in a community where natural childbirth is easily practiced. My body knows how to birth babies, like I did with my first baby."

A strangled cry of frustration rushes forward, "Can't we go home now?"

He nods. "I know you want to have a natural birth without an epidural, but what we're setting you up for is a common protocol, just in case. We may or may not have to use it. We will be prepared in the event there are any problems." He speaks with the everyday assurance of a news reporter, completely missing my points.

My voice shakes. "Let me go home. I can't think of any problems." I want to bare my teeth, "Do you know that before the onset of the industrial revolution, most women were supported to birth at home without medical intervention?" I want to plant my feet on the ground and roar, but I crumple, wet eyes, defeated, *paralyzed by shame.* I don't track now, it's too loud in this room with men invading all around me. *Does anyone hear me?* I don't name this violation for years to come. *Hospital rape!*

He leans toward me with his clipboard. "An epidural has been ordered. I'm ready to set you up. Sign here. Just in case." In the years that followed, I learn that "just in case" is a phrase used for a predetermined agenda. I don't dislike the anesthesiologist; I want him to trust me, rescue me—do the right thing. *Why doesn't he hear me? Where is Hank?* I press my hands against burning cheeks. I repeat back to myself what I know, it is Monday morning, I was promised state-of-the-art technology for an accurate read on the state and size of the babies; I am not having contractions; my midwife is not allowed to verify our course; I'm outnumbered. *Sign here.*

In the 1940s, it was not uncommon for women to be routinely sedated and for babies to be delivered by forceps—"knock-'em-out, drag-'em-out" obstetrics. I promised to never land in a hospital for labor and delivery. *Would it help if I remembered this now and hail praise for the male physician Dr. Robert Bradley, the father of natural childbirth? Would his famous contributions outweigh the threat of midwifery and impel the doctors to send me home?*

I lift my chin and stare blankly, without consciously identifying the blatant coercion to agree to a dubious agenda, man-made, in male hands, without a second opinion or informed options. "Right here, sign."

I am on their turf, worn down—conquered. I sob and scribble. As soon as I do I fall limp and non-responsive while a disbelieving voice wonders inside, *how am I going to push these babies free*? The next time I open my eyes, estrangement throttles, *Why have they cleared the room?* I don't spot a face nor do I scream. *How can I birth my babies if I can't feel them? If I can't feel me? When I am not safe?*

Breathe... Slow...Deep...Remember... Breathe... Slow...

An early habit sequesters me, either to comfort or crucify me. My chin drops, my hands cross and rest over my heart:

> *Hail Mary, Full of Grace, The Lord is with thee.*
> *Blessed art thou among women,*
> *and blessed is the fruit of thy womb, Jesus.*
> *Holy Mary, Mother of God, pray for us sinners now,*
> *and at the hour of death.*
> *Glory Be to the Mother, and to the Daughter,*
> *and to the Holy Spirit.*

The operating room ceiling is high with bright fluorescent lights, sterility fills the air; nothing feels natural. Strangers encircle my body. My eyes blink rapidly in search of a familiar set of eyes above blue masks that cover mouths and noses. I count five intense gazes that offer no comfort. Hank's blue eyes catch mine, brows furrowed. He stands behind me, his sweaty hands stroking and patting my head. It is not reassuring. Disturbed, I push his hands away.

Voices reach me, but they fade into the background. A word resonates, *Mother.* I'm in a forest, and all three babies are with me. We're held on a sturdy branch of a silver maple, untouched. The air is fresh, even moist, and rich with oxygen. I inhale deeply, savoring a moment of safety.

But I'm on a cold table like a slab of meat, I bite my lip. A voice echoes through my body—my womb. *Are you okay?* It is the mother voice eager to hold her babies but she can't feel them. Her yearnings are secondary, inconsequential.

Impatience fills the room—clicks, snaps, tapping feet. My body is on pause, quiet. I imagine ticking clocks, beeping timers, hands poised for action—achievements—progress. Nothing. My uterus is not contracting. Something else pervades the room, enigmatic with deep roots like my tree.

Thirty minutes of motionless stillness pass when the lead surgeon, Dr. Kramer, interrupts with a directive, "Pitocin!"

I heard it loud and clear and thought *WTF* before a part of me left to watch from above. *Pitocin (an artificial oxytocin) pretends to induce labor, to strengthen contractions when surgeons are frustrated because they are not trained to deliver babies—their expertise is surgery.*

Later I learn that in some circumstances the cervix may recoil, the process of dilation is not linear. But no one around me wants to know this or receive my consent to inject me with Pitocin. This is what I know: *My body and babies are not ready to birth.* This situation is insurmountable. I go to my tree. The docs are plunging forward, but really backward. They continue to guess that the babies are 2.5 pounds, *large enough* for a vaginal birth, to make it through the birth canal.

Oh, mother. *What are they thinking?*

The dose is strong. I fall off a limb, whip around swift curves and jagged edges as if my pelvis is riding a wild horse without a saddle. Hank's sticky hands are squeezing my head. I want him to stop. I want everyone to stop. *"MAKE IT STOP."* The mother part is still, watching. Another part yells, "It's not helping! Nothing is helping! Stop!" Hank removes his hands, "I'm sorry."

I know he is helpless like me. We fumble for each other like a football player missing a pass that rolls out of bounds and loses the game. A boundary has been crossed. We're out of our league. The trauma is mutual, and at the same time, a mother enfolds us.

All is quiet for a time, maybe twenty minutes pass. The Pitocin has not generated a single contraction. I'm not surprised. A surge of power flashes through me, knowing my body will not deliver. *Stay with me, hold us, keep us.* I trust the wisdom of pause in my body. *Why don't they?* The body doesn't lie, and right now it is overpowering the medication. I imagine the surgeon is not happy, unable to reckon that he is operating with diploma-led hunches based on my birth dates, not facts or instincts.

My body, my womb is winning but they won't let me. They don't even enlist the obstetric sonographer with leading-edge equipment.

Am I An Experiment? I worry about my unborn babies, aren't they absorbing whatever happens to me?

The air hangs heavy—a stunned silence. My body is relaxed, time passes. "We need to move this procedure along." Now my legs are strapped into stirrups like an upside-down cowgirl from the '50s. Dr. Kramer shouts, "Pitocin #2!" I imagine eyes prying into my uterus, waiting for a contraction, any sign of movement. But my body will not give over, *"No! No! No! My babies are staying. You can't have them."*

The dose is more aggressive, or its effect is cumulative. My pelvis throbs, spasming like a raging bull in a rodeo show. I ache for my babies. Mother is breathing strength from the tree above but my brain wants the epidural. This pain is induced—unnatural, unbearable like a searing muscle cramp. The anesthesiologist is eager to sedate me, to take away all feelings along with the mother instinct I hoped would push my babies free.

Amidst the unceasing throb, contractions, and dilation remain unchanged to support a vaginal birth at twenty-six weeks. *Will they cease and desist?* From my tree I watch, a woman rendered powerless without choosing. Hank's trembling hands on my head remind me, I am her.

It's 10:00 a.m. All feeling is gone, my womb anesthetized, invisible, like my babies behind a blue cloak of lies. Dr. Kramer has the power to decide, "We've waited long enough." The Pitocin has failed to perform. In other words, "A cesarean is required."

I do not feel the cut. I do not see the babies being scraped from my womb by the hands in blue gloves.

But I do know the moment they are lifted into this world. *Are they breathing?*

Baby A champions her first breath. She is 1.2 pounds, as tiny as a mouse, with multiple signs of stress. Her heart rate is beating above normal, her skin is black and blue. I imagine this is from Pitocin Whiplash.

Baby B is born two seconds later. She is received by a second team. She is 1.4 pounds, a hair bigger than her sister. She is not breathing. Her heart rate is slow, her body floppy, not moving. She is resuscitated twice and kept on a respirator. I watch this scene imprint on my mind—disoriented.

As soon as our babies are sectioned out of my womb I wither, lifeless, as if my body is on its way to the city morgue. I hear a voice, "This is the recovery room, where you wait." Unsure what we are waiting for or what recovery entails. I wanted to wait for my midwife, for my body and my babies to be ready to be born—at home.

I had hoped that all doctors uphold the Hippocratic Oath, prioritizing, "First, do no harm."

But now, in the recovery room, I want to lift my arms to reach Hank, but I can't. They are drugged and drained of energy, as are my legs. I tilt my head, Hank's face is visible, the blue cap still on his head. His hands pat my shoulders like a parent comforts a crying baby. Too numb to cry, I imagine we are wondering the same thing. *What the hell just happened? Now what?* He swallows, his skin pale. "I don't know," we say in unison.

The Apgar test assesses newborn well-being, and a score of eight or higher indicates good health. Test scores do change, an initial lower score doesn't mean unhealthy or abnormal. Our babies' scores are significantly low. Baby A scores four. Baby B scores one. This implies means immediate special care is required. Baby A is taken to the neonatal intensive care unit. Baby B will follow once her breathing is adequate with the help of a machine. We're given a hospital map and a social worker's contact to assist with resources for our unplanned lives. This includes the Ronald McDonald House (RMH), housing near the hospital for families with children who require long-term care.

Silence lingers before either of us can speak. When we do, it doesn't change a thing.

I'm given three days to recover in a single-family-style hospital room. It will take much longer. Hormonal resilience kicks in, burrowing instinctual injuries of this trauma into the background of my psyche, its magnitude unable to fit in the space of a recovery room. We meet our babies after two days. I need Autumn. Grandpa brings her to the hospital. I'm sitting at a table pumping breast milk when she arrives. Her skin is a delicate pink. Our verbal exchange is brief. She toddles to my bed captivated by the gadgets. I'm in and out of the bathroom, my body working hard to flush sorrows and assimilate incision inflammation that reminds me that my babies are gone. When I emerge from the bathroom, my adrenaline surges. Autumn lies on my bed, her shirt hiked up, belly pushed out to mimic pregnancy as if to say, "I'm like you, pregnant. Can I stay?" Enchanted by her performance, I melt beside her. I decide not to storm the Neonatal Intensive Care Unit (NICU) to rescue my babies. This baby needs me, too.

11
Second Nature

M y first impression of the NICU is bright lights, sterile chaos, and no windows. The second is olfactory; the place reeks of antiseptics, bleach, and medications, not to mention stinky diapers. I look around. The room is jam-packed. Along each wall are racks of beds that look like miniature gurneys; some are open and others are enclosed by plastic or glass. Each bed is connected to a network of monitors, some with flashing lights, intravenous drips of medication, and oxygen tanks. Most of the beds are separated by light yellow curtains that hang from metal rods. A lone cushioned chair stands beside each bed, facing away, toward the wall, looking like an alcove reserved for grief.

There is something odd about the room that calls my attention, but it takes me another look around for this to register. Against the wall to the right side of the door are cases of commercial formula from an affluent medical corporation. In the cubicle to the left side of the door sits a sullen young mother with dark circles under her eyes bottle-feeding a tiny infant wrapped in a soft blue blanket. Her eyes lock on mine; for a few moments, I enter her world. I am curious and bothered. *I wonder why this mother isn't nursing her baby and if that will be the case for me?*

An attendant wearing a blue mask and gloves is approaching. I stay with my new friend. She could be my daughter—I am twice her age. I press my lips together, place my hand on her shoulder, and tell her, "We can do this. We can nurse our babies." I gave her the information I was able to gather from a lactation counselor earlier. Her relief is instantaneous. I know that nursing does not happen easily for mothers, no matter how hard they try. The next time I see her, she is smiling and so am I. Her baby has successfully latched on and is getting stronger by the minute. We see each other daily for the next few weeks until her baby is strong enough to go home.

I continue to see our babies. We didn't plan for their names beforehand. The quickening of the events that led up to their unexpected birth pushed the idea of naming them to a corner. *We have plenty of time.* We call them Baby A and Baby B for several days. I had to take the nurses' word that "This is Baby A," and "This is Baby B."

Baby A came out fighting for her life. She has warrior wounds, and black and blue patches on her jaundiced skin. When I am able to hold her, I lean in, cautious. She is smaller than my hand. She latches on like lightning, sucking as a matter of life or death. Her lungs are strong. When I cannot be there, I am told her cry can be heard throughout the NICU. Each time the nurse hands her to me, I feel a confidence in her that I do not feel with Baby B. She has more girth than length, a robust suck—an irrepressible focus. Once she gets started, there is no stopping her. She empties one boob and is quickly on to the next. Her fingernails poke my skin like pins. More prevalent is the steady lock her eyes hold on mine, as if she is communicating an affirmation that she will hold me to, *We can do this!* She is sucking both of us alive.

I didn't know what a neonatal baby would look like. There isn't anything in our culture that prepares us to meet tiny fragile bodies struggling to survive. When I look at Baby B, she appears comatose. I see four limp limbs stretched out under bubble wrap material. Each limb is attached to an IV or monitor. Her skin is jaundiced and unclothed except for a plastic diaper suitable for a Barbie doll. Her eyes are closed. She has a tiny plastic mask over her face, intubated by a machine that is breathing for her.

"Is she OK?" is all I can say. I let out a forceful breath and lowered my head, noticing vacancy fill my heart. I want to be brave and offer myself the same conviction that I gave my teenage friend. *How will my nipple fit in the mouth of a baby mouse?* My legs wobble. I sit down.

The nurse tells me I will probably be able to hold her the following day.

A heavy thud presses on my heart. My thoughts are racing too fast for me to track them. I close my eyes to imagine holding her; the thought terrifies me. *I might break her! And she's already broken!* I cross myself and bring my hands together in front of my chest, *mother.* My face is wet, hands sweaty and bigger than Baby B. When I open my eyes; the nurse is gone. *I need to check for myself.* I take my driver's license out of my wallet and reach in through the hole in the top of the encasement of her miniature bed. She doesn't move when I set it next to the plastic that covers her. She is a tad longer than my license ID card. I want to push rewind, bring her back into my womb, and start over. I want to scream at the tops of my lungs, "This is not okay!" But I stop, sit back down, drop my face into my hands, and weep.

Friends come with flowers and food. Even though I don't want to see anyone, I'm glad they come. My birthday is around the corner, and they want to have a party for me. The last thing I feel is merriment and, somehow, I admit that connectedness with others may elicit buoyancy amidst devastating defeat.

I notice Hank and Autumn in the periphery of my awareness and urges to avoid a cauldron of emotions that throb within. I wander back and forth from our room to the NICU, wondering if I am here or not here. I am physically in the room, in the circumstance but not really. I'm looking on as if from a different tree, not held and not able to grasp or imagine this is my life. *Am I an apparition, inserted into a dream?*

The next day, I call my mom in New York. The last time she flew to California, she was stranded overnight in the airport in Chicago during a dreadful blizzard. "I'll never fly again." Near the end of our conversation, she reminds me, "You're strong. You've always been strong. If anyone can do this, you can."

Her words don't comfort me. I want to understand the primary emotion that is gripping me. It feels like burning anger mixed with embarrassment. I realize how difficult it is for me to ask for help, as though I am breaking a commandment. *Thou Shalt Not Need Help.* Amongst my seven siblings and alcoholic father, from as early as I can remember, my mother told me, "Nancy, you're okay, you don't need anything." She said it like a prayer. She needed me to be a strong child, a good mother's helper. *I worked hard not to need her, but all children need mothering.* I unconsciously internalized subordination to man, to the Church, and to culture. Now, blasts of red-hot energy surge through my system with an intensity that frightens me because even though I know how much women have historically been stripped of their power; this knowledge didn't help me to birth my babies. *What will it take to deconstruct a collective culture that has been painted and defined by men from birth to death?*

Messages from my mother swirl in my brain, "No, Mom. No. You're wrong. Not this. I can't do this. Not alone. I need help. It is larger than me. I need help. I need your help." Unlike every previous moment of pain I presented to her in my youth, this time, she is resourced enough to hear me. She sets aside her fear of flying and agrees to come.

Before she hangs up, she assures me, "We can do this." I want to believe her.

But shame grabs me. A brutal shrinking, hiding, that closes like a mussel. It tells me I have done something horribly wrong to find myself here, in this impossible predicament. *It's my fault. I'm so dense. Or is this one more dysfunctional system that fails to attend to humans when they are most vulnerable?* Regardless, a litany of Thou Shalt Nots passes through me, hopefully to unmask my instincts—my true voice:

Thou Shalt Not Doubt—Desire—Disagree
Thou Shalt Not Challenge Men with Power and Privilege
Thou Shalt Not Question
Thou Shalt Not Voice an Opinion
Thou Shalt Not Need Your Mother
Thou Shalt be Polite, Pretty, and Pleasing
Thou Shalt Deny and Disappear
Thou Shalt Remain Subordinate

While I have moments of grace assuring me that I'm doing my best, in my raw human moments, waves of dejection crash over me. There will be times when I involuntarily slither into a hurting, unruly dark place. I've basked in the light of transcendence many times. This is different than anything before. Like Inanna's descent down into the depths of the underworld, I will walk naked, exposed, lacking self-confidence. I will shatter with a full body ache, a cyclical churning upside down and inside out, again and again. *And I will reclaim, reconnect, and heal these fractured parts for me and my girls, and create my own female-centered commandments. Together with my girls, we will make a home—a nest for rest.*

On day three when I come to see Baby B, I don't feel more capable of holding her, but I do anyway. The nurse has me sit in a comfortable chair. I call it my grief chair, a place to befriend a river of sadness. She unhooks the tube from the oxygen machine. When she hands her to me, she feels inanimate, like an object, not flesh. "You can hold her for twenty minutes."

I barely slept the night before. I worried she was already dead. My mind was occupied with planning out how to tug myself up, and be calm and brave, no matter what. When adrenaline surges, I will leave the NICU. I will not break down. I will be strong. *I will nurse this teeny infant.* I remember the ease of nursing Autumn. I never had to think twice about it; it was second nature. I only needed to follow her lead. Babies know exactly what to do. *She will guide me, my body, to listen.* I try to relax on the chair. My feet feel less buzzy, and more solid on the floor. The impulse to run is fading.

Baby B feels like a newborn chick on Easter. She wears a pink crocheted bonnet that droops over her eyes—too big for her head. Her pin-like fingernails trace my chest. Beneath the white T-shirt she wears, her skin is murky yellow. My eyes fix upon the soft shiny glow on her face. Even though her eyes are closed, her faint breathing gradually synchronizes with mine. I feel warm milky moisture at my breast. I want to bring her back into myself, warm her, and give her more time to grow a sturdy sheath to protect her from the loud sounds that surround us. Within minutes I feel a flickering of movement. I soften my hold and watch carefully. *What is she doing?* Her little mouth is inching toward my left breast. *Wow, she is alive and wants to nurse!* Stillness envelops us like a magical cocoon. We enter a world of our own where the beeps, lights, and cries all around do not reach us. Baby B is sucking milk from my breast. Her suck is weak, but sure enough, she is latched on. *She knows what to do.* Milk is ready in both breasts; our bodies are talking to each other. This is my first sign of hope that she will endure this shocking beginning.

After three days in the recovery room at the hospital, we transferred to a lovely room at the Ronald McDonald House nearby. It is ironic to me that one of the institutions most responsible for preventable health problems—the king of fast food—seeks to help people facing critical health issues. The Ronald McDonald Houses are a prominent charity for this multinational corporation. But at this moment when I need support badly, I silence my critique and accept the comfortable housing and solicitous staff who want to help us. My loose jeans are rolled up below my waist, hiding and possibly protecting an incision that we don't talk about. I do not take the pain medication offered. I want to feel again…

I need all the help I can get to feel my body, my way through the jarring and unknown parameters of the neonatal intensive care unit. We don't think much about the fact that Baby A and Baby B are still nameless until Hank's Mom calls and asks, "What are you going to name the babies?"

"I can't wait to see them toddling around in soft frilly dresses," she spouts, anticipating their girlhood, before I answer. She's as unaware of the particulars of this unnerving situation as we are. What I know is my babies are in intensive care, barely surviving, with a dismal prognosis that will impact all of us for the rest of our lives. A condition that may not include toddling. I sulk, stuffing another "Shalt Not." The call does, however, expedite giving the babies their names. Hank's parents suggest several options. We settle upon Abigayle (Abby) for Baby A and Elizabeth (Libby) for Baby B. These names carry a sense of dignity, purpose, and an old-fashioned sound that might shape a medicinal remedy from the wise mothers before us.

Their middle names come later that week in a dream I have about the twins. Abby is crossing over a bridge to receive a rose from a beautiful youthful woman twice her height. I can't tell how big Libby is or if she has a body, but I know it is her. She is busting out in laughter that brings joy to all she meets. This dream rekindles courage and brightness like a premonition for things to come. Our twins are named Abigayle Rose (Abby) and Elizabeth Joy (Libby).

Eight days later, thoughts leap intermittently like frogs on a still pond in the night. When they jump, it's loud. I am awake. Autumn's heart is pressed dreamily against mine on our RMH double mattress, reminding me of our carefree life together, the simplicity, sensibility, and endearment I most love about her. Her second birthday is quickly approaching. I think about the odd and rapid change in our routine, from a natural life of play, yoga, good food, and friends to the constant medical inventions. Longings stir inside of me. I want to huddle with Autumn beneath the stars on our spacious rooftop, away from prying eyes and cries. I want to hold her hand, walk barefoot, and build a rock castle on the beach. One that will stand anchored amid strong wind.

Now it is Halloween, I am on the shuttle to the NICU to see Abby and Libby, with Autumn comfortably nestled on my lap. The thought of trick-or-treating on the children's floor of the hospital feels sad and disorienting. The joy that usually overflows for us at this time of the year is absent. Nevertheless, I paint my face like a clown and put on a cheerful facade for Autumn's sake.

———————

Something else tugs me in the night, my intuition confirmed. The doctor on duty tells me that Abby's intestines rupture in the night and are infected. The diagnosis is Necrotizing Enterocolitis (NEC). Immediate surgery is required. They called in a surgeon from Canada to perform the surgery that day. During the surgery, they will also tie a heart valve that did not seal properly. They tell me that the heart procedure is minor and carries little risk compared to the operation on her intestines, which carries enormous risk. They prepare me for the worst, suggesting that even if she does survive the surgery, her life span will be short. She will need to receive artificial nutrition through a feeding tube, along with medications that will lead to a liver transplant and a compromised immune system. If the liver transplant doesn't kill her, infection will. *Holy Christ.* Typically, on a one-pound baby like mine, they have a short forty-five-minute window to cut her open to expose her insides and perform surgery using the tiniest instrumentation. The surgeon they have called is regarded as the best in the field. To date, this surgery has not been recorded as successful.

"Wow. Anything else you want to share at this moment?" I say, in my haughty spiritual-but-really-afraid voice. I have no time to think. Everything is happening so quickly. I need a diversion.

My girlfriends are eager to host the Blessing Way they had scheduled for December. A Blessing Way is traditionally a Navajo ritual created to spiritually support and empower the new mother through her birthing journey to motherhood. Even though the twins arrive prematurely, they want to offer provisions for this grim passage. Today, I wonder if it is more appropriate to order a tombstone and plan a funeral. I don't know if I'm joking or bracing myself for the worst.

As much as I want to kick, scream, and run, I splutter a few words to the doctor who delivers this bundle of news. I tell myself to shut up and push on. I sweep Autumn up into my arms, amble through the door of the NICU, quiver down the hallway, and out the front door. I jump on the shuttle back to the RMH and run into our room, still carrying Autumn on my hip. I call Hank at work. He listens. I speak rapidly, telling him everything I know. After hanging up the phone, I slump over, unable to grasp the silence on the other end. Without hesitation, I sit down in front of my milking machine and pump. Autumn is perched in the chair beside me. She takes off her shirt, holds the second set of plastic cups to her flat chest, and, like the little engine that could, huffs and puffs as if to say, "I think we can. I think we can. We can make it over this slippery slope." This is when waterworks stream down my face faster than the milk from my breasts, without a plastic cup to contain them.

That night, after work, Hank joins Autumn and me at the hospital. We each take turns holding Libby. Her situation hasn't changed much. She remains intubated, only able to come off oxygen to nurse. Her suck continues to be weak but steady. Her skin is less yellow. She is gradually gaining weight. I'm not told this at the time but the birth trauma and lack of oxygen caused extensive brain damage that will impact her ability to function for all of her life.

Abby comes back from surgery alive. The good news is they removed all of the infection. The heart valve is cinched. The bad news is they took out all of her small intestine. The possibility of recovering the ability to digest food is minimal. This merciless news includes a new regime of artificial nutrition and medications. I am told this will inevitably lead to a liver transplant, assuming that a suitable liver is available to transplant.

Breathe.

Hearing this is scarcely easier than seeing her post-surgery. She is sprawled out on an open preemie bed like a punctured bag, a bruised life desperately reliant on oxygen and meds from tubes attached to her limbs the size of worms. She is on life support. When I push myself to look more closely, I see her abdomen covered with loose gauze puffed up like a purple balloon about to burst; I nearly vomit. I see the colostomy bag full of dark greyish-blue fluid and quail, "What is that?"

"The color of her excretion will change once we put her on formula; for now, she is only receiving pain medication and fluid," says the nurse attending to her full-time, in a soft compassionate voice.

I immediately like this nurse. I imagine we are close in age. She has dark hair pulled back in a long ponytail revealing gentle brown eyes that are level with mine. Her name is Akira. I want to hug her. I want to hug anyone who is brave enough to attend to these tiny creatures. Noting my frail state, she invites me to sit down.

"You can stay as long as you like. All through the night if you want. I can bring you tea and something good to eat," she smiles. I agree, feeling a wave of calm from her soft, protective demeanor. Hank is with Autumn. Kym Ann and a few other friends are taking turns holding Libby. My mom will arrive soon to spend a couple of months with us. She is not yet privy to the extent of what we are dealing with. *What if she's not up to it?*

I thank Akira for the warm mug of mint tea. She reminds me of a fond memory from Rumi. I sit, remembering these words inside of myself. I want them to comfort me:

> This being human is a guesthouse.
> Every morning a new arrival, a joy, a depression, a meanness,
> Some momentary awareness comes as an unexpected visitor.
> Welcome and attend them all
> Even if they're a crowd of sorrows,
> Who violently sweep your house empty of its furniture,
> Still, treat each guest honorably.
> He may be clearing you out for some new delight.
>
> — Rumi[10]

"Thank you," I say again, leaning into the chair, glad it is facing the wall. I want to absorb the meaning of this verse. I sit for a moment, noticing that my

---

[10] Jalaladdin Rumi: a 13th-century Persian poet.

body is trembling with energy. Instinctively, I close my eyes to follow it. I feel myself being absorbed into a space of quiet within. It is as if the words of Akira, the nurse, are fostering a direct transmission from my friend Rumi. Sensations and feelings peak in my system, and for the moment, I feel them. Sometimes I interpret this energy as self-blame, rage at the doctors, fear for my children, or jealousy of my friends. Interpretations that cause me to obsess about Western medicine protocols, injustices to women, and insidious patriarchal imprints. Now, it's just energy. I can let it burn. It feels more like my heart and body are cracking open to digest what is happening. Allowance opens, which encourages me to stay in this situation. I don't like it but I'm here—feeling. My instincts forewarn me to stay awake, and listen for the next best thing for my daughters. *Is it possible to allow unimaginable hurt—the deepest cuts—to open us rather than disempower us?*

My perspective is shifting. My feelings are accompanied by bodily sensations. My skin is cold and, at the same time, I feel sweat dripping down my back. Some thoughts catch my attention while others keep passing by. One that stays is about the changes I see in Autumn. Viscerally, I know that she needs me. *How will little Autumn carry on a night away from her mommy if I choose to stay by Abby's side?* She isn't yet two and prior to this hospital crisis, she has always been with me. Intimately close to my body, like a chrysalis in her cocoon, fixing to fly off when her wings mature. My attention to her will have to wait.

12
Mother's Milk

R ight now, I inwardly feel (almost hear) Abby calling for me from beneath the plastic tubes that sprout from her lungs and mask sound. It's a strong pull, not like the sound "mommy," but a cry that means the same and calls for the womb of the mother. Inside, I know what is being revealed to me—all infants need their mother—and all mothers need our Earth Mother. Our relationship is reciprocal. This knowing pulls me toward Abby. I need to be at Abby's bedside, prepared to hold her the moment the doctor says I can.

First, I go outside to sit under a tree so I can feel Mother Earth beneath my feet. I sit and listen to the messages that are rising from the ground up into pockets of my body. I know it is critical to keep my attention drawn down in my body, to earth. She is offering me a wordless transmission. When I arrive at Abby's side, I do not allow myself to be distracted by the intensity of beeps, bells, and cries that fill the NICU. Suddenly, my breasts are wet and leaking onto my blouse. I hear these words speaking over and over in myself: "Mother's milk; mother's milk; only give her your milk." This is the medicine I trust, resounding from Earth within every fiber of my being. I open my eyes, glance over at Abby Rose, and seek out Akira.

I tell her, "I know what to do!"

"What do you mean?"

"I mean I know what to do for Abby. Doctor Wagner requires that Abby be given commercial formula once her incision heals a little more. I disagree. I don't want her to have the hospital formula. She must have only mother's milk, my milk. If she is going to have a chance to heal, she has to have only my milk. All natural. No chemicals or processed products. It has to be holy, fortified, like Mother Earth."

"He isn't going to go for it. I know he will be concerned about weight gain, and they always use formula for rapid growth," she says pensively.

"I don't care. I feel strongly about this. She is my child. It really matters to me that I am empowered to choose what is right for me and my baby. After everything she has been through, her system is compromised. She will need a super-duper immune system." I had researched the difference between breast milk and formula. The American Academy of Pediatrics (AAP)[11] considers breast milk "natures perfect food, brimming with live beneficial bacteria, antibodies, and enzymes." In our modern culture where mothers are not afforded maternity leave, may be single parenting, or have a host of other contemplations, what matters most is what works best for mother, baby, and family. Conventional formula feeding can also be a healthy choice for babies when a mom isn't able to provide breast milk. Some of the reasons I want Abby to have my breast milk is that it contains the nutrients that she requires for healthy growth, and antibodies to ward off illness and infection. She needs something that is easy to digest, given the fragility of her intestines. Studies also show that breastfed babies have higher levels of cognitive functioning. Given the extent of her trauma, I hope this is true. More than anything else, holding Abby in my arms is good for me. It reminds me to eat well so she can have quality nutrition.

Akira's mischievous smile and the light in her eyes tell me she agrees. When Abby was constantly crying when I was not able to be with her, I showed some of the nurses the practice of kangaroo care and left one of my baby slings. Akira was the first to wear Abby in a sling across her chest. She noticed that she easily slept when she was being carried. She is able to continue to attend to other patients and barely notices she is carrying a tiny creature on her chest. She knows about my visits with the young mothers in which I tell them to "never say 'never', we can do this," and remind them, "It's never too late to nurse. It's the best thing for your baby. And you need the oxytocin love cocktail." Akira is the nurse who advocates for kangaroo care[12] in the NICU. When the babies are held close, they feel our heartbeats, their oxygen saturation levels increase, they sleep better, and they gain weight. This

---

[11] Webmd.com/baby/breastfeeding-vs-formula feeding
[12] Kangaroo care is a method of holding babies' skin-to-skin that came about in the late 70s as a response to the high death rate of preterm babies.

simulates a womb. "Change doesn't happen quickly around here, but I'm willing to stand with you on this one," she tells me.

"I want to talk to the doctor with you," I say with optimism. I do not know anything about hospital births but I know how to nurse babies. Mother nature is a clear teacher.

We speak to him when he comes over to check on Abby. At first, he is reluctant, given Abby's dismal condition. Soon he sees that I have done my homework. I present realistic, intuitive knowledge about the benefits of mother's milk, especially the ability to build her immune system to prevent further infection. Akira feels like a sister. When I can't be there for Abby and Libby, she is a mama bear. I pump bottle after bottle of milk; she labels them with a big black marker "Abby or Libby." She clarifies in the nursing notes that they are fed only my milk and not formula.

Akira lets me know when she is off duty. I take up the mama bear role. I call the NICU at shift change to remind the nurse on duty that there is plenty of milk in the refrigerator for Abby and Libby. When a substitute nurse comes in, she or he may not read the entire report. She might fall into the routine of opening a can of formula, pouring it into a tiny plastic bottle, placing it in the bed, and letting the infant suck it down. All of this without picking the infant up. I know this won't work for Abby. I am triggered when I call and a nurse tells me, "You're being irresponsible. If you want your baby to reach three-and-a-half pounds, she needs to drink formula. It has all of the nutrients she needs."

"It's artificial nutrition, difficult to digest, and can't compare to mother's milk," I say, about to hang up. Panic tempts me to say, "Don't you dare, you unscrupulous witch." Then I take a deep breath and say, "Don't feed her; I'm on my way." I leave Autumn with my mom. I run the quarter of a mile from RMH to the hospital without stopping. When I enter the hospital, I am winded and red in the face. I imagine, judging by the look on the attending nurses faces, that I carry an air of righteous intensity. I strut over to Abby's bed and see a familiar nurse unhooking her from monitors and preparing her to nurse. She stands shorter than me, in floral scrubs; her name is Bonnie. She respectfully passes Abby to me like a newborn kitten, "You came just in time. Abigayle just woke up." I soften on the spot, sit down, and thank her for consoling my baby. I bring Abby's two-and-a-half-pound body up to my chest and feel her latch onto my breast as if it is the last source of oxygen on the planet. After reviving herself, she does what she does every time she nurses. She locks both of her bottomless black tourmaline eyes onto mine as if her soul sees mine. Her will is impressing upon mine. Her life is attached to mine. She speaks to me through her eyes. In these clear moments, I feel relief from fear. We are bonded—joined. We will climb this mountain. She will do more than survive. I see it in her eyes. I am here to do all I can to help her thrive.

Three months after Abby's surgery, the Canadian surgeon returns to take out the stitches. (The scar is the shape of a smile). When he comes to speak to me, he is stunned in disbelief. "We've never seen anything like this in the history of NEC surgery on a one-pound baby. Her entire intestine has grown back. This is impossible."

"Hmmm," I say, not feeling super surprised, but happy as all heck. The spirit of Abby and Mother Earth told us this. Nurse Akira generously helped us, Abby provided the impulse, and I was able to listen. Together we are stronger. The goodness of nature—mother's milk—became a remedy. The doctors did not see this coming; a mama bear desperate enough to challenge their artificial treatment protocol. Imagine if the corporations that provide the canned formula to the NICU invested in kangaroo baby carriers. Imagine a breast milk bank next to the NICU with lines of volunteers ready to nurse these babies and hold them close to their heartbeat. I imagine these babies thriving, with deep roots in Mother Earth and branches spreading in the sky.

We emerge. "We" means Hank, Autumn, and me. All of us processing this situation in our own way. Hank has a full-time career to attend to. My attention is on reclaiming my instincts to navigate an uncharted rocky road, giving myself permission "not to know," and learning to ask for and receive help. "We" also includes a friend, a volunteer, my mom, and new friends we make at the hospital.

We ebb and flow like this, in and out, back and forth from RMH to Stanford Hospital, with hope for an early release from the hospital. The doctors tell us that the babies need to have steady weight gain and reach at least three-and-a-half pounds for us to take them home.

My mom, Camille, arrives three weeks into this ordeal. This is a tremendous help that allows me to spend more time at the hospital. Autumn is happy to stay with her at times; they get on quite well together. Mom is a natural cheerleader when it comes to children gaining independence. She lights up, "It's time to potty train Autumn." I hadn't thought about it, trusting that her imitation of me at the pump would carry on into the bathroom. It has, but it isn't quite regular enough for Camille. Being the optimist that she is, she thinks giving Autumn her own little throne will seal the habit. I came back from RMH after my morning visit with the babies to see Autumn sitting on her pot with a bright grin on her face. Her rapture is so focused that she doesn't notice me come through the door. I unobtrusively look on. After a moment her eyes glow, her face glitters, her mouth the shape of a big O. She bounces off her potty, turns around to look at her deposit, and cheers, "Gamma, look!" Like a miner discovering gold, she is beaming with pride.

My mom, a natural cook, is fascinated with new recipes and access to all sorts of healthy food in Palo Alto, not easily found in her hometown. Hank can rest more at our home in Santa Cruz at night to replenish his reserves for his work. He doesn't say so, but I sense that the stress is getting to him. His constitution is growing weak. In the midst of round-the-clock care and unpredictable occurrences, our conversations continue to be short and narrow. Over time, friends visit less and less. They have their own lives to attend to. With my mom and Autumn around, I have someone to talk to. It is lucky that I do, because what happens next nearly shatters me entirely.

Three weeks into the NICU period, the chief physician requested a conference with Hank and me. *Oh no, not another conference!* This time it includes an eye specialist. All of the babies in the NICU are constantly undergoing a variety of exams to recheck their Apgar scores in order to rule out or find dysfunction. Immediately following Abigayle's major surgery, I sign for another surgery to put a deep line or portal in her neck. Her veins are so tiny they are not able to hold the needles from the intravenous fluids and pain medications. By the end of the week, they need to put another one in the other side of her neck. On top of all the medications, she had two blood transfusions. At this time, her torso is swollen dark purple. She is wider than she is long. She is crying more often. I imagine the pain medications are wearing off. She recognizes when she is not with her mother, which is the place where any baby, small or large, needs to be in order to feel safe and develop—and grow. Babies this small need extra protection to develop myelin sheath, the protective layer beneath the skin that supports healthy neurology and brain synapses that protect us from absorbing external stimulation. Libby is seriously compromised, yet has not required the same surgeries as her twin. She is in a semi-comatose state, marked by unresponsiveness, and drinks at a much more leisurely pace than Abby. It is as if all of her energy is required to sleep and grow. Motionless, she sleeps like an angel.

Amidst the trauma and turmoil, Abby communicates to me through her eyes. I feel a certain connection through her eyes. The moment she latches onto my breast, I anticipate and cherish the transmission between us. On this day, however, the vision specialist tells me that she has retinopathy of prematurity. That both of her eyes need an operation in order to save any vision that she might have. I found out later that the eyes need more oxygen than any organ in order to function well. Due to her extreme prematurity and low oxygen levels, the doctor decides we need to go along with this, or else, "she has a significant risk of blindness if we do not do this operation now." I am worried about signing something I do not understand—again.

Later I learned that the National Library of Medicine reports that sixty-nine percent of patients completely trust physicians to put their needs above all other considerations (October 13, 1998.) The American Board of Internal Medicine Foundation conducted a survey of trust in the U.S. healthcare system. Ten percent of patients believe their doctors do not give them all of the correct information. Fourteen percent of patients believe their doctor does not know or listen to them. Thirty-three percent of patients believe their doctors do not spend enough time with them. Only forty percent believe the hospital puts its health above profits. (NORC 12/29/20 – 1/26/21).

The doctor tells me: "This operation will save her eyes." The anxiety I feel makes it hard to listen as he continues to rap on about advances in technology.

I only need to sign.

What the hell? I talk with Hank; he is equally clueless. We have no idea what to do. *What? I don't get it. What will be next?* This will be the seventh or eighth medical procedure for Abby (I lost count), most of them surgeries: tying the valve at the heart; the complete removal of the small intestine; two deep lines inserted in her neck, two blood transfusions, now laser surgery—not just to one eye, but both. Not to mention two dosages of Pitocin before the C-section trauma that just happened. *Bloody hell. And this is the baby who was doing the best at birth!* I began to worry more about Libby, the one who did not breathe at birth and had to be resuscitated twice. The one for which Dr. Falkner pronounced, "She will be fine; she just may not be able to use her legs." An immature voice yaps in my head. *Oh, just her legs. Who needs the use of legs?!* Mistrust intensifies in my system. I want to leap out of this situation but I can't. I'm horrified and don't know what to do. I need time and more information to process what is happening. I want to understand. Now you are requesting to perform laser surgery on both eyes. I can't see past this situation. *What else?* I'm told that without the surgery, she will most likely be blind. We can't tell, but if we postpone this surgery, we may lose the chance for her to have any vision at all. *Is this another "just in case" situation?*

I'm scared to death that this isn't going to work out, whether we do the surgery or not. I put my hands on my head, bunch my hair into a fist, and yell, "Christ Almighty, I don't know!"

Dr. Cho assures us he is a well-trained physician. *How am I to know the right thing to do?*

My chest caves in and I sign again. The wait time for this surgery is perpetual agony. I hold Abby tight one last time before surgery. She bolts onto my breast, empties it dry, and moves to the other, the entire time her onyx eyes fixed on mine. My heart pace quickens, while at the same time, Mother Earth hugs my legs to the ground, whispering steady calm. I want to steal my baby away, make a wrinkle in time, and honor the internal rhythms that connect us—but we're logged to a schedule. *Why does everything in this hospital feel so urgently timed?* After emptying the second breast, she falls asleep for about five minutes before it is time to put her back in her bed.

I can't stand it. I have to go out. I have to get away from the endless buzz of monitors and announcements over the intercom. *Shut up! Shut up! Shut up! SHUT UP!* I yell to myself in an empty elevator heading up to the top floor. I dash onto the roof, where a few other people are airing their thoughts, pacing back and forth, some smoking.

"Can I have one of those?" I say to a rather gruff-looking fellow.

"A smoke?" he says with a long face. I recognize him as one of the parents of a child diagnosed with cancer.

"I met your boy Tommy the other day. He seems delightful and so brave."

"A lot braver than me." He hands me a cigarette.

Honestly, I don't smoke. I'm just feeling crazy anxious. "Do you have a beer?" I ask, trying to crack the air with some levity. He has already returned to his pacing. I join the pace but in the opposite direction. I stop to look out over the hills and do a few hara squats as loudly as possible, not caring what anyone thinks. (Inhale up, exhale down with a "HAA!"). I pace to visit Autumn and my mom. I stumble to Libby—nervous. I speed back and forth from the roof to the second floor, sputtering and struggling to see if Dr. Cho is done. No, *but Dr. Cho is a good doctor,* I mutter to myself with the immature, critical, derisive tone that implodes when I'm humiliated, flinching with wrongness. *Why did you sign? Idiot. Idiot. Idiot.* I stare at the ground, squeezing my arms over my damp breasts, desperate to see her eyes. *This is taking too long. Where is she?* I should have taken her home days ago. *Idiot.*

Finally, I heard my name over the intercom. I dash to the NICU. Dr. Cho is standing by her bed with another doctor. "The surgery is complete. She is going to sleep for several hours. She will be very tired. The patches won't come off for three days. Then we will know how successful the surgery is."

"What did you say? Say it all again, please, more slowly." I breathe to quiet my heart so I can hear past the unruly voice in my head. *Patches on her eyes for three days? No. I have to see her now.*

Three nights pass with Abby nursing more ferociously than ever, her eyes concealed. I check on Libby through the night from time to time. She continues to sleep, waking for short periods to nurse. My mom is running out of ideas to keep Autumn entertained. Their comfortable exchange is more and more like a bumpy monologue, "Where's Mommy? I want Mommy." Autumn persists, trying to be a big girl, imitating me at the pump, and perfecting her potty training. I feel her struggle to adjust to the hours I spend away from her in the

NICU. When she speaks, her eyes are moist, wide, and strained, her words tangled.

The patches on Abby's eyes are layered thick with white gauze. My mind vacillates between hopefulness and gloom, even though she is safely sleeping in my arms. We will trudge on, regardless of the outcome. We will know each other. She will find her way. We will find our way—together. Trailed by caving in, pangs of terror pulsing through my system like sheets of glass. It is the strength of her suck that wakes me from this all-consuming shroud as if the life in my arms is lending compassion for the part of me that is terrified, that creeps over me unannounced. Her tender breath grips my focus and for a moment softens my worry. "We'll be okay." *Is it possible to feel smothered in pain, and like a safe, underground current is steadily carrying us at the same time?*

I don't know. I consider living with a disability and the collective historical memory that has influenced how disabled people are perceived; heroic, comedic, mysterious, angelic, tragic—disposable. My aunt with one glass eye, was uninhibited and living strong in her eighties. I remember the old blind man who operated the candy store on Main Street where I lived as a child. It was next door to the YMCA on the upper half of a historic office building downtown. My younger siblings and I skipped over there after swimming practice. He sat on a stool in a square booth, with windows across the top on all sides with a cash register at the front window. Rows of candy, newspapers, and magazines stack the lower shelves. We were naïve, not convinced of his blindness, so we tested him by snatching candy. We'd barely touch the candy before we heard his booming voice, astonishing us like a magician. "That will be ten cents for the Snickers bar, young lady." My little sister wet her pants once. *How did he know?*

Day three finally comes. I arrive early to the NICU, clutching my jaw, stomach empty, and eyes twitching. Akira is on duty today; she reaches for my hand. I'm thankful for her tender touch.

"Dr. Cho made his rounds this morning. You can take the patches off now," she assures me with a gentle smile. My voice choked with tears, "Me? I can take them off?" I blink at Abby. She is in her tiny bed, kicking her left leg, and bandages are over her eyes. My voice shakes, "I'm afraid to look. I want to know, but I don't want to look. I don't want to know, but I have to know." I agonize.

"Do you want me to take the patches off?" she coaches, sensing my ambivalence.

"No. I can do it. What if I sit down, and you put her on my lap? Can we do it together?" My breasts are leaking. "Why does this feel like such a big deal?"

"She's your baby. You have all the reason to be concerned."

I take Abby onto my bosom. She latches on and is off to the races. Akira slowly peels back the tape over the left eye. "It is there," I whisper. "She is looking at me." My body breathes, settling more into the chair, breathing to my belly. Abby empties one breast with the grit of a warrior, she is onto the next.

Akira carefully pulls off the right patch. My mouth drops open and hangs like dead air. Only the white of her eye is visible, the iris is turned in, crossed to the left. Gravity weighs on my body and splits open my heart, pushing me underwater. I tread for air, to swallow, to breathe. Mixed with this splitting pain tearing through my heart, vicious, harsh, with no end in sight, is an unbroken wholeness connecting between baby and me. I flutter through sensations, unable to digest what I see.

I want to stay, sit here, and nurse her forever, with both of her deep charcoal eyes looking into mine again as if to say, "Mommy, I see you. I see you." And I want to scream! *No, no, no! Not fair! NO!* "Where's Dr. Cho?" I plead to Akira. Hunched forward, high chin, flaring nostrils with fire in my eyes, I search the unit for an explanation.

I railed off in one long fluster, "Her eyes have a murky layer of substance. What is it? They look swollen. They are not the same. Her right eye is turned inward. I can't see the pupil. They are very different. She's not looking at me anymore. Our eyes are not meeting each other. This is not okay!" Dr. Cho is wearing a Hawaiian floral tie and a light blue shirt under his white lab coat. He stands tall, confident, examining Abby's eyes. *What would Abby say, if she could speak, if she could choose? Would she have signed up for this?* She is the vulnerable, voiceless one who matters.

"Can she see?" I roar, unglued.

He shoulders away from us, looks at his chart, rubs his eyes under his glasses, and replies with less poise, "Her eyes are sore for a few days, a little watery from the procedure. The procedure went very well. The muscle is weak but her eyes are okay."

"No. Her eyes are not okay! She is not looking at me!" I strike back, he will not erase my words.

"She was not able to see. Now her eyes will get better," he says with absolute certainty. "I'll come and check tomorrow. Everything will be okay." He heads out of view.

I want to shake him and say, *"A mother never forgets her child's gaze. Never! Three days ago, she was looking at me. I know it!"* Instead, I rock and howl, like a wild, brave person in a psychiatric ward in the '50s who knows she sees blue, and the psychiatrist professes in a pompous voice, "No, dear, you saw red." My instincts are easily challenged when faced with serious decisions. *Am I gaslighted?* I doubt myself and yield to the expert. In the years to come, I will find out that it is not unusual for vision to be delayed in preemies due to lack of oxygen. I learned that vision can improve with movements that help oxygenate the visual center of the brain. The surgery performed by Dr. Cho has weakened the muscles that support eye movement. Her vision is uncertain. Hypervigilance continues. I pace, read, and research.

Abby is not the only one who needs me. The critical nature of the twins' situation dictates more energy than I could ever imagine. Autumn feels the impact of my intense focus on the other babies. When she can no longer manage her needs as secondary to the twins, she shows me a natural solution.

Amidst the unexpected, I don't think this through or know where this notion came from. I thought it was impossible to produce enough milk to nurse three babies at once. I planned to nurse Autumn until she weaned herself, as I learned was possible from other mothers and books I read, a healthy natural course to follow. I don't know anyone who has nursed more than two babies at a time (with twins in critical condition) but I trust the natural intelligence in our bodies to honor and complete an attachment bond to wean from mother when secure and ready.

Autumn endearingly imitates me at the pump. She toddles along for a short bit without nursing. But I know she isn't okay. She is trying to be big—brave. Something is different about her. She muddles her words. She clings tightly to my side, unable to relax her grip. Her spirit is dimming. I feel her stutter as if her heart is missing a beat. She needs her mommy—as much as the twins do. It begins here for Autumn, the challenge to express her needs amidst the amplified screams of her sisters.

The next morning, she is having a rough time, fidgeting, not eating, adhering to my leg, eyes blinking as she struggles to speak. We are about to take the shuttle to see the babies; she tugs my pant legs many times and finally looks up at me with eyes like saucers.

"What is it, Honey?"

She keeps tugging; her mouth is working hard but words lag. I sit down on the carpet to scoop her onto my lap, "Tell me." There is a long pause. Momentarily, any thought of getting to the NICU dissolves. I am here, in this moment with Autumn, joined to her challenge, her ache. Then she stutters, "Ma-ma-ma-mom-ma-my, can I pa-ple-ee-eas-ee na-na-na-ur-se?" My eyes fall into hers. Her need is my need. I am unable to turn from her. We are one ache—one longing. Even if all the studies in the world say it is impossible to nurse three babies at the same time, my body, the innate wisdom in my mothering capacity speaks loudly, "Yes, of course you can, Autumn." I hold her close, "Of course you can, Honey." She latches on like Abby, like a shooting star. Her well-structured skull is three times the size of Abby and Libby's put together. Milk is pouring into her. Later I learn that it is the activity of sucking that produces milk. My job is to keep up with calories and fluids, oxytocin will do the rest. It is less than a month since the birth. I am twenty pounds less than the forty pounds I gained during the pregnancy. I will never forget nor can I express the angelic glow of satisfaction that lit up Autumn's face when she puckered off into a serene nap.

———

It is shortly after Christmas when Libby is transferred from the Stanford NICU to our local hospital in Santa Cruz. Libby's time in the NICU has been fairly uneventful, without the surgical complications that Abby has undergone. Her current task is to gain weight. She has slept most of the time, intubated, not moving or making a sound. The NICU needs to free up her bed. As far as the doctors are concerned, she will be served well at Dominican Hospital.

I ask the doctor whom I facetiously name Dr. Sunshine, "How is she? She is barely moving. What do we need to know about her?"

"She had a rough beginning but she'll be okay." He speaks casually, as though to begin life intubated, cannulated without sound or movement is a common occurrence. "She's already reached three pounds, so we're going to let her finish her weight gain at Dominican Hospital," he says in an official we're-clearing-the-shop voice.

"Oh," I croak. "What about her sister? How will we manage visiting babies in two different hospitals along with my toddler? Wouldn't it be healthier to keep them together for visiting?"

"I understand, but our unit is full. She doesn't require anything more than weight gain. We need to transfer her."

Anything more than weight gain? I say to myself, incredulous. It doesn't occur to me to ask for instructions. I don't realize it at the time but I'm ashamedly inhibited by the power differential that subjects me to remain complicit within what seems to be an obstetric production-assembly line nature of a healthcare system concerned more with financial gain and less with my babies' weight gain or the well-being of our family. My subjugated instincts scream, *How can disconnection—separating my three children from me, their mother—lead us to heal? Won't this encourage further dis—ease by pulling us away from what is most natural—The Mother Connection?* I sweat beneath powers stronger than my instincts, erasing my cries. "Do not challenge medical authority. Do not question specialists who have earned their rank." I'm facing extreme medical challenges. *Is it possible to receive practical support? Don't twins placed together gain weight faster?*

Later, I discovered the historical origins of separating mothers and babies is a "new" practice that emerged in the 1890's, when incubators were invented. Incubators were used to regulate the temperatures of preterm babies, and formula was introduced shortly after to facilitate calories in the absence of the mother. This led to a protocol for faster discharge. (National Library of Medicine, 1/9/2019). Studies on the developmental consequences of separating mother and baby and lack of human contact only began in the

1970's (Kangaroo Care Study). In the 1980's, the advent of government HMO's and cost-based care shifted attention to billing rather than patient care, and prices skyrocketed.

Dr. Kenneth Ludmerer, professor of medicine and the history of medicine, sheds light on the impact of this system on residency training for doctors. In his book *Let Me Heal*, he describes the "turnstile" effect: "In all specialties, residency training came to be dominated by an overriding goal; discharging patients as soon as possible. House officers were instructed to begin discharge plans on day one of a hospitalization, sometimes even before meeting the patient." He notes how the late David Kipnis, MD, former chairman of the Department of Medicine at Washington University School of Medicine, stopped teaching residents in the 1990s because house officers only wanted to talk about discharge and not about treatment. Ludmerer believes that "the requirement that residents see as many patients as possible in a short time is a major cause of "burnout" among house officers."

I fade further into a grey place. Dr. Ludmerer's prize-winning research had yet to be published when the lead OB-GYN, Dr. Kramer, arrived at the end of my hospital bed early Monday morning, October 21, without an introduction. The stranger with our lives in his hands, likely indoctrinated by the "turnstile" mindset, who announced, "It's time. We're going to the operating room."

The three-hour drive to two different hospitals is daunting, especially for Abby. While Libby is released from the hospital after reaching the required weight of three-and-a-half pounds, Abby's weight gain is slower. I visit her every other day in the NICU, but this arrangement is not sustainable. I'm worried, Abby isn't gaining weight. On the days I am with her I put her in our kangaroo sling, she nurses, sleeps, and gains weight, giving us hope. But the weight is lost on the days I cannot be there, as I am nursing Libby and Autumn.

When a friend drives me, my thoughts are nearly kind. When I drive alone, I strain for the life of my offspring as if they are an endangered species. I envision myself driving to the hospital, creeping into the NICU to steal Abby like a thief at a bank. "Put down your syringes! Unhook the monitors! Give me my baby now, and no one will get hurt!" I must have absorbed some crazy ideas from the TV dramas that are viewed on every floor of the hospital. I certainly feel nuts. In hindsight, I realize my imagination is working hard to protect my girls and myself, to help me gain control in a situation in which I feel utterly powerless.

Sometimes, without consciously choosing, my body settles down. I breathe wide and root like a mother tree. An epiphany strikes me with an idea to propose a logical plan that a logical person like a doctor will, with any luck, agree to. Once I get the doctor's attention with my stunning performance of a confident mother, I show him my evidence; it is well charted. "Look, Doc. The day I am here, she gains weight; the day I am not here, she loses it. She needs to be home with me." I paint a picture from a memory. "In the not-too-distant past, home visits happened all the time. We can do that, right?" I pause. He's looking over her chart. "She needs to be with me every day. I am sure once we get her home, she will gain the required weight and keep it on." He warms to me, "If you can get an agreement from her primary care physician to come and visit her daily until she gains weight, you can take her home."

I speak with Dr. Magarian at Dominican Hospital, he is very happy to come to our house to weigh and check in on Abby. "He will make sure we stay on track." The doctor pauses, examines the records again, turns to me, and nods, "I will call Dr. Magarian in the morning to arrange the release of Abigayle's care to him."

"Great!" I say, giving him a big squeeze.

"That is if he agrees," he cautions.

It will be a full month before Abby is released to come home. Each twin comes home in her own stocking. At Christmastime, a volunteer grandmother group crafts a stocking for each baby at the NICU to go home in. I imagine a circle of beautiful crones sitting around a cookfire, singing while weaving a pouch to transport infants' home where they belong. This illuminates a part of my psyche. I feel warmed, held, and hopeful. We still hang Abby's and Libby's bright stockings on the wall at Christmas above a statue of Kali, the ultimate expression of Mother Nature, who represents transformation, the cycles of birth and death, which create and devour. We hang them as a reminder of this very strange time in 1996 when we spent all of our birthdays, Thanksgiving, and Christmas in the NICU at Stanford Hospital. As we continue on the long journey ahead, I hope to remember the medicine of our elders with this grandmother song from Sheffy Oren Bach. Original source unknown:

I hear the voice of my grandmothers callin' me
I hear the voice of my grandmother's song
She says, "Stand in your power
Women stand in your power
Listen, listen. Listen, listen."

I hear the voice of my grandmothers callin' me
I hear the voice of my grandmother's song
She says, "Give birth, give life
Mothers, give birth, give life
Listen, listen. Listen, listen…"

In the month leading up to Abby's homecoming, I nurse Autumn and Libby, while pumping milk for Abby. It amuses me to see Autumn's big head next to tiny Libby's, both latched onto my boobs. I'm quenched by Autumn's comfort. Gradually, I prepare her for Abby's arrival, assuring her that she can continue to nurse until she feels finished. She responds, "Okay." In the meantime, we thoroughly enjoy this intimacy. Quite magically, on the day Abby is to come home, Autumn puckers off my breast, looks at me with her bright eyes, and matter-of-factly declares, "Mommy, I'm all done."

And just like that, Autumn is weaned at two years and three months old.

I celebrate these moments of success amidst countless trials. Life can easily wipe out the best-laid plans and dreams any one of us may have for ourselves or our children. I seldom thought about what I wanted for my twins; I assumed everything would go well, as it did with Autumn. *What the hell?* The reality is my babies are three months premature with brain injuries that will impact our lives—*forever.* It's incomprehensible. I grapple with shame and isolation for all of us. And I sense the wisdom and guidance of Mother Earth as I continuously learn to trust my intuition and embrace the unexpected.

I'm only beginning to realize how important it is to ask questions, listen to my body, voice my opinion, and trust my intuition. When I listen to my children, I feel a portal to wisdom open in my body, guiding, informing, and restoring possibilities. Other times I feel as if I've suddenly stepped back into the 1950s, where every move a mother makes is judged and mediated through society's eyes. I refuse to be confined by narrow definitions of "normal."

All my life, yearnings have lived inside of me. I don't want this dark episode to overshadow the progress I've made to mend and recover from earlier traumas. I want all of us to feel whole and thrive beyond hardship. I want to listen and let every murmur become a roar.

13
Coming Home

On the whole, life at home is an improvement over life in the NICU, for three reasons: I can turn out the lights, open the windows, and snuggle with all five of us under one roof. We relish the quiet without the interruption of hospital interventions and strangers. Kym Ann and a few other friends continue to hold the babies and make us delicious meals. We are fortunate to have volunteers support us for several months.

Among the volunteers, an Italian couple stands out, arriving every Friday with a song on their lips as if entering a party. They effortlessly prepare a feast in our kitchen, their presence only known by the aroma of garlic, basil, and rosemary drifting through our house. They make pasta and tomato sauce just like my mother. The sauce is thick with green vegetables, filling our plates with love. When they announce their final visit, "The garlic bread will be finished in five minutes; everything else is on the stove and waiting for you." I reverently beg, "I will pay you to return weekly." They understand how to be in a family's home without boundary intrusion. Although they must decline, we carry their kindness in our hearts along with gratitude for many others who have reached out to us with baskets of nourishment.

I long to be outside. Soon I discover a way to simultaneously wear two baby slings. With Abby and Libby slung to my chest, Autumn happily skips alongside us as we hike to a nearby park. I feel a sense of normalcy in our unique lives when all four of us can explore nature together. As I sit on a park bench, Autumn runs in the sand or up and down the slide, yelling, "Mommy, watch me!" When I am not watching Autumn, I bow my head toward my sleeping bundles, mesmerized. Their faces glow, part of them intricately connected to earthly existence, and another to a soul realm. They suck enough milk with each passing day to grow stronger.

In six months, we arranged for nursing services through a local agency. Our first nurse is exceptional, a mother of nine children, including two sets of twins. She is a comfort to have around, offering exceptional support. This gives me time with Autumn and to delve into research. I am determined to understand my twins' condition and do the next best thing to help them along.

In the first six months, Libby mostly sleeps, she doesn't cry like Abby. During Libby's intubation period at the NICU, a powerful sedative was added to the intravenous fluid that dripped into her pin-size veins. She was semi-comatose, until now. She screams abruptly—inconsolably; her body twitches and her eyes blink incessantly. *Perhaps the sedation has worn off and this is a delayed trauma response?* She struggles at the nipple, latches on for a moment, startles, and wails. Concerned about her agitation and weight loss, I reach out to our doctor and a lactation consultant for help.

Our primary doctor councils against sedation and encourages swaddling her like an infant. Despite my desire to breastfeed, she isn't gaining weight. We switched to nursing her with a tube. I diligently pump milk and put it in a plastic container attached to a tube that I insert into her mouth with my finger. She sucks anxiously, receiving milk, but more often than not it spurts out like a missile. She cries and projectile vomits—persistently. She reacts to even the slightest stimuli, day and night. There are brief moments of rest when she is wrapped snugly like a butterfly in a cocoon. We try various methods to soothe Libby; rocking, walking, or bouncing her on our mini trampoline. Stress escalates, as doors close, horns honk, utensils clack—life. I imagine she can hear a pin drop. Fraught, I consult our doctor again. He confirms my research, "Her nervous system lacks the myelin sheath required to protect her sensory receptors and filter sound." He referred me to a neurologist, Dr. William Schultz in San Francisco. Unfortunately, each visit leaves me more frustrated, as I receive no new information, only new prescriptions.

Dr. Schultz speaks assuredly with a distinctive East European accent. He is cleanly shaven except for a thick pepper mustache shaped like a worm atop his narrow mouth and square jaw. He wears dark-framed glasses that tip over his stout nose. I am a good foot taller than Dr. Schultz, but a lot less confident. He acknowledges the obvious, "A weak neurological condition, not thriving, and seizures. I have medications to treat this." *I know this, she's eleven pounds. Breathe.* At a subsequent appointment, he suggests a brain scan to investigate increased *clonus*[13] despite already following his three-month treatment plan of medications. I figured out that Libby's inability to latch on or keep food down is due to the continuous frequency of her seizures, even though the duration of the spasms is short.

Dr. Schultz is a pediatric neurologist, but he doesn't like crying. He insists that Libby and I wait in the lobby until the medication kicks in. "A quick poke will sedate her." Libby is fast asleep by the time he pokes up to thirty purple needles into her scalp for an MRI. "Best to increase her Phenobarbital and Topamax to three times a day." These medications were meant to heal her clonus, calm her nervous system, and promote weight gain. But they have failed.

"What?" I give him a long incredulous stare before I close my eyes and think, *Western medical surgeons section out one-pound babies, perform liver transplants and blood transfusions, and take brains apart, but do not have a way to comfort a significantly underweight baby who cries persistently?*

After he removes the needles from Libby's head, he tells me, "The MRI indicates more gray than white matter in her brain. That's very abnormal."

"Hmm," I say without surprise. "Is there anything else we can do to help her brain?"

"No. There's nothing else that we can do," he asserts with a faint grin.

"In other words, the best you can do is to consult the inside of your head, refer to your medication manual, and send me home with one drug after another for my fragile baby," I mumble, not caring if he hears me.

"Any pharmacist will fill this for you," he declares, while I swear and mutter about this insane solution. *Is he listening? Did he already confidently write a prescription before we entered the room?* I want to punch him.

---

[13] Clonus is a series of involuntary, rhythmic, muscular contractions and relaxations. It is particularly associated with upper motor neuron lesions and in many cases is accompanied by spasticity. The frequency may last a few seconds to several minutes.
Kenneth Ludmerer, MD. *Let Me Heal,* Oxford University Press, September 1, 2014

"You're quite sure about this? There is no other course of action or knowledge to obtain through another source?" I plead in my mama voice.

"Absolutely. I've been practicing neurology for over twenty-five years," he brags.

"How do you come by this assurance?" I roar, fire in my belly.

"Medical school, fieldwork in hospitals, fellowships," he continues.

"That's what I thought. Has any neurologist ever looked outside of medical school or hospitals run by medical schools?" I ask, knowing I will not return to his office.

"We know it's not there," he claims.

"Prior to looking, you mean?" I say, enjoying the probe.

"That's right," he says, defending his turf.

Not a very scientific approach for such a scientific profession. Am I on a dead-end street? He doesn't give a hoot about my curiosity to explore options. I've learned about alternative health care all of my life. There must be an alternative healing treatment for my daughter. He has earned his rank. I walk out with Libby sleeping in the sling around my chest and another prescription in my hand, knowing I will not make it to the pharmacist.

At that moment, I have a visceral awakening in my body. For the first time since this debacle, I am actively challenging a man-God to his face. I am owning my lived experience that positively confirms another authority—my instincts—Mother Earth.

Why bother to fill her already compromised system with the same medications that have not shown one sign of improvement? I'm skeptical of animal-tested, synthetically derived, profit-generating, side-effect-promoting formulas that benefit pharmaceutical companies and medical institutions. I read up on neurological development and learn that gentle, repetitive motion will settle her and allow her to manage to suck and swallow her milk.

I will continue to look outside of prescribed boxes into alternative treatments like diet, acupuncture, oxygen, and time in nature. A sense of relief fuels me. *We will find our way.*

One moment everything seems fine—she nurses and assimilates her food—and then in a wink, her body stiffens. She projectile vomits every ounce. Washing clothes, floors, walls, innocent bystanders, and myself are standard procedures. After a few more months of vigilance, I am able to anticipate her pattern within a matter of seconds, but I find that comprehension keeps pace with bewilderment. I know by now that I am not dreaming about someone else's life and that Libby has more complications than Dr. Sunshine from the NICU led us to believe. I don't yet know what this is or what it means for the longevity of our family.

I have not come close to unpacking the multiple layers of trauma-induced upon us. I have no inkling if Dr. Sunshine knows more or less than we do about taking care of premature infants, but I do want to return and ask this question: *What happens when the sedation wears off?*

Sedation—a side effect of being captive of a Western civilization that is more or less compelled to go on heroically saving life, and then destroying it in order to advance a growing pharmaceutical industry *and deny women the wisdom inherent in their bodies.*

I'm on autopilot. It's familiar. I dive in with fierce determination to understand my twins' conditions and offer them the best support. I yearn for another capable adult to share the emotional and physical intricacies of this household. As a woman raised in the '60s, I learned to attribute my worth to serving the needs of others. Caregiving became my specialty, yet the momentous responsibility of parenting falls disproportionately on the backs of mothers without giving financial assistance, positive validation, or societal support.

I set out to meet with our primary physician. We are referred to the San Andreas Regional Center (SARC). SARC is a private, nonprofit corporation funded by the state of California to serve people with developmental disabilities as required by the Lanterman Developmental Disabilities Act. After numerous developmental screenings, Abby and Libby qualify for intervention services due to their high-risk medical conditions, developmental disabilities, and the likelihood of additional disabilities. Their prognosis is indefinite. *Indefinite.* Their conditions include cerebral palsy, blindness, and developmental delays in all areas. We are assigned a service coordinator for ongoing individualized program planning (IPP). Occupational therapy and vision services begin in our home weekly until age five. It is the start of support but also introduces an influx of strangers into our home *indefinitely*.

14

Healing Triangle

I learn about a neurological acupuncturist in our area named Dr. Zhu. A friend of mine works as his secretary and encourages me to check out his medicine. The twins are about fifteen months old when we go to his clinic on the east side of Santa Cruz. Dr. Zhu holds an open-room clinic. All of his patients are treated in the same space. After checking in with his assistant in a small front office, we walk into a medium-sized room with earth-tone walls and four or five chairs spread out around three walls. There are lines of tape on the floor to practice walking. One wall has a ballet bar for exercise. To my surprise, when we arrive, Ram Dass (a famous international spiritual teacher) is sitting in one of the chairs to the left. He is being treated for a stroke and is working hard to lift his legs into motion. He watches Dr. Zhu treat Abby and Libby with a big smile on his face. I smile back and recall his famous words, "Don't think about the past, don't think about the future, be here now." I'm encouraged by the compassion I feel in this space. My breath sinks a bit more into my body as I wonder how he is navigating a stroke and the impact this might have on his public teachings.

Dr. Zhu wears a white jacket and wire-rim glasses. His shiny black hair is lined with grey. He squeezes my hand with a tender gaze at the twins as he leads us to a chair. I like him immediately. Abby and Libby are snuggled in slings crossed over my chest with their tiny heads popping out. He is quick to treat them—gingerly, skillfully. First, he puts about six needles in Libby's head, saying, "The next time, we will give her more. Let's leave them in for twenty minutes." I like that he is taking time to see how her body reacts.

Then he gives Abby the same amount, assuring us this will help her eyes. He waltzes around the room like a good fairy, adjusting needles and encouraging the movement of the limbs of several other patients. Dr. Zhu is eager to help us. He invites us to come for three visits a week for the price of one weekly visit. I accept his generous invitation, knowing that the expenses of choosing alternative treatments outside of insurance coverage will require ingenuity and careful planning for out-of-pocket expenses. *Be here now. One day at a time. Don't think about—indefinitely—for life.*

Libby responds well to these treatments. When she receives the needles, her eyes stop fluttering, her head steadies, and she becomes calm. Within a few weeks, her condition improves significantly. The frequency of seizures decreases from one hundred to about twenty-five per day, and she gains weight. Dr. Zhu advises that for acupuncture to treat her brain injury properly, we needed to come soon after the injury for optimal results. He guides against medications. Libby needs all of her energy for growth and development. I choose not to accept prescribed medications, having experienced their effects on myself. I adjusted the dosage to match my body weight which led to a foggy, gloomy, lethargic state. This could not be beneficial for my daughter. Despite doubts that arise, my instincts align with my choices, and I trust them.

"As her system develops, the clonus will eventually stop," Dr Zhu reassures us with an attentive smile. I feel supported by his expertise.

Dr. Zhu's open-room clinic offers a refreshing perspective on healing. He believes in a healing triangle, every branch of the triangle holds equal value—the doctor, the patient, and the community—each benefits the other. Sitting in his clinic, we feel connected to a larger healing community. In this clinic, everyone shares experiences with brain or spinal cord injuries, strokes, or other neurological conditions. Each part of the triangle plays a crucial role in the healing process. If one part is absent, the healing becomes difficult. This is different from traditional doctor-patient hierarchies that lead to discomfort, isolation, or submission from individuals who are otherwise proactive.

I cherish the moments sitting in Dr. Zhu's clinic three times a week, where empathy and camaraderie create a vibrant exchange of energy that holds us together. We learn from each other's struggles and feel empowered to carry on with the hard journey of healing. I will carry this treatment jewel forward, along with the treasured interactions that fuel confidence and curiosity as I strive for a sustainable lifestyle for my family. Sadly, in a couple of years when Dr. Zhu relocates his clinic an hour away to San Jose, we feel a huge loss. Given the intensity of our daily schedule, traffic, and the typical requirements of managing a household with young children, we are not able to travel that far. Little do I know that later I will forget this triangle, feel isolated and overwhelmed. I will ache to the bone, fall into despair, and overlook the other people facing similar hardships.

15

I'm Staying

It is March 1999, after Spirit carried baby Libby and me away from that steep edge to home. Daffodils are blooming cheerful yellow. Sprinklings of peace are sprouting in our home like morning glories. The electrified ocean wind of Hera that mysteriously steered my distraught hopeless body and baby Libby home on that horrific dark night is fiercely etched into the core of my being. *"You're Staying."* Nursing my babies calm both of us and reminds me that some of their fetal cells (called PAPCs) migrated into my maternal organs during pregnancy—connecting us forever. Even though I am carrying them, they also carry me. I am the embodiment of my children, we're growing—and loving together.

Still, at times, I feel like I ride as a passenger in my own body, fretfully looking out onto strange land. My body is working, but *will I make the right turns, will I stay on course, will I...?*

I look in the mirror, desperate to revive my tired eyes and drained body. My mind continues to push ahead, seeking a routine, predictability, and some semblance of structure that I can relax into—while another part of me clamors for my former life—a deliberation to choose personal time, friends, and work that provides the security of steady income. I see how living within ashrams, where the rules were neatly outlined, gave me a surface sense of security. Eventually, if I didn't agree with them, I chose not to comply. I took what I liked and left the rest. Soon I will recognize another remnant from the past to excavate as I come to understand the hurdles a mother must climb on a regular basis, while wearing an invisible backpack, to access true belonging, safety, and connection.

We buy a bigger house with three bedrooms a few blocks away. The prior occupant, a long-distance truck driver, left her dogs inside and a slew of chickens fenced in the backyard while she traveled for weeks at a time, so the place requires a complete overhaul. All the rooms but the kitchen have oak wood. We refinish each floor but the front room, which is trashed. There is a benefit to wooden floors saturated with dog urine: when refinished, the color is unmatched—beautiful mahogany—no smell. Later visitors will ask, "How did you get your floors this awesome shade of brown?"

We're a couple of blocks further from the beaches. I still hear the sea lions and smell the briny air in the distance. I steadily open and unpack boxes that are scattered around the house. The babies have been out of my arms for fifteen minutes. I wake to my own snoring, snuggled next to Autumn with Roald Dahl's *Matilda* opened on my chest. As usual, I conked out before she did. I creep out of her bed and tiptoe to the front room, light a vanilla-scented candle, and turn off the house lights. On my way to my rocking chair, I admire the elaborate tiny house that Autumn has shaped out of wooden blocks. I don't touch it. I'm aware that she, too, is reconstructing her life. I sit down and feel the warm sturdy wood against my back. I rock slowly, meditatively, savoring the larger space within and around me. Although I am exhausted, I hear my heart whispering, *you can do this.* I imagine myself organizing the kitchen, bedrooms, and bathroom, building a wheelchair ramp, and converting our garage into a playroom where my girls can learn and grow. Five mouths to feed instead of just my own keeps me going. Cooking fuels me, with each recipe I feel more anchored in my feet, more deliberate in orienting myself in a life I would never have imagined. A bit of order comes with sacks of groceries, yet my schedule is unpredictable day and night: when I sleep, who I see, where I go, or when I will have time to connect with friends or recover professional interests. Like most mothers, I'm not easily given the occasion to drive off to a scheduled job or advance in my career like Hank does.

Hank has never been physically violent to me. Without a doubt, emotionally he has not been present. We're both stumbling around in the wake of expulsion from a long-term membership immersed in a spiritual community. He initiated this expulsion with a letter from both of us and signed my name without my consent. I want to choose for myself. Prior to now, Hank preferred to confide in his guru. This was his go-to for all things spiritual, including the historical versions of Eastern yogic or Christian traditions that permit men to renounce, enter a monastery, or walk away from family obligations. I wanted him to speak with me out of respect as the woman who was carrying his child. I'm not saying this to hang out his laundry; that is not my place. Albeit, his actions didn't help me to trust him.

I learn about a long-standing and rising statistic. The divorce rate is eighty percent for couples with special-needs children. After the initial life-changing diagnosis of a child with a disability, parents encounter a shocking reality. Learning that your child or children may face a disability *for a lifetime* is impossible to digest quickly. The dream of wellness, functional achievements, and easy celebrations is lost to us like death. When I consider the past three years, I recognize both of us are attempting to process loss and protect ourselves while we learn to adapt. It's persistent in the same way traumatic grief is. I am on my feet cooking dinner and suddenly I'm butchering bread like it's a block of beef, or puffing myself up like a peacock as if to say everything is gorgeous and light. All of the stages of grief are present: denial, anger, bargaining, depression, and, with any luck, acceptance. I feel hopeful yet unable to imagine what recovery will look like.

I don't blame Hank. Neither one of us knows how to communicate about what happened on October 21. Before Hank, I was deeply scarred by relational trauma. My tendency was to flee and avoid relationships altogether. In my heart, I long to love and be loved. I reckon I've had little practice developing skills that fortify relationships to endure the highs and lows of time. I do realize that my years of numbing, self-sabotaging, celibacy, or barricading my body did not allow me to get messy, work through conflicts, or take the steps required to build trust. It's different this time around; children are involved. I'm not going anywhere. *I'm choosing to stay.*

All parents know that personal sacrifice is necessary; now it is multiplied by medical and therapy appointments, hiring and training support providers, and interacting with a range of agencies for advocacy and support to navigate a world designed for able bodies. The best-committed relationship is susceptible to disconnect; ours is compounded by the unpredictable cycles of traumatic grief. We are as endangered as the leatherback sea turtle.

The one ginormous thing that had defined the relationship between Hank and me is no longer holding. Another feeling burns in my gut that isn't singular to Hank. Maybe it is betrayal, or unfairness, or both. The care of babies often lands on the lap and in the hands of women, although the choices a woman makes about her body are often not her own. If a woman chooses to renounce external responsibilities like children, she is severely shamed, judged, and suddenly excommunicated or injured to the point of death. This choice is one of the many options not afforded to women. It is imprinted in our psyche. We carry the babies, we birth them, we raise them. Obviously, we don't make them on our own.

I want the decisions about our babies to be shared. *Aren't they meant to be?* I'm still often tongue-tied around men, having internalized the age-old adage that men are superior to women. My rational mind knows this is not true, my scar tissue tells me otherwise. Now that I am a mother, I am surprised when I behave in similar ways to my mom. The suppressed emotion, silence, and turning the other cheek. I promised myself, *I would never be like that. I will never let a man define my place or who I am.* Awkward, I know. I don't remember one in-depth conversation with Hank, like the many I have with my friends that I call brother or sister. The vulnerable talks where you peer into each other's eyes and feel words that don't need to be spoken. *I hear you. I see you. I'm here for you.* I remember wanting this—often.

The hypervigilance drives me like a locomotive without brakes. I want Hank to join me in the promising treatments I learn about for Abby and Libby. This usually isn't a good thing. Every time I approach him with exciting discoveries, I feel another brick cementing the wall between us. He is pooh-poohing my optimism. My intuition tells me there must be a way, but his mood crashes my stamina. Like strangers on a ship passing in the night, he tells me, "I have limited energy. I'm lucky to keep my job." I notice his skin is blaring with red rashes. I've seen this before, and whenever I ask him about it, he brushes me off. It seems worse but he's not saying so. Instead, he bemoans Libby. He wants to have her institutionalized[14]. I'm horrified by this

---

[14] "In the first half of the twentieth century, parents were encouraged to institutionalize their disabled children; those who kept their children at home were likely to be told that they were depriving them of therapeutic and educational services. (Leiter, 2004) A parent's movement in the 1960s and 1970s worked to obtain community-based services and was followed by a wave of activism by disabled adults and later collaboration among adult, parent, and professional constituencies."
Gail Heidi Landsman, *Reconstructing Motherhood and Disability in the Age of "Perfect" Babies.* Routledge, NY. 2009.

suggestion, while at the same time, I'm aware that we're both in need of buoyancy.

I decide to contact a family and marriage therapist for help. I go alone. Hank isn't interested. They are trained in *Hakomi therapy[15]*, a body-centered somatic approach to psychological well-being. After many sessions of unpacking myself on the floor, body shaking, and grief releasing, my therapist asked me if I'd be willing to try an experiment. "Wait, I'm not done," I plead. I need more time to discharge. I have been pretending not to know what I know. I want to do my best for our children and I'm not willing to drag someone along if they aren't willing to step up and get messy. I agree to an experiment—next session. They set it up carefully, with props, as if I'm entering a laboratory. I put on a make-believe purple coat (white doesn't work for me).

The first part of the experiment is to imagine raising my children without Hank. I sit, following the instructions to envision myself in our house, more alone. I'm guided to pay attention to how I feel, and the energetic sensations in my body. *Lightness. Open. Bubbly. Fire. Aliveness. Fear.* I leave that place to imagine raising our children with Hank in the scene. I sit, immediately feeling *sad. Tight. Heavy. Caged. Fear.* Like I have a fourth child, but not in a good way. And there it is—*shame.* Like I've done something wrong. Fear is present. Telling me that, either way, *I won't get it right.* The sensations in my body are crystal clear. It scares me. I'm afraid of the unknown aspects of this situation, but when I lean in, beneath shame, beneath fear, I'm able to ground in my body. I feel okay. I choose to muscle up and lean into the unknown, single. I'm not brave. I can't carry his weight. *Am I being selfish or self-preserving? Or is this the ultimate labor of love: giving birth to myself as a mother?*

It turns out to be a mutual decision. Hank and I work out an agreement with two mediators, who help us with the parenting aspect of the separation agreement, and emphasize that the role of a parent cannot be enforced. *Am I*

---

[15] The Hakomi Method of Experiential Psychotherapy, a body-centered approach developed by Ron Kurtz, combines somatic awareness with experiential techniques to promote psychological growth and transformation. Hakomi theory holds the body to be a window to unconscious psychological material. Hakomi integrates principles of Eastern philosophy, emphasizing concepts such as mindfulness, loving presence, and empathy.
Kurtz, R., Feb, 2009, Goodtherapy.org, Feb, 2018

expected to accept this? The idea that a parenting agreement can't be forced makes me so mad! It's not about enforcement. Our children exist! I'm on the floor. *Oh, does he get another free pass for a medical condition?* Hank will only be involved with the two most-able-bodied children (Autumn and Abby) one evening a week and one Saturday a month—even less with Libby. The counselor calculates this to be three percent of parenting time. *Ouch.*

16
Forgotten

N ow I am free to call upon a strategy I know well: self-reliance, the twin to hypervigilance. I plunge ahead into the countless books about parenting. I'd give anything for a manual on parenting brain-injured children or anything that comes close to depicting our lives. I have three uniquely dissimilar children, each with specific needs for their level of development. When I consider my fully functioning, able-bodied Autumn, all of these books make sense. Now I am challenged to foster a suitable life for my disabled twins and grieve the life I will not have with Autumn or abled-bodied twins. When I'm driven like this, it doesn't mean I have a well-thought-out plan. I don't.

I find comfort in meeting a fairly progressive mom with twins a year older than mine. Her daughter doesn't have any visible challenges. The boy can use his upper body, although the use of his lower extremities and speech lag behind. Donna has been trained in Western medicine, but is actively pursuing nontraditional measures. She gave me the book *What to Do About Your Brain-Injured Child* and is already implementing a home therapy program based on the tools she gathers from this book for healing and growing the brain. She sees good results. Her son has learned to feed himself, although haphazardly, but he manages to get food into his mouth. It is a joy to watch. I race through the pages eager to learn. It makes sense: In order for the brain to grow, it needs oxygen, movement, neurological stimulation, and sensory integration.

After reading this book, I'm motivated to learn about the plasticity of the brain and the 'vagus nerve' that acts as a superhighway through the body, carrying information between the brain and organs to help the body respond, rest, and integrate sensations. The research indicates that my daughters' conditions are not stagnant. They can achieve higher levels of function if given appropriate stimulation. Donna lives near her mom, who volunteers to help implement a daily, three-hour neurological movement program. She encourages me to do the same. Donna is in the process of separating from her partner. I'm not surprised; it's a rough road to travel. I had several conversations with her husband. He is similar to Hank in many ways—a good man with honest intentions, yet unprepared for this insurmountable task. He tells me, "This is by far the hardest thing I have ever faced. I can't do it."

I want to know more about Donna and how she manages. She looks fairly rested and continues to work part-time as a physician's assistant. Her mother is retired and lives nearby. She takes care of the twins while Donna works, and maintains Daniel's home therapy program. The twin sister attends preschool. It sounds like a wonderful arrangement—an arrangement I long for. Instead, I am in the midst of integrating the daunting reality of raising humans alone. But I have made a good friend in Donna, who understands me. This. Us. 1999.

I ride as a passenger inside my own body, looking out our front window as if on a ride, watching, watching. This is what hypervigilance does. It's a driving force, an elevated state of alertness constantly censoring not only me, but the four of us until collapse happens. I isolate. I'm unable to motivate myself to leave the house. I have my children reminding me of our existence, but I wonder who our people are. *Who would call on me now?* I am fading, like a forgotten Polaroid. To be forgotten is the worst sadness of all. I miss communal spiritual practice. Dark, doubtful thoughts return. I'm unsure where we belong as a family. I'm determined to implement the patterning and neurological stimulation program for Abby and Libby. Each patterning session requires three people to guide their bodies through a twenty-minute course to wire their brains for movement. I have sporadic nursing help and volunteers in and out of the house like a drive-thru restaurant. My life has zero resemblance to my tidy life of accomplishment and proficiency. Unchecked to-do lists and tracking people defeat me. *Why do I fixate on making things better?* Friends who were so strong with us during the pregnancy of my twins and the four-month hospital phase have moved on with their own lives. Most of them don't have children. I imagine we have less and less in common.

Sitting in the red chair at the kitchen table, I lift my head and notice an invitation to a baby shower on the table—RSVP required. I didn't send one. The party has already passed. Lucy is one of the pregnant moms in my Mommy and Me yoga class. She was pregnant with Hannah when I was pregnant with Autumn. She is much younger but we had a lively connection and our toddlers became natural playmates.

When the invitation first arrived, I imagined Lucy ready to birth a full-term baby, Hannah playing at her side. I saw Lucy untying packages decorated with colorful bows and lifting up lace dresses and rain boots to stomp in puddles. Our mutual friends reached out their hands to feel the soft textures. They sat in a circle and took turns passing toys from one to the other, saying, "Isn't this darling?" "Oh my God! I love it!" or "I can't wait until all our girls are holding hands and running on the beach together." It reminded me of the alien trajectory I find myself in.

Shit. I didn't even call her. I forgot how to have a coherent conversation that isn't interrupted by crying, and an onslaught of thoughts about my messy, fragmented, unfinished life. No matter which way I turn, I feel raw and exposed. I already let two helpers go because they made Autumn cry on several occasions by entering her room without permission. Like myself, I feel her outcry for boundaries. Hank has moved to his own apartment on the other side of town. I struggle to reconnect the threads of our life. I want to know where the finish line is.

17
Motherhood is Dharma

A loud knock at the door disrupts my napping. I had fallen asleep with my head on the table.

"I'm coming!" I yell, shaking myself like a warrior.

It is not the cry of a child. It is a sturdy knock at the front door. *Am I parked illegally? Who did I piss off? Who would call at this hour?* I look at the clock that hangs above the kitchen sink overflowing with dirty dishes. It is 8:35 PM—only fifteen minutes into alone time.

I groan and drop my head to the table.

"Go away," I yell.

Apparently, whoever it is does not see the "Do Not Disturb" sign on the front door; I already dismantled the bell, involuntarily digging myself into a hole, and sealing myself off. The knocking becomes more persistent. Then I remember a particular phone call I didn't answer.

It was Cathy on the answering machine, her happy, annoying, spiritual voice saying, "Pick up. I have something to share with you. I want to come over."

I press the erase button. "Sorry, not in the mood for sharing."

If this is Cathy, she is as brave as a hungry tigress. Now, I have no choice. If I don't answer the door, the knocking will wake up the babies. If I do answer the door, I might say something I will regret and cause her to fall off the wheelchair ramp. I trip over *The Pink Fairy Book* and my wooden clogs on the way, as if I'd been drinking shots of Amaretto.

I squint my left eye, forcing my right eye open, and recognize Cathy on the other side of the peephole. She is smiling and holding a brown paper package.

"Ugh," I groan, yet a still small voice within me urges me to welcome this friend who has always put her hand in my hand to walk together, a true sister.

When I open the door, Cathy prances in like a breeze of ocean air.

"Come in," I say, after the fact, pretending to be glad. As I clear a seat for her on the sofa, I begin to feel how I've missed her.

"Please; sit down, friend," she says in a honey voice that eases my discomfort.

I flop down on the sofa next to her.

Over the years, I had come to confide in Cathy. Her daughter, a little older, was a playmate for Autumn. I wonder about my abrasive tone. *Why do I cut people out?*

I am disappointed in myself. *Have I lost the spiritual connection that I deeply felt before the twins were born?* I remember my first visit with Eunice in the fall of 1976, when she became my guide, and later when she said "Get On With It!"—insisting that I do not abandon my soul purpose.

Is Cathy here to do the same, to help me remember?

———

It's just over three years since the twins were born at six months gestation. Sitting with my friend Cathy, I consider how much my life has changed. I meekly scan the clutter of therapeutic apparatuses I've acquired for the girls: wheelchairs, sensory integration devices, wedges, bolsters, and scribblings on paper of ongoing tasks. I notice a spiritual confidence that I used to tout at the ashram, perhaps to hide my insecurities. I wonder: *What is samadhi? Is it real, does it matter?* I feel a shake inside, not different from when Alice told me about RW—someone who could help me. I'm listening, but unable to look my friend in the eyes.

I don't want to hear about anything that sounds like the all-pervading bliss of enlightenment. I have a bookcase stuffed with spiritual teachers and teachings. I feel disillusioned with spirituality. Even my well-worn "bible" that sits by my bedside—*I Am That, Talks with Sri Nisargadatta Maharaj*—does not penetrate my quandary. I want something that speaks to the core of being an embodied woman, a mother, beyond a healthy meal plan or how to clean just about anything. I didn't recognize it at the time but have come to realize that since receiving guidance from Eunice, the bulk of the teachings I'm exposed to are written by men, perhaps for men. Problematic, I know.

"I brought you a tape to listen to."

"No, thank you." My chest tightens.

"This teacher is unlike any teacher I have ever met. He is down-to-earth." *She's sure.*

"An enlightened teacher who is down-to-earth. Did he put away his ochre robe?"

She giggles. "He dresses in plain street clothes. You know the clothing doesn't matter. It's about our presence." Her tone makes me feel like I am missing an opportunity to have tea with Oprah. I might perish if I don't attend. She continues while my bullshit barometer is tracking.

"He's not shielded in claims to enlightenment or selling tickets. He's straight. His talk is actually disturbing, very human—real. He's addressing the human condition. Most everyone fell asleep. We're not used to this kind of discourse in public meetings."

"No," I say again, feeling like a stick in the mud, letting Cathy hear my self-doubt.

"There is subtle yet refreshing humor in his words. He speaks about dark nights and human challenges." She delicately places the cassette on the table like a bouquet of flowers for my dying life.

"Really," I tingle, raising one eyebrow, which is very hard to do when you're dog-tired.

"Yes, really, but that's when most of us fell asleep. No one talks about dark nights," she says, admitting her difficulty with the topic.

"Hmmm." We sit quietly for a few minutes. I feel myself breathe and soften; my shoulders drop. Quickly I steer off intimacy and jeer, "Sorry, Cathy. I'm not up for a shot of nirvana from the spiritual marketplace. You can leave now.

My hands are full." I say, folding a tiny onesie from a load of laundry on the coffee table in front of us.

"I know you aren't," she says. "That's why I bring this to you. I see what you're up against. I see you. I know you. Remember, we're friends. I'm your sister."

"Thank you," I nod, looking at the cassette on the table, folding with my hands.

She quietly gets up, opens the door, turns around, and says, "I'll be back." *I know she will.*

That's how much I have changed. Three years earlier, I would have run to answer the door, let her in with open arms, and graciously taken her package. I would have offered her a cup of tea and something sweet to eat. That was when my life was blissfully wrapped around one sturdy finger—*Soul Purpose—my claim to samadhi*; before I was hijacked to Stanford Hospital. When I was certain of myself, on fire with purpose, empowered to hoist my enlightenment flag. *I was on top of the mountain. I had arrived.* Before my honeymoon with Autumn snug in my sling, happily attached to me, inoculated to the misfortunes of human life, before I forgot what it felt like to start the day with a sun salutation. Before I fell prey to former patterns of doubt, stubborn self-reliance, and the seductive, insidious psychological mind games. Thoughts that tell me a Frappuccino will get me through the day.

I open the package that Cathy placed directly before me, eager to listen.

I read the title on the cassette. *The Mysteries and Thresholds of Christ:* by *Adyashanti*[16].

Adyashanti has a nice ring to it. Oh crap! My chest is softening again. "He talks about dark nights." *Maybe this is like the spirituality Eunice represented.* I don't want my old life back. I don't want a spiritual life cloistered with paraphernalia, rules, attitudes, and teachings that superimpose an image on top of our messy humanness. I thought I left the house of patriarchal fathers—

---

[16] Adyashanti, meaning 'primordial peace' is an American spiritual teacher and author from the San Francisco Bay Area who offers talks, online study courses, and retreats in the United States and abroad. He is the author of numerous books, CDs and DVDs and, together with his wife Mukti, is the founder of *Open Gate Sangha,* Inc.

confinement. I recognize I've hit another bottom. I didn't realize listening to Adyashanti speak about dark nights would bring me comfort. I learned that rigid dogma doesn't foster critical thinking, and therefore overlooks our creative potential. Eunice planted seeds within me. There is more gardening to do. *Will Adyashanti's message address the challenge of trauma and relationships, raising children—the life of a woman, caregiver, or householder?*

"What the heck?" I speak aloud to myself. "What do I have to lose?" I tear open the bag, put the cassette in the player, sit down, and listen.

My body softens a little more. *Oh no!* I feel a tingle in my toes. My spine shivers. I am not sure if I am excited or afraid.

"Spiritual awakening is just the beginning... It's getting your foot in the door. It's the beginning of a mysterious unfolding akin to the thresholds and mysteries of Christ." I imagine he is speaking about all Christian mystics, as far back as Catherine of Sienna, the peacemaker, or Hildegard von Bingen, a Benedictine abbess who received divine visions as a child and would later make significant contributions to medicine and music. Or Saint Teresa of Avila, who wrote the prayer of union. Therese de Lisieux, affectionately named 'The Little Flower,' believed that children have a gift for adults to model. She trusts that what matters most is not great deeds but great love.

I listen with my hand over my mouth, reminiscing about praying with cloistered sisters at a hermitage I visited near Maine.

At a certain point, I have to pinch myself. *Am I really hearing this?* When I hear, "the dark night of the soul... and the feeling of utter abandonment by Spirit," I have to pause the cassette and get my headphones so I can turn it up. My attention intensifies with a resonance that quivers through my body. "Christ asked that his cup of sorrow be taken from him."

I swallow hard, gasp, and listen without a blink.

I feel my heart ache; longing is ignited. My throat unleashes garbled sounds when he talks about challenges—dark nights—the temptations that arise after awakening. *Holy Mother of God!* He is referring to the heroine's journey—the descent of the Sumerian goddess Inanna to the underworld. He continues about the threshold of resurrection and the possibility of new life. *New life.*

Listening maddens me with inner reflection. I am being called to the task of moving through the darkness of the underworld. Cathy disrupts my resistance, a guide like Inanna's sister Ereshkigal. *Am I at a stressful threshold—a rite of passage to perform a funeral for my former life? Is it possible that the life I have been given is the exact dose of medicine for the transfiguration of new life—soul purpose?* If I can resist clinging to the old, the past, and feel this stinging sorrow, "Die to the old—Love will wear your face.*" Love will wear my face?* True transformation is exactly as Julian of Norwich points out: There is only one thing to learn well: Love. *Who shows you love?* Love. *Why?* For Love. It's all here in this recording, sparking my remembering of Inanna. Shining a light. Forming a bridge. Not only is love possible, but it is also already happening. *It is happening.* My old life is being crucified. I am at an essential crossroads on love's journey to love.

Cathy tells me people in the meeting had fallen asleep listening to these words. *I feel seen.* The shackles of my life are falling away with the perspicacity of this message. I am at a precipice that needs to be traversed for the spirit of love to mature. What I have thought to be an insurmountable crisis is now lit up *like a gift.* I have been arguing about the wrapping paper.

"Awakening is the first threshold, the moment we long for all of our life. It is the beginning of embodying and enacting a path to a wholly new life, the life of divine love on earth." He continues to talk about temptation and the other thresholds that follow. At a particular point in the discourse, he says, "Every spiritual revelation is followed by a corresponding ordeal." He continues, "This is the part that no one likes to hear about because it is where the spiritual rubber hits the road."

HA! I giggle, wide-eyed and ready for more. It is music to my ears, aligning with all I've learned from Eunice, the Goddess, and the women mystics who have come before. My cup is filling. How did I let it run dry? *You're strong, you don't need anything* (that voice). *I do need. I do long. I want to connect to this person.* I am ready to shed this miserable state. He directly addresses my ordeal without bypassing any part of our humanness. He offers a guidepost that makes perfectly good sense.

I call Cathy for directions and apologize for my clenched fists.

Adyashanti offers a meeting the following Wednesday called Zen Satsang. I learned that this name was coined by his teacher, Arvis Joen Justi, one of the first women that we know about who teaches Zen in America. She is married with five children. I'm encouraged. Come hell or high water, I am going to make it to this meeting. Hank and I agree that Wednesday night is my night out. He arrives at five, along with Sally the nurse, to take care of our children. I take a shower and read a story to Autumn before I leave the house. When I am getting up to go, she fastens her arms around my leg.

"Stay, Mommy. I don't want you to go. Take me with you."

It is at least a one-hour drive over the two-lane Highway 17 to the Unity Church in Palo Alto. The traffic over the hill is unpredictable. I don't want to be late.

"Your daddy is here. I'll be out for a few hours and come right back home."

"I want you to stay and tuck me in." She is gripping tight.

"I will tuck you in again when I get home," I promise. Hank picks her up, assuring her that I will return.

"Come on, Pumpkin, let's look at the fish," he says, opening a children's book.

I grab my purse and dash out the front door. I jump in the driver's seat of my blue Toyota van. My heart is pounding when I pull out of the driveway. For some strange reason as I drive past the front of the house, I turn to look. Autumn is standing in the big picture frame window with her arms thrashing in the air crying, "Mommy." I keep driving. *I'm a terrible mother. This is unpardonable. Why is she so sad?* I keep driving. Hank is with her. *She will be fine. I have to go.* I can't turn back. I drive. I think about what the flight attendants say before takeoff. "Put your life jacket on before assisting your children." I'm putting my life jacket on.

When my mind isn't busy with worrisome thoughts about how Autumn is getting on, I continue to reflect upon the mystics, the how the teachings infiltrate my current situation. I realize that I have been working like a steam engine to fix the condition of my children. I huff and puff for a different life. I want to wake up early in the morning to make blueberry pancakes and call up to my three daughters, "Breakfast is ready, come to the kitchen." I want to hear their little feet patter down the wooden stairs to the kitchen, half-dressed. I want to hear little Libby sing, "Let's go the beach, Mommy." And Autumn chimes in, "On bikes." And Abby yells, "Me, too!" I want to remain neutral and not have to instruct every helper or nurse about the choices I make for the care of my children as if I don't have rights in my own home. And I don't want to live in the paradox of leaving my children in order to love them or myself better.

I come to admit that a conditioned part of me had fallen prey to the common belief within patriarchal parlance that spiritual awakening looks and behaves a particular way. My life does not fit the collective stereotype image of an evolving spiritual person. I remain curious: *Do I believe that awakening is devoid of feminine nurturance, mother connections, trauma, challenge, hardship, depression, or paradox? Do I maintain blind loyalties to dogmas of separation, written by men, taught by men, for men?*

I make it to the church ten minutes early. There are about twenty or so people sitting quietly in chairs and a few in the hallway lingering when I get there. I make a donation and head straight to the front row for a seat on a meditation cushion. I sit in silent anticipation. As I sit, a ferocious lightness rises from my belly, and my chest caves open. I've felt this before—deep listening—sensing inside. I don't notice Adyashanti walk in or hear him sit down. I look up when he begins to speak. He is sitting in a comfortable chair, wearing ordinary street clothes. He speaks in a casual tone, as if spiritual awakening is as natural as breathing. As I listen, I notice something that I had not noticed in anyone before. He doesn't seem to need or want anything. There is an absence about him that doesn't need personal veneration, agreement, or compliance to him or a dogma. I feel the absence of performative spiritual attributes and behaviors. I learn that he and his wife, Mukti, formed an organization called the *Open Gate Sangha*, a gateway to liberation. The gate is always open, come and go as you please, with no rules. Soon, Mukti will become a dear friend.

Several meetings pass like this. My breathing appears and disappears. Form appears and disappears. *I savor goodness*. I sit hollowed out like burning amber, my mind is gone in a good way. I resonate with Adya's transmission, not the image he presents. I am drawn into a presence that feels impersonal— universal. *Is this what it means to abide within the collective consciousness?* I feel relaxed, spacious, and still while moving. These words will remain with me as a conscious reflection: *Form is emptiness—emptiness is form.* My experience deepens like this for months and years to come, guiding me through the power of unconditional meditation. I arrive a few minutes early, sit down in the front row, and feel words fill space. Heaviness is lightening. Body space is expanding, space that is all-inclusive without an inconsolable ache. For the first time in my life, my body registers safety with a male teacher. I realize how much I've wanted this—needed this. I feel old patterns creep in from time to time, but they don't lead me to believe Adya will exhibit power over me. A missing piece of nourishment lands in my body, fulfilling a sense of personal sovereignty through practice. Later, I will understand more about why this spiritual friendship is so important. If I had to name this, I'd say healthy masculine energy is supporting my psyche to heal and find balance with my feminine soul. For now, I relish no need to perform a song, a dance, a spiritual image, a list of accomplishments, an identity—anything. I am free to take up space in my body as I am. I tell Adya I understand spiritual awakening to be self-authenticating. He tells me that when awakening is genuine, it does not require external validation or proof. This seals our friendship because we both know inner freedom is not confined or decided by outer circumstances or external authority.

When I drove home that first night, my car hit autopilot. I sat behind the steering wheel, astonished by a reverberating hum. It was disorienting to be in the form of a body sitting in the driver's seat and not steering the car. At the same time, I knew where I was going and where I had been, and I knew that these places were not separate, they existed within the interwoven fabric of consciousness appearing differently yet with equal value.

Adya is a straight-talking guy, obviously not the sugar daddy type from my past who grooms women as adornments to puff themselves up or satisfy distorted whims. He points to the truth, the truth he learned from his Zen teacher, Arvis, mother of five. He maps out the territory of awakening, urging each to look within. No one can do our shadow work or travel through the underworld for us. When I walked out of that Satsang meeting, I walked into the Dharma of life, with my children front and center. The life I have— beckoning me to show up to the nitty-gritty details.

When I arrive home, I go directly to the bedrooms of my little girls. I lunge in full prostration, overflowing with fiery sweetness from my heart. My bow to

Adyashanti at the end of Satsang is pale in comparison to the gratitude I feel for my three little teachers.

I never imagined that my daughters would become my teachers, and that motherhood is dharma.

Our trials will continue for the rest of our lives, though I no longer frame my life as a single parent with three very unique daughters as an insurmountable tragedy or lost samadhi. The grief of loss and heartbreak is still with me, yet a new way of living is unfolding. I'm learning to lean into the messy edges of my life and to be kind to the hypervigilant part of me that switches on to fix, change, and make things better. I welcome space that includes my children as they are, innocent, beautiful, carefree, precious, vulnerable, and unmanageable at times. I hope to learn to live outside the lines of what our culture holds up as "normal" or "perfect."

What I can now say out loud is that trauma makes you want to build a fortress around your body. When an unexpected occurrence pounces upon you, it is a shock. Transitions are hard for me. I can feel unhinged by uncertainty. *Who do I allow to cross over the bridge to our fortress? How do I build bridges? How do I care for myself and my children when I burn bridges because my internal compass for safety fluctuates?* I often need time to think, to consult someone, and to reflect on a decision that was required yesterday. I see my tendency to want to get things right. It depletes me. I want to know when it is safe to be vulnerable, to let my needs be seen, open a door, and close it in time.

18
Prajna – Heart Wisdom

A new name found me—Prajna. I witnessed most of the residents at Kripalu receive a spiritual name. It was a big event, with bodies shaking and tears flowing as the guru named his disciples. I might have been interested until I saw how he behaved in his home when I was there to provide therapeutic massages for his wife. Something felt off yet familiar, the man of the house subjecting his wife to abuse. I had not learned to speak up against violence toward women, I kept silent, through the conditioning of my familial name Nancy. Now I am undergoing an inner transformation from an old identity or way of living in the world to—one of becoming—*prajna.*

Prajna came to me in many ways before it stayed. I heard instructions in meditations, through dreams and mystical images. I used the tools I gathered to decipher meaning. As I sat with these messages and images, I felt energetic impulses—enlivened instincts that conveyed *prajna* as a way to help me smell danger, pay attention to the sensations in my body, and listen—to be able to respond with curiosity, care, and confidence. *Prajna* would teach me to trust my instincts to align with the forces in nature as allies—friends, at my feet supporting me to stay, to root, and speak up in the face of danger. I could become dangerous in the best way—messy, unkept, and wise with sharp edges, unable to be taken advantage of. Later I learn that *prajna* is a means to develop psychic knowledge that is not of the overculture or consensus reality but comes from the cosmos in supernatural ways—through our connection to Mother Earth. In this way, *prajna* would teach me to live in the middle, the liminal space between worlds; here and not here, interconnected—not separate. This is exactly what happened on September 11, 2001. I was stopped in my driveway. I felt something horrible trembling—cracking through my body but it was much larger than my body. The same unlocatable voice that I've heard many times before told me to sit still and invite others to sit with me to meditate. *It was a powerful call to sanity, one that I chose to listen to.*

Another time, I heard the word *prajna* on a day retreat with my friend Adyashanti. He gave a discourse on the *Prajnaparamita;*[17] as I listened, I was shown that *prajna* as carries a sharp sword of discrimination. A sword that sees through lies and cuts through to love and truth. *Prajna* can teach how to live without inhibition, pretense, or lies. The lack of training in discernment and critical thinking has been problematic for me. In my home healing practice, I visualize standing at the gate to our fortress. I hold a sharp sword, able to access critical questions and ask them—unapologetically. I get to choose who enters and why. I am able to ask questions that I wish I had asked earlier in life. I learn to react less and respond from a grounded, fertile place. When I tell Adyashanti about the name that came to me, he nods and hugs me like a brother would, an equal, an ally. *"Prajna* suits you." I feel the benefit of a healthy relationship with a wise male. He calls me *Prajna*, with a blessing for others to benefit from my dharma.

I remember a Buddhist nun who once told me that *prajna* means 'heart-wisdom. In simple terms 'to take no shit.' When I was very young, instincts were available to me. I listened and was guided to protect or help others. Over time, I learned to discount my instincts. *I was not able to be a protectress for myself and my girls. Prajna* is not regulated by protocols, social constructs, or sets of instructions, but learns to utilize what is most beneficial at the time. *From this day forward I vow to honor everything in life as a treasure with undeniable inherent value, especially at the most vulnerable moments of birthing and dying.*

Prajna is not about intellectual mastery or the accumulation of more knowledge, material possessions, or power over others. *Prajna's* home is the soul, a space of equity, belonging, curiosity, and care. *Prajna* or Wisdom also means Sophia—the female or feminine aspect of God with maternal qualities. *I call to learn with Sophia.*

---

[17] Prajnaparamita: Prajna is the sixth paramita (perfection). The term Prajna is from the Sanskrit: "Pra" which refers to "that which is before," and "jna" which refers to knowledge. The compound of these terms then means "before knowledge," "root knowledge." It is often translated as intuitive wisdom. *Prajnaparamita* is depicted as a beautiful feminine deity with four arms. Two arms are folded on her lap in the classic posture of meditation, and her other two arms hold a sword and a book.

Wisdom is not a result of how many years you have gathered. It is different than that; it is a cultivation, a harvesting, and often times—a wrestling. Reclaiming instincts and connecting to myself as mother—becoming crone, not separate from Earth Mother and all beings. The practice of being a Mother has the possibility to bring our world to balance. Children give us cues, challenges, and messages to grow us. As Therese de Lisieux said, children are natural representations of the preciousness of life, showing us that all of life has intrinsic value—Spirit in action. I still yearn for places of belonging that acknowledge, include, and celebrate disability, and make the invisible caregivers visible as the weavers of life. I will share sacred feminine healing practices for Mother Earth to connect, thrive, and celebrate amidst tremendous loss and undying love—to mend our world and create spaces to feel safe, held, and sustained in deep care.

19
Arms Wide Open – The Village School

T he Village School Is born, late summer 1999. Once I read *What to Do About Your Brain-Injured Child* from cover to cover, I can't rest until I try everything. I read over and over again: "The injury is in the brain, not in the body. The brain requires oxygen and movement to heal. Duration, frequency, and repetition are the key elements for neurological growth." Our bodies produce one hundred thousand new brain cells every day until we die. When our brains take in more oxygen through movement, we increase function in our bodies. Injury limits us but the neuroplasticity of the brain is not limited.

I administer therapeutic treatments to give the twins' brains the information they need to grow. I have a specific patterning table and vestibular equipment built. I research and design sensory integration tools that are spread out all over the house. Our living room and kitchen look like a neurology gymnasium. Teams of volunteers are in and out of the house three times a day helping to implement a twenty-minute "patterning exercise." It takes two volunteers and me to move Abby's or Libby's body through a series of patterns: one at the head, two on opposite sides of their bodies, moving the head and the limbs in synchronicity. I feel compelled to bring my twins as much function as possible, and the sooner we start, the better the chance for recovery in all areas of brain function.

The children are doing well, our circle of support is expanding, and people are finding a pleasant relaxation restored to our household. People whom I might have pushed away are returning. It is a welcome relief to be able to receive life with open arms, and my energy is increasing. I feel encouraged and more alive for the task.

With volunteers and friends, we develop a not-for-profit organization, which hosts an inclusive preschool that integrates developmental movement with Waldorf education. Our program becomes an overnight success, with full enrollment shortly after we open. We reserve 30 percent of our placements for children with disabilities. I hire a Waldorf teacher and train everyone on a course in developmental movement. I play the roles of mom, head cook, trainer, and grant writer. We receive every grant I write, for building a classroom and playground to develop our program and serve twenty-four children at one time. Soon we expand to include parent education, support groups, yoga, and Satsang.

Satsang for women takes place in an open space above the classroom. Marlies, another student of Adyashanti, lives in my neighborhood and uses our meeting space. Once a week, she leads a circle to explore spirituality as women and/or mothers. The size of the group varies; more and more mothers begin to attend when they learn we have a play school and they can bring their children with them. Four of the women have daughters close in age to Autumn, Abby, and Libby. They become great playmates. I remember one time finding them in one of our bedrooms bouncing on a double-size bed like a trampoline. Abby isn't able to stand on her own but there is a girl on either side of her holding her hand and supporting her to jump to play *Ring Around the Rosie*. I watch for a while, relishing in the explosion of laughter when they all fall down and stumble to get up again. Even though the bedroom is off-limits, I let them continue. *Who cares? They're having a blast. And Abby is included.*

Marlies opens the meeting with silent meditation, followed by a suggested theme and time for questions or to share about our lives. A space is cultivated for us to connect with our bodies, our voices, and our knowing, and to honor the unique way of women's wisdom. Marlies is kind and wise, with an endearing capacity to create safety. I savor these weekly meetings, knowing my girls have playmates. It takes some time for me to be vulnerable. Each week I feel more comfortable sitting with these women. Sometimes, I feel an enormity of grief burning in my chest and fear if I let it out, there will be no end to it. I let it seep out bit by bit, feeling held in a circle of sisters. I come to discover that each time one of us is vulnerable, this gives all of us permission to be more tender and honest. There isn't any drama, rather we are unleashing suppressed, wounded parts, decoding conditioned imprints, and finding our common ground. A ground that empowers us as women awakening to rise together in fierce, wild love with compassion for our unique journeys. We cry, laugh, celebrate, and ponder together, acknowledging that the way of woman and motherhood is not easy. We have wombs. There are sacrifices to make, difficult decisions afoot about food, vaccines, media, and the hardest of all— self-care and honoring our bodies.

I attend one silent retreat per year, whether I think I need it or not. This is a deliberate boundary I set for myself. Sitting in silence is a great source of nourishment, often better than sleep. For me, it is essential to my health care, like a lubricant that massages my soul. I learn to bow to the intelligence beneath my shoulders, in my body. A learning that will continue. During these early days of practice and exploring my direct inner spiritual experience (where I am more confident, as I am not as dependent on an outer source), I still check in with my friend Mukti and her husband Adya. I value friendships of mutuality that honor direct experience. One I am told is "Sahaja," the natural state of peace that liberates the worry of worldly concerns; another is "The Tao," the unchanging principle of the universe. I'm curious to discover how spiritual experience will unfold and integrate life with my children. *Will my inner experience hold true and strong amidst the most challenging aspects of motherhood?*

In our school organization, we have two nurses. Both are incredibly supportive and loved by all of us. We refer to them as family, Aunt Carolyn, and Grandma Alice. In the summer of 1999, with their help, I am able to attend a ten-day silent retreat with Adyashanti at the Vajrapani Institute, a Buddhist retreat center in the Santa Cruz Mountains. We have multiple silent sitting periods each day and a Satsang at night. The absorption in silence nourishes my bones; my mind isn't sticking to thought. I sit in the meditation hall with about forty other students, each of us on a cushion facing the wall—ten sessions of forty-minute sittings per day. During the evening meeting, we face the front of the room and listen to a dharma talk followed by an open dialogue. Before the lights go out and we return to our cabins we have another silent sitting. On this particular retreat, during the meditation periods, I sit next to Mukti. The hall is dimly lit and still, like a clear full-moon sky. About halfway through the sitting, a bat darts in through a window and whips through the room, stirring the quiet. Suddenly there is an uproar of screams, heads ducking, and people falling to the floor. Mukti and I remain still, not flinching. I know a bat is flying overhead but it doesn't disturb a deeper sense of equanimity. Eventually, the bat flies back out the window. There is an uproar of laughter and relief. My life feels more and more like this. There are disturbing, unpredictable events that take place and I have less of a reaction. I'm more resourced and able to respond with kindness, humor, or intuition rather than fighting what is. My nervous system is harmonizing.

Each day frees up my instincts and brings new discoveries. The most pronounced is "I'm here and I'm not here." Another, "I am what I've always been—nothing new has been added and nothing can be taken away. I'm okay, just as I am." The wildest recognition for me is walking in nature and realizing that I am everything: the streams, the forest, the mountain, the lake, the animals—the earth. Most important is the discovery that my children do not subtract from spiritual practice; in fact, they bring gifts and trials that acknowledge the dharma of woman as nature—the womb of life.

Our school is thriving; Abby and Libby are making developmental gains, Abby more so than Libby. The integrated classroom works superbly for Abby. She isn't able to walk yet like the other children, but she manages to keep up with high-speed crawling. This is how she gets to know our visitors. When they park their shoes at the door, she puts them on her hands, creeps around the room, returns them back to where she found them, puts on a new pair, and is off again with another set of shoes.

A one-room classroom turns out to have multiple advantages. Abby rarely misses a beat. The children tend to climb up on the big oak table near the cooking area to help with measuring, chopping, mixing, shredding, stirring, grating, peeling, or blending together all sorts of ingredients for our meals. A favorite is our bread-making day when several children mix and roll out their dough all at once. Abby will mix and roll out dough for hours at a time if we let her. She skillfully imitates the other children, saying, "Can I add cinnamon and honey and make a twist for Grandma?" She doesn't have a wide vocabulary yet, but when she speaks, we are always surprised at what comes out of her mouth—like, "Did you calculate the ingredients?" Or "We're getting reacquainted."

Our toilet area is part of the open space. It is enclosed by a short half-wall with a privacy gate that easily swings open to enter. The handwashing seat is stationed on the outside wall with a stool to climb up for washing hands. Two girls, the same age as Abby (four) are adorably kind. They help Abby in small ways and don't mind waiting for her to catch up. Abby is infatuated with their toileting routine. One day, after watching them swing in and out of the toilet, Abby is crouched at the gate. She rises up on her knees, like a whistling tea kettle, and announces, "I'm going to use the toilet now." Her little friend Katy follows her in. "I can help you." Abby is sitting on the little throne. The room is quiet until we hear tinkling. I resist clapping and fussing. *They got this.* Katy helps her pull up her pants and leads her out the gate. I hear Katy whisper, "Let's go play in the sand." Abby tells her, "I have to wash my hands first." Since Abby can't stand up on the stool to reach the sink, she and her friend devise a plan. They move the stool away; Abby climbs up on her friend's knees, reaches the sink, and pulls herself up with Katy supporting her from the back. Up until that day, before watching the other children, I had little success guiding Abby to the toilet. She has fewer accidents but still wants to wear panties like the other kids. She can feel sensations in her upper body but doesn't easily feel when she needs to pee. Her issues with leaky gut syndrome are not yet under control. I imagine this is embarrassing for her. Now, when other children express their urges to get to the potty, Abby joins in, "Me too. I have to pee." At the beginning of this phase, Abby spends the bulk of mornings in and out of the toilet area, proud that she can do what the other kids do.

I am thankful for the natural kindness these children show in our inclusive space. I remember as a child watching children climb on and off a small yellow bus. I was curious about these children, *where do they go, what do they do, why aren't they with us?* Later I found out that they had disabilities and required a different environment. Perhaps when children experience other children with differences early on in life, their natural tendency to be kind and inclusive is not conditioned out of them.

We hang a hammock swing for Libby from the ceiling in the corner of our school room. She does not have any voluntary movement, speech, or vision yet. She loves being in the classroom surrounded by the sounds of children. A volunteer named Julie comes a few mornings a week to help Libby paint outside on the sidewalk area. She holds Libby in her lap close, sitting on the ground. Libby makes a different sound to indicate her choice for red, blue, green, or yellow paint, dips her left foot in the paint, and spreads the paint over a large canvas. Her foot swishes back and forth, splashing a colorful design across the canvas. It looks like a burnt orange sun setting at the edge of the ocean.

Once a month on Fridays, we perform a play for the parents based on one of the stories we read and modify during the week. Every child acts the role of a character or the environment. We make the scene for Grandma's cottage and costumes with support from several parents. Our version of "Little Red Riding Hood" is a favorite. In this play, little Red (Molly) is not tricked by the wolf (Stevie), she stays the path according to her mother's (Eileen) wisdom and makes it to her grandmother's (Katy) cottage safely. Several trees inform her to make haste—a hungry wolf is following her. The children with language act the parts that require speaking. Abby is the fireplace—she is staged near the back wall and wears a red cap, charcoal eyes, and an oversized flaming orange top that covers her entire body. Libby sits in her wheelchair at the end of the trail of friendly trees at the entrance and faces the audience of parents and grandparents crowded together on the floor. She has a ring of bells strapped around her wrist. Julie assists Libby to shake her wrist, indicating first Red, later the wolf, at the door. Libby's chair barricades the door so the wolf cannot enter. The cunning wolf decides to sneak in through the fireplace. Abby hears the wolf and vigorously rumbles on cue, destroying the hungry wolf. Grandmama and Red invite the audience to enjoy the basket of goodies that the children prepared the day before. The audience is delighted.

When Autumn turns five, she leaves our program and attends the Santa Cruz Waldorf School for kindergarten and grade one. The campus is situated at the entryway of a redwood grove with trails that reach deep into the forest. Each classroom is artistically designed like the house in *Little House on the Prairie* with hardwood floors, handcrafted doorways, windows, tables, and chairs, and richly lazured (a painting technique with watercolors) walls that support the developmental age of the child. The campus is surrounded by an oak grove, a playing field, and a designated school room for music lessons.

Autumn thrives in her classroom with about twenty peers. It has its own kitchen, woodworking area, and art space. She readily becomes more capable in her body—climbing trees, making art, and carving toys out of wood. I imagine she feels relieved to be out of the house, where Abby and Libby consume copious attention. She is quick to rise as a stellar student, in a way that she will later describe as a little bit obsessive. She enjoys self-mastery and completing whatever task is placed before her to perfection. A few kids from our neighborhood go to the same school. A couple of blocks from our house they have a bus stop that I walk Autumn to each morning. Even though I am thrilled that she will have her own school separate from the twins, I will not forget the tears that pour down my face as she leaves on the bus. I still cry inside when I feel how fast life passes by and the accumulation of missed mother-and-daughter experiences with her. Her educational journey separate from me has begun. Sometimes I wish I could turn back time to how it was before I was helicoptered away from her.

After in-depth research but without lengthy contemplation, we (actually I, as the primary caregiver) decided to turn the responsibility of our school over to the head teacher. I rented our home to her and her family and move from Santa Cruz. It's 2002, Autumn is soon to be eight. Abby and Libby are six; it is time for them to enter traditional grade school in order to receive special education services. I explored the local school, and talked with many parents regarding services in the area for grade-school children with disabilities. I find there is not a program that focuses on neurological development, functional movement, or even physical therapy. These are aspects of our program, alongside typically developing peers that exhibit success. As much as I love the community that has developed around us, I don't want to give up on an education that includes therapeutic movement for the twins. The sooner we address their injuries, the better chance of achieving independence.

My experience and research led me to continue with a program similar to ours that offers both developmental movement and a Waldorf curriculum.

We learn about a Waldorf developmental school in Colfax, California, from a teacher at our school who was employed there. She highly recommends that we try it for Abby and Libby. I contact the school, we apply and are invited for an interview. We drive up to Colfax, anticipating the beginning of a new life not too far from home. The director is at the trampoline pit when we arrive. I sit with Libby on my lap in a sling with Abby next to me on a bale of hay. We watch her coach her students through a variety of movement routines. I am impressed to see them jumping, crossing midlines, and repeating verses out loud as they move. They aren't distracted by our presence. *I want this program for my girls.* The director walks us by the animal grooming station on the way to the office. "This is where the children attend to the animals." "Wow," I say. "How perfect." The interview is short. The director, a sturdy woman about fifty-five years old, has been running the program for a couple of decades. She sits down on the sofa next to me. She tells me with tired eyes, "I can't take them. Bring them back when they are walking."

I feel like a birthday balloon suddenly poked with a sharp pin. "Oh," I breathe.

She turns her eyes away from me. "I'm sorry."

When we are heading back to the car, we meet her husband coming up from the swimming pool area. He must have seen my long, sad face. He stops me to say, "You know, she used to be able to work with children like yours, until she lost her own. It's too close to her heart."

"Oh, I'm sorry," I say, wiping tears from my eyes.

On the ride back home, I wonder, *how am I going to get my girls walking? Isn't it the movement program that will stimulate new development?* I sink inside, questioning, *what's next?*

Then I remember that the director said there is a Waldorf School in Pennsylvania specifically for children with special needs, and they might accept non-ambulatory children. I have several conversations with this school, and they agree to accept my daughters. There is also a traditional Waldorf School nearby for Autumn to begin grade two. This entire process is quick but soon everyone has a placement.

We prepare to take on the task of moving across the country to Pennsylvania. Packing up our house, transferring the responsibility for the school, saying goodbye to friends—all flows very smoothly until the final days. I don't know who panics more, Autumn or me. We have a going away party for her with her classmates on the beach. Her teacher comes because she is very fond of Autumn, and is sad to see her go. She has an idea to form a circle and sing, "Make new friends, keep the old, one is silver and the other gold." This doesn't go over too well with Autumn; she runs barefoot down the beach crying, hides in a tent, and we don't see her for a good twenty minutes.

When she finally comes back, she says, "I don't want to say goodbye; I want to stay here."

Next, a group of friends from our school and our Satsang meetings surprise us with a huge going away party. I am floored by the number of people who show up: people from Thursday-night African dance class, friends who helped us when the babies were tiny, volunteers, families from the school, and people I don't even know. We have a larger circle of support around us than I knew. I am also moving away from Open Gate Sangha and my women's circle. Many times, I will ask myself, *what is the next best thing for all of us? How can I know?* I don't see a better plan and can't imagine not trying.

There is nothing glamorous or easy about moving a family of four. A good friend spends three full days with me, sorting and organizing our household into piles: sell, give away, or pack. I transfer our school program to our classroom teacher, who will attend to the families we serve. We pack up our special equipment specifically for the twins that are expensive to replace. My brother Joe is on his way to California from New York to drive our moving truck across the country; Autumn, Abby, Libby, and I will fly.

At the side of our house, we have stacked a collection of children's toys and clothing to donate to the Goodwill store—the giveaway pile. Over the years, friends gave us all sorts of miscellaneous items, out of warmth or pity. We call a collection agency to come and take these things away. Goodwill Industries sends a truck. We are loading it in the driveway when Autumn comes home from a playdate. Just as the driver is getting ready to jump in the truck and drive off, Autumn appears on the scene with a distraught look on her face. She spots a doll that she hasn't played with for years.

Quickly, she decides, "That is my most favorite doll in the world; you can't take it!"

She climbs onto the truck and clutches the doll to her chest. "You can't take this. Go away. You are ruining my life!"

Then she starts pulling out other toys, yelling hysterically, "This is mine. You can't take it!"

I'm gutted.

I try to coax her off the truck by giving her the doll. "Of course, you can have this."

Her eyes speed over the truck; suddenly, everything is the most important thing. "It's mine, all mine! You can't take this from me."

And so, it goes. The lady driver claps her hands like a dog trainer.

"Would you get a handle on your kid? We're on a schedule."

I secretly pass her some cash to buy us more time. She sticks it in her jeans pocket and rolls her eyes. I feel Autumn; she is triggered, and for good reason. She isn't ready to let go of her home, friends, and school. She needs time for transition. A phase I do not offer myself. Little by little, we roam the truck and make sure she has all the things she can't live without. I carry her and her tattered toys past the boxes in our close-to-empty kitchen and let her finish her outburst with a good cry on the sofa. As she cries, I cry too, inside, considering: *Am I doing the right thing?* At the same time, it feels as if the adrenaline in my system is spitting fire. *Go, go, go!* I don't see how I can attend to Abby's and Libby's medical injuries without the support of a good school program to improve their functional skills. And I feel like I must. I'm sure I don't consider all the options or know what they are. Memories of this community, being in our house, with the people here, pull me to stay, but the part of me that drives forward is on autopilot. *Am I unable to accept that this might be as good as it gets?* I'm driven and can't find the off button.

Later that night when I am reading to Autumn and tucking her in her bed, she asks, "Mommy, do you still love Daddy?"

I sit quietly by her side for a while, then whisper, "Honey, when people come together, sometimes they drift apart, but when two people love each other, they love each other forever. The circumstances may change, but the love remains."

It is quiet for a while. I imagine she is asking, "Does Daddy love me?"

"Your Daddy will always love you and visit you often."

She opens her eyes wide. "Why doesn't he ever want to do what I want?"

"What do you mean?"

"We always do the same thing: bookstores or music stores."

"Hmmm," I respond. "How about telling him what you want to do?"

"I can't do that."

"Hmmm. Is it hard to ask?"

"Yeah."

"Why not try?"

"I know what he'll say."

"What will he say?"

"We'll see or maybe." Hmm. I am familiar with that response but withhold.

Then she openly ponders, "Why don't you stay with us on Wednesday nights?"

"It is your dad's turn to be with you, and my turn to have a free night."

"But I want to come with you."

"How about if we plan a night for just you and me to do whatever you want?"

"Yeah."

After I listen to more of her concerns, she relaxes. I read to her until she is in a deep sleep. I'm unable to sleep, considering the journey ahead of us.

20

Ancient Language – Connection

M y mom meets us in Pennsylvania to help us find a house and unload. We are able to rent a house in the 200-acre Camphill Village for adults with developmental delays, just a few miles from the school that Abby and Libby attend. It is a beautiful three-bedroom, 100-year-old farmhouse with a nice flat yard, garage, and fruit trees, situated directly across the road from a bubbling brook. The floors are made with wide wooden planks upstairs and down. Our backyard stretches across the farm with views of the barn, biodynamic garden, and a herd of cows. The living room is spacious with a grand stone fireplace, but the kitchen is tiny with low ceilings and barely enough room to pass each other. All of the appliances, including the washer and dryer, are squashed together near a small table with three chairs under the window near the back door. After the kids are settled in school, I do what I always do—organize, paint the bedrooms, polish the floors, make curtains for the windows, and color-code specific areas for Abby to navigate our new home.

Autumn rarely mentions her dad. When he calls, she more or less listens on the phone, nodding her head with a "Yes" or a "No," cautious not to expose her emotional needs. Her dad comes to visit several times over the year. I sense unexpressed emotions blocking their connection. The wall between Hank and me is more transparent. Our transactions are amicable with complicated topics floating to the surface, feeling like a messy business deal with both parties in the red.

My initial plan is to return to California every year for a silent retreat and for the kids to visit their dad. For two years in a row, Autumn prefers staying in Pennsylvania and going to a summer camp with her new friends. When I ask her about going to California, she stammers, "I'm not going, and you can't make me!" Intuitively I know something needs healing, and trust that whatever needs to happen will do so in its own time.

It's fall 2003. Libby and Abby are accepted to the Beaver Run School in Pennsylvania, the only Waldorf school in the country that is considered a public special education school by the state of California. Since we are from California, Abby and Libby do not need to pay tuition; it is covered by the state. Abby travels back and forth to kindergarten each day. Libby is a part-time boarding student who lives with a family of four and a few other students during the week. She is home with us for weekends, holidays, and vacations.

Libby, now seven, expresses herself in many ways, yet not with words. She has her own language of sound and movement: giggling, laughing, crying, moaning, or kicking with squeals of excitement or aches of disappointment. The greatest of all her sounds is silence. Libby teaches me that this is the space where we are connected, where sound reverberates from. She has a perspicuous way of teaching me to read her cues and meet her needs.

When it is time to go off to school, she either kicks her legs with excitement or sits very still with a thoughtful look on her face, indicating she is eager to learn. When she doesn't want to do something, she seals her lips over the tip of her tongue. This is her "no" or "I'm done."

One day I feel an echo of sound in my body; it compels me to call Libby at her school. *She needs me.* I feel a strong pull to be with her. I stop what I am doing and call her houseparent, asking if I can pick her up early for her weekend visit. I give no thought to how I will manage to pick her up with my other children in tow—it is an instinct that I don't question. The houseparent reports that Libby has been crying inconsolably, which is unusual.

Libby can be miles away; I still feel her and hear her voice. She shows me that beneath language, labels, and interpretations, we are connected. Libby and I are latched just like a nursing mother who—whether she is at the supermarket, jogging, or giving a lecture—feels her milk start to let down as soon as the baby begins to cry. She knows it's time to go home and be with the baby.

Before I leave to collect Libby that day, I discover that Abby has a high fever. My mind chatters. *What if Libby catches Abby's fever? What if Abby cries all night? What if the cat meows all night? What if Autumn can't sleep?* Memory forebodes a broken record of what-ifs: *What if I do not get any sleep at all?* Despite this litany of concern, my body keeps moving toward the car to pick up Libby. A gentler voice nudges, *are these thoughts true? How can you know?* The worry seems silly and it subsides. I'm in my car unconcerned— laughing but not alone like a passenger on autopilot—trusting this movement.

I arrive to gather Libby, and she does what she always does when she feels me approaching—she squeals wildly. She knows the sound and rhythm of my walk. She is already kicking herself out of her chair before I reach her. The scene is familiar: Her eyes wander around the room. With earnest focus, her eyes gradually meet mine and she reminds me of why we're here. In this moment—in this profound moment—we meet each other's gaze. I am never sure what Libby sees; she is legally blind, yet at this moment—one light is shining. There have been many of these moments, flashes shorter than the time it takes a lightning bug to glow when Libby looks deep into my eyes—yes, Libby, who has been diagnosed as blind since birth, sees. And in those brief snaps, I see a place, an exquisite, peaceful place that pulls me deep inside myself, while simultaneously I am removed from my ordinary awareness and my perception opens to the vastness of this mysterious life.

Libby teaches me to tend less to the voice in my head. I'm becoming aware that much of this mental and emotional chatter is part of how conditioning works. Even when this voice in my head is in complete contradiction to the movement of my body, it is easy to follow the chatter and discard the intuition in my body. Libby is a tuning fork. If I disregard my instincts and the feelings in my body, I am cutting myself off from responding to her needs and what I know deep in my bones. Our collective unconscious gathers an accumulated momentum that follows patterns of thought. I feel how this postpones, denies, or ignores the quiet impulses that lie beneath thought and reside in our hearts and bodies.

I don't want to miss this opportunity. I have to wonder: *Is it possible to follow a call deeper than our human-made dramas?* Libby teaches me again that when I only give attention to surface images, I miss her—Libby—her language of love and the only communication she knows. My relationship with Libby helps me to listen to quiet spaces. She assures me that life is managed by this underlying connection. It is in a call-response relationship with itself. Libby is calling. I'm to respond. All I need to do is get out of the way and listen, rather than feel drained by the ifs, ands, or buts that float around in my mind like clouds obscuring the clear blue sky. My energy is lifted.

Libby giggles all the way home. When night comes, *guess what happens?* Not a creature is stirring—not even the cat. Everyone sleeps like newborn babies nestled in their mother's resilient octopus arms.

As for me, I rest, knowing that the ancient language of Libby is alive. Perhaps this is how we attend to our cherished children regardless of how they appear. *Perhaps she doesn't need fixing?* I know her love is not injured, tainted, or absent in any way. More and more, I learn that adhering to limiting labels that have emerged from the Western medical complex (that I can't seem to separate from patriarch systems or capitalism) teaches us to disconnect from our underlying essence, the connective tissue of love. *How do we name something in a way that is helpful and does not adhere to a descriptive limitation or social construct?*

Abby is seven years old and attends the same kindergarten as Libby, but travels back and forth each day. The classroom is decorated in soft colors and silks, a dreamy atmosphere like a fantasy world. Abby's overall development has steadily improved at our program in Santa Cruz. I believe she will receive movement therapy here. She receives gentle stimulation, makes toys, and learns songs, but she doesn't overtly work on functional movement skills. I see her crawling around on hands and knees and, just like at home when she puts people's shoes on her hands; she is getting to know them.

After a semester of attending this program, I am surprised to find that they allow her to sit in *"W-sit"*[18] while she has braces on that cover her feet and ankles. Apparently, the teacher isn't aware that this is detrimental to the shape and development of her hips, legs, and feet. There is a physical therapist who attends to the children in the classroom once per week. I am concerned that she does not recognize the danger to Abby's body. I can't unsee what I see.

---

[18] W-sitting is a position of sitting on the floor. The child sits on their bottom with their knees bent and rotated on the floor behind them in the shape of a W.

My intervention triggers a rift in our communication. This makes me sad, as I respect this program and the dedication of the teachers.

I see the social and creative options offered but I'm hell-bent on functional development, especially walking. The teachers tell me developmental movement will not begin until first grade. Everything in my body cries, *no!* We don't have time to wait. I remember all that I read about brain stimulation. *The sooner we address the injuries, the better, and the first seven years are critical periods.* I'm anxious. I am not sure what to do.

Two moms at a yoga class in town tell me about the Family Hope Center and are connected to the doctors who wrote the book *What to Do About Your Brain-Injured Child.* I am relieved and eager to explore it.

The Family Hope Center program requires a hefty commitment, it is rigorous and comprehensive. Once I learn more, I decide to homeschool with this new program: six hours of activity a day, six days a week. This includes a crawling and creeping program and directions for a walking track. The walking track we build is twenty feet long with a medial support in the middle of two tracks that resemble a cross-country skiing trail. The track teaches lateral walking; the height forces her heels to reach the ground and the brace pushes her knees open with every step.

We gather our tools, make the equipment, and set up our workshop in the barn. We turn crawling and creeping into a game. Abby and I chase each other on our bellies on the hardwood floor; for creeping we wear kneepads. We make an arm brace to support her right arm so it doesn't overextend at the elbow. We maximize breathing and oxygen intake between our laps around imaginary tollbooths to different countries we pass through.

The vision program is interspersed with creeping and crawling. By now we know that eyes require more oxygen than any other organ to develop and function well. Abby receives several rounds of *light stimulation therapy*[19]. I present hundreds of sight words in big red letters on oversized index cards. I flash the cards in front of her; she memorizes the images, and after a few months she is reading hundreds of words. As the weeks progress, I notice more energy in her body. She is more focused and determined to do her schoolwork training. One day she decides she needs to get something from her room

---

[19] *Light stimulation therapy* is designed to help improve the speed, accuracy, and efficiency of the eye.

upstairs. She holds the railing, leads with the left foot, and climbs one step at a time. I linger behind her, just in case. It's fabulous to watch. Not every day goes so smoothly, especially in the winter. There isn't heat in the old barn. We warm up by pretending to chase chickens around the yard, stretching to music, reciting verses, or making up pure nonsense songs to keep the marathon going. Abby is no longer using her wheelchair. She is able to walk alongside me by just holding my hand. Our regular routine fosters forward momentum.

The first sign of spring brings more warmth into the barn and sun into our garden. The warmth invigorates our schedule. We often finish early. One day, when we get through the routine quickly, I take Abby for a treat. I feel proud walking into the store with Abby. She leads us to the frozen dessert section and picks out a vanilla Rice Dream sandwich. On the ride home, I notice that Abby is looking out the windows. Normally she keeps her head down and pays little attention to the landscape. *I wonder what she sees.* Golden wildflowers and purple lilacs are blooming everywhere amidst the fields of growing grasses. I drive down the long, stone driveway that leads to the back of our house. I park by the garage. I see Abby through the rearview mirror. Her face is relatively clean. She still holds a napkin in one hand, seemingly conscious of a drip on her face. She licks and wipes, licks and wipes. This is a new behavior. Normally she does not take the initiative to clean herself. She is attuned to herself and the environment in a new way. She needs a little help getting out of our van and spouts, "I got it! I can close the door myself." I let her.

I hold her hand as we walk down the narrow sidewalk to our back door; her grip and stride are strong. Something is strikingly different, yet I cannot pinpoint it. She isn't looking down when she walks. She is holding her head high and looking around the yard. Then she stops and stands still for a moment, announcing with sheer excitement,

"HEY MOM, LOOK! THERE ARE FLOWERS IN OUR GARDEN!"

I take in a long deep breath. "That's right!"

"They're yellow!"

She is absolutely right—and clearly not blind. That is the day she let us know she is seeing much more than her early prognosis. She is perceiving shapes, flowers, and colors. She can see!

Abby's brain develops the equivalent of 2.3 years over a seven-month period. We are so grateful, yet Abby lacks social opportunities. We work hard at home by ourselves. I talk with some folks and decide to apply for grade one at the nearby Kimberton Waldorf School, the same school Autumn attends. She is accepted into a class with a very open-minded teacher and given provisions for a classroom assistant. The resource teacher stands in Abby's court, rooting for her success. Abby is given eurythmy lessons, a system of rhythmic physical movements to music used to teach musical understanding and offer therapeutic benefits. In the morning, Abby and Autumn wake up at the same time and race each other to the breakfast table. Abby enjoys picking out what she will wear. She needs some help getting dressed. What a treat it is for me to make their breakfast and send them off to school together. They walk through our backyard, and down a trail to our neighbor's house to catch the bus. Abby wants to keep up with her big sister, announcing, "I'm coming. I can do it!"

It is time for the Rose Ceremony, a well-established tradition at the Kimberton Waldorf School near the start of the school year. During the first week of school, each first-grader is matched with a twelfth-grader or senior buddy to usher them onto their journey through the grades. Sarah is an occasional helper at our house and knows Abby, as well as something about her special needs. She chooses Abby to be her buddy. The day before the ceremony, Abby comes home singing, "Mom, do I have a special dress to wear tomorrow?"

"Let's go upstairs and look," I say with a huge grin for the girl who was told she would never walk.

As we go through the clothes in her closet, it is like a light has turned on and she is seeing them for the first time. "I like this. I don't like that. I want to wear this; it's orange."

She chooses an orange cotton dress dotted with pink flowers and white tights. "I like the flowers," she smiles.

The leaves are turning bright yellow and orange when Abby, Autumn, and I hop into the van and drive off to the school for the Rose Ceremony. It is the first period on a Friday morning. The auditorium is quickly filling with students from all grades and many families. When we arrive at the school, the parking lot is full. Parents who do not have a student in first or twelfth grade enjoy participating in this event. I park at the creamery nearby and hustle over. The five-petaled rose to pass from senior to the new student represents the dawning of a new destiny. I quietly walk in and find a seat that isn't reserved for students. I can't see over the many heads. I decide to climb up and watch from the bleachers, happy to have my glasses with me. The seniors file in like kings and queens celebrating their merited turf. The first-graders follow, adorably, in a single file with enthusiastic chants from a captive audience. The twelfth-graders sit in front of the left side of the auditorium facing the audience. The first-graders sit on the right facing the stage. Once everyone is seated, the orchestra stops playing and two seniors take the podium to introduce the event.

"Today commences our last year of high school… and is an initiation for the first-graders to cross the rainbow bridge and embark upon a spirited journey through the grades… each will receive a rose … for abundance and support."

I hear intimate nose-blowing grace the hall. I imagine the speech evokes nostalgic memories of youth for most of the parents, myself included. The two classes' teachers stand up front and begin calling out the names of their students; grade one follows grade twelve. The first twelfth-grader is called, stands up, takes a rose from her teacher, and walks a few steps to meet their first-grade buddy at the center of the platform to give away the rose. The ceremony continues; several sets of names are called. My hands begin to sweat the closer they get to Abby's name. I watch a number of first-graders confidently climb the steps, receive the rose, hug their buddy, and turn around to walk back down the two steps and to their seats. *She can do it. Relax. Abby will do it by herself, as she did the day before at practice.*

I hear Sarah's name. Sarah stands up with the red rose and ambles to the platform while the first-grade teacher calls, loud and clear, "Abigayle Ginty." The room falls silent like an empty cavern. Abby is not moving, her thick pink-rimmed glasses steady at her nose. After an infinite moment, it is as though a little birdie whispers in her ear, "That's you!" Surprise flashes over her face, as if to ask, *Is that me?* My heart hammers. *Will she stand up? Is she going to crash?*

Will she receive the rose?

I'm on my feet cheering in my head: *You can do it, Abby. Get up; it's your turn. Go. Take the rose!* In a moment, my ache to rescue her is reeled back to a lake of stillness. Tears rain down my face and soften my worry. Sarah waits patiently. Abby stands up. The audience exhales in unison. She steps toward the platform in slow motion. Her awkward gait is overshadowed by her exuberant smile, shining like a perfect sunflower. As she climbs the final step, she reaches for the rose and collects it, but stumbles slightly. Sarah catches her mid-flight just as the audience inhales a collective gasp. Abby pops up, still gripping the rose like a dog does a bone. They hug for a moment, restoring Abby's dignity. She turns around with a smile as big as her face and heads toward her seat. Sarah consciously slows her pace, supporting Abby to take her time. Abby lands on solid ground and marches back to her seat with her gaze held high. I want to set aside my wet tissues and clap for a thunderous victory. It is a fantastic beginning, and it is a finale. On that day, I stopped wondering: *Will this community accept Abby? Will she find her school-age community? Yes, of course; why not?* I feel that the heart of community prospers when unique children like Abby are given the opportunity to touch our humanity. As waves of euphoria ripple through the air, my faith in humanity spreads to a new dimension of hope and resilience. The ceremony culminates like a wedding of hearts. Beneath the image of difference, this demonstration alights upon the truth of our connectedness, our oneness, and how much we benefit from each other and our unique expressions.

After the ceremony, I slip out the back door—crying. The front of my shirt is ridiculously wet. I am not sad or suffering. It feels like honey is oozing into every cell of my body. Maybe my body is releasing the effort and tension that brought us to this moment. I feel contentment as if receiving the rose is the reason we are here. Abby reminds me of the simplicity and richness layered in the rose as it passes between us throughout our life journeys, accentuating our cyclical nature of beginnings and endings. No wonder—Abby's middle name is Rose; she's playing her part well—she is a bridge.

21

Tell Me You're Kidding

I t is late spring, early summer 2004; we are driving in our family Toyota van along the rolling hills of Montgomery County, Pennsylvania, lush green foliage surrounding us in the cool damp air, the sky a hazy blue. Nine-year-old Autumn sits beside me in the front seat, her hands skillfully crocheting a green and yellow book bag, her eyes eagerly scanning to spot the bold red heart on the Variety Camp sign, a charity-funded camp for children with special needs and medical conditions. Glancing in the rearview mirror I check on Abby and Libby, who, if all goes well, will soon spend a ten-day adventure at this overnight camp, at no cost to us.

Imagine that. Ten days.

As I drive, I'm lost in a magical daydream—ten days free from Abby's and Libby's arduous therapeutic routines. Ten glorious days for me and Autumn, a chance for her to have alone time with her mommy.

I have a squirrelly habit of adjusting the rearview mirror to keep a watchful eye on the back seat. I need to be ready if Libby's head tilts and obstructs her air passage. Libby always sits diagonally behind me. No matter how many precautions I take with straps and cushions to prop her head, she manages to slip her mouth beneath her neck harness, barely able to breathe. I'm prepared to pull over at any moment, unbuckle, and swiftly adjust her position to ensure she can breathe freely. Driving alone with my three girls on a busy highway feels like a high-stakes game, constantly living on the edge. Today, my options are limited. Do I ask Autumn to unbuckle and assist Libby before she turns blue? Do I trust Abby to push her sister's head up, not down? Do I navigate across the busy highway and risk everyone? Or, stay home—alone—isolated?

I choose not to rely on prescription drugs for my daughters. Instead, I nourish their growth—both brains and bodies—with a special food and supplement diet, and alternative therapies. This approach may cause many Western medical professionals to raise an eyebrow. Many prefer we adhere to strict, structured, and time-consuming routines. But it frees me from the hassle of constant doctor visits for prescription refills, and the worry over side effects like anxiety, irritability, rashes, reflux, loss of function, or unexplained behaviors, including seizures. I'm relieved to leave the "current medications" section on school or camp registration forms blank boldly marking N/A: NOT APPLICABLE.

I've listened to the heartbeat of my children since before they were born and feel a natural connection to their needs. My intuition guides me in discerning what truly supports their well-being.

Knowing my daughters are not drugged gives us a sense of empowerment. I don't want to engage in battles to prove pharmaceuticals have not helped us.

Behind me, Abby—who has a sophisticated ear for song and story—is leaning out through her booster seat straps toward Libby and loudly mimicking an episode from *The Berenstain Bears*. Even though she doesn't track words visually, she easily memorizes songs and storylines. Today the theme is camp.

Libby does not utter a single audible word. She expresses consonants, like ga, ka, hun; or vowels, like eeeh, aaah—connecting in her own way. What Libby is not able to express with words, Abby makes up for in imagination, sassy details, and elaborate babble. Twins through and through.

"I see it; there's the red heart!" exclaims my copilot, Autumn.

"Good eye." I slowly turn into the long stone driveway.

The parking lot is empty except for a blue Ford wagon and a yellow Beetle bug, and it's nice to know that we have the exclusive privilege of a parking spot. I pull up to the "Accessibility Parking" rectangular sign and park between the designated blue lines, turn off the engine, and place our shiny blue placard in the window.

"Can I push Libby's chair? I want to push Libby," bursts Abby.

Abby is on constant alert for a chance to assist her twin sister, even though her gait is unsteady. Holding onto Libby's chair provides her with some stability and, I imagine, boosts her self-esteem. Meanwhile, Libby squirms in her chair, aware that we have arrived.

Autumn helps Abby out through the sliding side door while I lift Libby's wheelchair from the back of the van. Abby like an excited and playful Labrador, eagerly latches onto Libby's chair, ready to roll. Autumn coaches her to settle down. "You have to wait for Mom to get Libby," she says, with a hint of impatience. I know that she, like me, can't wait to settle the twins so we, the older girls, can embark on our adventure.

Abby continues to bounce with anticipation. I undo Libby's straps and buckles. Instantly, she propels herself into my arms, and bangs her head against my forehead, while emitting an ear-splitting squeal. Shaking it off, I pry Libby's stiff legs apart, straddle her thirty-six pounds of dense weight onto my broad left hip, and shuffle her into her chair.

"Autumn, is the brake on?"

Autumn steps on the red lever to secure Libby's chair. I shimmy her into her cushioned seat, adjusting her position. I flip the black bolster between her knees, fasten the harness over her torso, position her head in the neck cradle, secure the forehead strap, and tighten the torso and waist belts. All the while, she kicks rhythmically to Abby's elated bouncing. As Autumn instinctively wipes the drool off my right arm, she hands me a fresh bib for Libby. My shirt is already soaked with slobber.

But I don't mind. I fantasize about the sunny days that lie ahead, unscheduled, our trip back home to California to visit friends. I imagine driving in a rented convertible along the beautiful northern coast. I wear a drool-free coral blue summer dress that is tucked away in my closet. Beside me, Autumn sits in denim shorts, a yellow spaghetti-strapped top, sunglasses, sun hat, happy for her mother's attention. Our hair is dancing in the warm sea breeze. We sing her favorite songs from school, share stories, solve riddles, and sip ice-cold lemonade without a care in the world.

As the four of us roll along with Libby's chair toward the director's office, Abby takes the lead, pushing ahead. Autumn walks beside the chair, secretly steering Libby over sidewalk cracks, bumps, and around corners. I smile at

Autumn's finesse as she dodges every puddle, boosts Abby's buoyancy, and determines the pace of our course.

The acting assistant director, Jennifer, warmly welcomes us. She's a slim, athletic-looking woman in her mid-twenties. Standing in front of the sign, VARIETY CAMP HAS BEEN SERVING MEDICALLY FRAGILE AND DISABLED CHILDREN SINCE 1949. She wears the traditional white Variety Camp T-shirt with a bright red heart. After introducing herself, she receives high-spirited greetings from Abby and Libby, while Autumn offers a shy hello. Our tour commences.

Jennifer leads the way, sharing information about the camp as we pass the mess hall and kitchen. They are known for providing a fun, safe, recreational experience that fosters greater independence and opportunities to participate in adaptive, age-appropriate, peer-group educational programs. A wave of relief washes over me, hearing that Libby can participate fully regardless of her physical limitations.

We enter a vibrant arts and crafts center, where Abby shouts, "I love to paint!" "So does Libby," adds Autumn.

Jennifer points out the medical building where medications are administered to the campers. I take a deep breath and mention that Abby and Libby do not require medications.

"Oh, really? You don't give them medication for their cerebral palsy? All of our campers take medications. Isn't that unsafe?"

The familiar dance begins anew. "No," I respond. "Actually, I'm relieved not to manage the side effects we've encountered from medications. Libby is more alert and content. She sleeps and eats better because her neurological function is better organized. Abby has progressed in all areas of functioning."

"Really. How unusual. This is news to me. What is your approach?"

Jennifer's doubts echo that of many others—parents with special-needs children to diploma-flooded medical professionals. For eight years since Abby and Libby were born via C-section, I have had to explain my choices repeatedly, with each new nurse, caregiver, helper, school personnel, therapist, or specialist. Constantly defending my parenting and wellness path, "outside of pathology" is draining.

I want to close my eyes and not have this conversation again, but here we are, at this wondrous camp, on an exceptionally beautiful day.

We sit in her office, and I share my research and collaborative efforts with a neurological acupuncturist, osteopath, and cranial sacral therapist. "The results convince us to stay our course."

"Tell her about the hyperbaric oxygen chamber," boasts Abby.

"Here in Pennsylvania, we found the Family Hope Center, where the directors taught us to treat the brain injury directly, rather than the symptoms, with organized movement, hyperbaric oxygen, and sensory integration. Abby is walking and seeing. Libby eats and senses much better. We've seen so much improvement."

"Really?" Jennifer wants to know more about eating organic food.

Autumn proudly shares about a nearby health food market, as if she is boasting about swimming medals. The conversation centers on how to build immunity and stay healthy during flu season. Jennifer listens and responds attentively when her slang prompts a contagious fit of giggles from Abby and Libby. I ignore the fresh puddle of pee at Abby's feet.

Autumn takes center stage, grabbing an orange cone-shaped cylinder as her makeshift microphone. Marching, she announces, "Attention, campers, please return to your bunk house. It's time to song up."

Libby is still, captivated by Autumn's song about her when Abby bursts in with high-pitched volume. "Sing about me!"

Jennifer wheels Libby around in a circle. Abby squeezes my hand, indicating she wants to jump. I grit my teeth, amazed at the strength of her muscles. Eventually, I got her to the restroom.

Autumn skips away in a circle, arms stretched out like a wide-winged bird, once again fortifying us with unexpected comedy.

Jennifer catches Autumn on the rebound and confirms our plan. "Please take a menu, supplement what you want, and call me if you need anything else."

We've completed our interview and tour of the camp for Abby and Libby. Autumn and I will soon be flying across the country.

"This is too good to be true." I pinch myself.

After reading to Abby and Libby, all three girls are asleep. It's 11 PM. By no choice of my own, hypervigilance kicks in. *Am I being overprotective or reacting to birth trauma?* I meticulously organize their specific diets with instructions, sticky notes, and supplements in sandwich baggies for each meal—for ten days. I cook, puree, and store Libby's meals in glass jars, and freeze them. I open Libby's capsules and mark, "dissolve in water then plunge through her tube." I convince myself to set aside oils and skin brushing. They'll survive for ten days. I exhaust myself with details.

On Sunday morning, I am ready to load up our van with our checklist in hand. Autumn stands at the edge of our stone driveway, like a flight attendant doing a preflight check: Diapers; Wipes; Plastic gloves; Bibs; Meals; Toiletries; Wedges; Bolsters; Extension tubes; Backup feeding supplies; Check... The sisters hug and say goodbye to each other. My stomach churns as I drive off, realizing I've never left the twins anywhere for this long.

The campgrounds are bustling with activity as we arrive. A friendly camper reaches for Libby's hand. Abby is curious. "Who are you?"

"I'm Katie. I'm a camper."

Together we head to Mr. Wilcott's office (the director), sign a few waivers, and we're on to Cabin 8 to meet the counselors.

Suddenly I feel an ache in my belly when Mr. Wilcott says, "Then go to the nurse's station to check in and drop off their medications."

"Ah, I don't have any medications. Jennifer signed off on this." I worry, *Will I be asked to take them home?*

"I know. You have to check in with the nurse anyway. Routine."

The counselors, Sarah, Liz, and Monica, greet us warmly beneath a rainbow-painted banner that stretches across the full length of the cabin, announcing

WELCOME ABBY, LIBBY, MARIE, JODI, ROZY, AND EMMA TO CABIN 8.

We unpack the van, go over the details for each day, and chat comfortably for a good hour before I venture to the nurse's station. The counselors are undaunted by my lengthy instructions. "No big deal. We'll manage just fine, won't we, Abby and Libby?" My belly softens with relief.

I make my way to the nurse's office, where I see other moms signing medication forms for their children. The stacks of large plastic zip-lock bags filled with opaque brown bottles make my stomach clench.

The nurse, clearly exhausted, without looking up, instructs me to put our medications in a plastic bag and fill out the emergency-release forms.

"I don't have any medications."

She looks worn out. I imagine she has already spent over eight hours following protocols. I'm edgy. Her tired eyes meet mine; she glares at me like I'm imposing upon her turf.

"You don't have medications? Let's see here. Twins with cerebral palsy. Libby with a seizure disorder and no meds?"

"Libby hasn't had a seizure for over three years." I knock on the wooden table, hoping it will shake her mood. "My daughters have a well-documented health care plan. I've spoken with Jennifer, Mr. Wilcott, and their counselors. I am told we are good."

"They must have medications!"

I meekly plea to call in the director. She agrees. They have a rather long chat, arms flying in the air. Ten minutes later he walks over, "You can leave."

I stagger to the mess hall, it's lunchtime. A counselor is feeding Libby her pureed meal. Abby is entranced by an older boy at the next table who is banging his cup on the table. I decide to disappear before the noise escalates. *They're in good hands.*

I am ten minutes away from home when my cell phone rings on speaker mode. "Hello, Mrs. Ginty? This is Mr. Wilcott. We need you to come back to camp. We're not going to be able to keep your daughters here."

I nearly skid off the road. "Tell me you're kidding!"

"The intake nurse is not comfortable with Libby's seizure disorder. She wants medication."

I explain, "She doesn't have a seizure disorder. Her diagnosis has changed!"

"You have to come back. I can't override standard medical practices."

Tears stream down my face. *What am I supposed to tell Autumn?* We have to catch a plane at 6 a.m. *Come hell or high water, we're getting on that plane.*

I drive back to camp.

Over the past seven years, I've encountered diverse perspectives on healthcare and parenting, learning enough to fortify my choices. I recognize that each person is shaped by cultural and medical conditioning, every child is different, and every family is limited by their resources. I hold myself accountable for the choices I make with the resources I have. *Why is it so challenging to feel autonomy from medical systems? Can a person feel empowered to chart a different course?*

For some strange reason, I name the woman in front of me Nurse Bullwrinkle. We barely know each other and we're fighting. Urgh.

I trudge up the ramp where Nurse Bullwrinkle sits surrounded by trays of medications. Her wrinkles deepen as she squints at a stack of prescriptions.

As soon as she spots me, I imagine steam pouring out of her ears. She rises, kicks her feet back a few times as if to gain traction, and raises her voice.

"I told you. You can't leave these girls here without their medication! Where is their medication?"

"I don't have any. They are safe."

She points to the supplements I provided for the counselors. "What is this? Calcium, magnesium, elderberry syrup—these aren't medications? Anything that goes into your child's mouth that isn't food requires a prescription. Where are your prescriptions? What if your child has a seizure and we do not have a prescription to give her Valium? What then?"

My guard is up. "Valium! You're not giving my child Valium."

"All children with seizures get Valium or Phenobarbital."

I want to wave a red cape in front of her, try to dizzy her like a matador. "Libby used to take those drugs and she became deathly ill. We're not going there. She's healthy and seizure-free. We have a tried-and-true treatment plan."

Nurse Bullwrinkle insists, "You need medications to treat illnesses. What's with this special food? We can't take this. We don't know what it is!"

I swear under my breath. "The counselors are happy to follow their diets."

As scores of children roll up the ramp, corralled into a line, Nurse Bullwrinkle tells me to sit in the other room. "Don't leave," she barks.

I cannot sit. I pace, calling Autumn's caregiver to explain. I'm mortified, anxious, angry, and loud. Nurse Bullwrinkle's puffy head looms through the door. "Please keep your voice down. I have sixty more children to get through this line before bed. They need their medications."

Slam.

I want to duct tape my mouth before I retaliate with something I will regret. *Am I a prisoner of a faulty medical system? Who gets to make decisions for my children?*

After an hour of pacing, I slip out the back door to cabin 8. Liz sees me coming. "Sarah is reading bedtime stories. Your girls are a riot. Thanks for bringing them here."

I want to fall into her arms. "The director called me back. The nurse won't let me leave."

"Oh no. Our regular nurse canceled at the last minute, due to a family emergency. You have a sub... Don't worry, we'll take care of your girls."

I slip back inside to face Nurse Bullwrinkle. I feel compassion for her, she is obligated to enforce a medical paradigm. She doesn't know that a parent could learn proper care for her children. She is waving two stacks of paper in front of my face. "Mrs. Ginty. Complete these forms. List each supplement, dose, frequency, precautions, and your doctor must sign."

My body tenses. "I can't get hold of our doctor on a Sunday night." I want to scream. "I've been sitting here for three hours and now you ask me to fill out more forms?" I scribble through the pages.

I'm on form number five when she charges at me again. "I can't get hold of your nursing agency. Before you can leave, they need to fax us Libby's nursing schedule. If a nurse doesn't show up, I'm calling you to pick up your child."

It's dark outside. *How am I going to get a signed schedule on a Sunday night?* I see her fangs, urging me to obey. *Where's the duct tape?* I'd best shut up. I imagine she scorns me. A soft voice tells me she's just doing her job; be kind.

Still, I pace, wearily pushing numbers on my cell phone, desperately searching for a doctor. Twenty minutes later, Mike, the supervisor from our nursing agency calls back. He's already privy to Abby's and Libby's treatment plan and assures me everything is sorted. He will have the doctor fax over his signature the next morning.

I want to reach through the phone and embrace him tightly.

It is 2 a.m. when I collapse into bed. The alarm sounds one hour later.

I'm exhausted, grumpy, and battle-scarred from yet another clash with the bloody horns of Western medicine. Despite any victory, I'm at odds with mainstream culture's institutionalized protocols. The best-laid plans always end up in nasty drawn-out confrontations. My hypervigilance is never easy to shake. I long to press a button that will rejuvenate my energy, lift my spirits, and center my attention on good-humored Autumn.

Our friend Bill drives us to the airport on time. Autumn wants to read books together and draw during the flight but I can't keep my eyes open. Upon arriving in California, we rent a convertible as planned. Autumn wants the top down. I want everything closed tightly, to curl up and release the sorrow of injustice, for both of us. I want our life back—before my twins were injected with life-threatening complications. I crave sleep. A week ago, I was ready to do whatever Autumn wanted. Now I'm exasperated. *Oh my God, is this what nine-year-olds listen to?*

Gradually, a sense of spontaneity returns. It is not as cozy and joyful as I wanted, but it is our time together. We stay at Marin Headlands, hike along the coast, build sandcastles, and play chase. At night, I poop out long before Autumn. We visit cherished friends, go to the boardwalk, and spend time at Kiva Retreat hot tubs. We charge into Grandma Alice's swimming pool, have underwater tea parties, play follow-the-leader off the diving board, and do bellyflops off the side of the pool.

I envision Abby and Libby happy, thousands of miles away.

One day Autumn catches me staring into space, my mouth in a frown. She sees through me and says, "Mom. Are you thinking about that nurse?" Her eyes squarely catch mine. "You know, you can let it go. Just let it go."

Her words touch me. *Can I let go? Can I allow myself to soften?*

In that moment, possibility emerges. I'm not proud of my intensity but Autumn reminds me that I can unburden myself from devastating thoughts. What is done is done. *Can I let go of my endless agendas to fix the twins and heal their brain injuries? Can I let go of my wish to have my three daughters playing together in the sand, gathering coral and shells, dancing barefoot in the warm sea breeze?*

Through her sagacious words, Autumn freshens the moment. I'm not going to bluff and tell you I can let go automatically. I can't, but she reminds me to breathe. I feel spaciousness arising that cradles life exactly as it is, the embrace I crave. When I feel held, the onslaught of harsh judgment, should have, could have, if only relaxes. I'm aware of narratives that loop. *Can I let them pass? Can I unfurl myself? Can I reframe my narration?*

It's easy to forget that I can change my perspective when I sense danger for myself or my children. My brain automatically fixates on the worst-case scenario, blocking out all other possibilities. I'm not being hijacked into a helicopter anymore. Breathing, I recover myself and remember all the times I did not leave, cave in, give up, or passively allow myself to be coerced into something I know is not right. Now, I get to choose. I may not always sound nice or kind, but for the first time, I recognize that when I am uncomfortable with rigidity or fierceness, I'm actually being brave. I'm building my courage and muscle memory to choose differently, to challenge the status quo. I know that I will continue to make mistakes and be messily imperfect as I learn to speak up for what I believe in. *Am I being disrespectful or becoming more honest and braver?*

Through tears, anger, resistance, laughter, anguish, and rest I allow myself to feel all of it. And in allowance, I am kinder. I reframe our lives and know deep in my heart that we are whole, not broken, regardless of the hardships we face.

In Autumn, playfulness blossoms without protocols, agendas, or 'fix it' plans. *Thank you, my little teacher, for reminding me of the preciousness of each moment.*

22

The Feminine Soul

I'm invited to Woodstock, New York, to offer a weekend Satsang Intensive. The host told me *Gangaji*[20] is a regular teacher there. They have an established group interested in non-dual teachings. I'm unsure how I will manage, as I'm busy offering meetings in Delaware, New Jersey, and Pennsylvania, alongside the clients I see in my private practice when my children are in school. Getting out of the house to meet people and explore truth nourishes me yet I straddle two very different worlds. Each requires a different energy; Libby's and Abby's need for constant care and Autumn—my whispering owl—all are unique expressions. My nervous system is slow to calm and sleep is sporadic. Often, I'm like a short-order cook, sweating to respond to orders. Satsang requires a different type of response. When I am able to relax into the backspace of who I am, I'm able to respond freshly—*but now, amidst my strange life?* Still, I say I will come.

I drive to Woodstock on a Friday afternoon. The previous week at home is bonkers. Abby's typical six-hour therapy program, Libby has the flu, and I volunteer to chaperone Autumn's field trip to a yogurt farm. I'm dragging. I gather the directions and estimate travel time but I don't account for Friday turnpike traffic. I arrive at my friend's house at 6:40 p.m. Satsang begins at 7 p.m.; it will take twenty minutes to get there. In the shower, eager to change out of my grubby mothering clothes, I realize I forgot my clean beige blouse that is hanging in my closet, 95 miles away. I want to escape out the window, hop into my car, and drive home. I call out, "Laurie, I forgot my shirt, do you have a top I can borrow?" She is extra small, I'm not. *F**k.* I hear Laurie and

---

[20] Who is Gangaji? Gangaji: (born Texas, 1942) is an American born spiritual teacher and author who offers Satsang internationally.

her husband whisper in the hallway. "You can borrow one of Jack's shirts; he doesn't mind." *Oh great, I'll show up in a cowboy shirt.*

Reluctantly, I accept the plaid flannel with a collar that buttons down the front. I feel disoriented, somewhat choked by the collar. Despite feeling frazzled and out of place, I face the unexpected. As we arrive, I notice cars parked along either side of the building. My hands are clammy, I swallow, clear my throat, and wonder, *why did I say yes?* I imagine the audience waiting for someone like Gangaji to waltz in with flowing elegance, smiling from a reservoir of silence. My thoughts are loud as I walk into the quiet Satsang hall, wearing Jack's cowboy shirt and sandals. Even though I wobble, I can't help but laugh at the irony of the situation. I sit in front of a peaceful group of about sixty people like I just came in from milking cows. I'm reminded that life doesn't go as planned. I attempt to switch into dharma mode, "Welcome to Satsang." *I know, faking is awkward.* I want to moo myself home like a cow.

Other times, amidst my chaotic and unconventional life, I would close my eyes, take a few deep breaths, let my heart beat fast, ground through my feet, and remember my purpose—why I am here—and speak honestly. I'd say how fucking hard life can be at times. I'd talk about our shared humanness, sleepless nights; how I wasn't going to come but I'm here because I love truth—the commitment I made in 2001 when I was called to offer Satsang. And I wonder, *why do I hold myself to an image?*

Respected guides like Eunice, Adya, and the few female teachers I know, emphasize teaching from your lived experience, with honesty and curiosity as your compass. Doubts flood my mind, as I try to form a bridge between family life and spiritual teachings. *Can I clear my mind, let myself be vulnerable,* and allow a real teaching to emerge?

I'd like to tell you that I got over myself. I don't, not yet. I imagine discussing the realities of family life will place me on the periphery again. I'm also learning to be kind when things fall apart. Becoming real is a continuous journey—one that I currently suck at. I long for conversations within spiritual circles that discuss the beauty and the hardships of motherhood. Most spiritual teachers I've encountered are single men, or without children, with apparent personal liberties. *Can I non-apologetically speak about the nitty-gritty details of everyday life?* How to embody peace amidst broken appliances, family conflicts, single parenting, the heart-wrenching experiences of domestic violence, infidelity, or caring for the ill, disabled, or dying? I want to create circles that invite curious explorations that wonder how we mend our heartbreaks, see our struggles as initiations, and empty ourselves for greater acceptance and courage, that celebrate rites of passage. I know people talk about these things; I'm a therapist. But not everyone can afford private therapy. Gathering in circles gives us the opportunity to be witnessed which rinses shame, mends isolation, and brings us together in community.

I'm torn when spiritually educated men self-assuredly discuss common experiences like trauma or emotions and are held up with great value; books get written. Women have long attended to the messiness of our human existence; their stories and work often go unnoticed.

On the drive home from Woodstock, I feel relief. I realize that sharing real-life holds immense value. I don't mind being shabby. Traditional Satsang follows a model historically dominated by men, one that women who are able to be carefully kept, polite, and pleasing may hold allegiance to. My urgency is to unearth who I am as a woman and a mother. Perhaps forgetting my shirt is a metaphor for stripping away the spiritual trappings that are unbecoming of my time. Perhaps I am at a threshold of a firsthand discovery, a decoding, an undoing of spiritual imprints that unleash the way of women, the feminine soul—the Mother.

As much as I am nourished by Satsang, I finish off the rest of my scheduled meetings and close shop. I want to cultivate ways to express these life-giving discoveries—starting with me, my body, my life with my children, and the deep knowing of my feminine soul.

The following week I lend my car to one of our helpers. Whenever he borrows the car, he adjusts the seat to a slightly reclined position. I wonder how he drives like this, as I feel like I'm falling backward. Surprisingly, as I sit in my car after my Woodstock revelation, it doesn't feel strange. I pause and sit for a while; it's actually quite relaxing. From this vantage point, I can see through the rear-view mirror and my hands rest comfortably on the steering wheel at 9 and 3 o'clock. The seat is situated directly in the middle, neither reclined nor tilted forward. I have an epiphany; I am the one who's been adjusting and pushing forward to the future, hurriedly steering myself to the next place. I am the one racing into the future to get things right.

I see my tendency to jump ahead, to rush into things before I am truly ready, without sensing or listening in, unable to turn off hypervigilance. I see my anxious desire to establish a professional life that my colleagues without children seem to have. I think about all of the arranging and rearranging I've done and continue to do to find the next cure for my babies' condition since their birth. *Wow.* I'm sitting in my car, relieved and bright with revelations.

Quiet envelops my body. It's odd, as I realize it's okay to do nothing. I don't need to adjust my seat, or strive to be somebody or somewhere. Right here, in the middle—is balance. I don't need to race ahead to get to a better place for myself, my children, or anyone else. *Life may be teaching me to drive in reverse to undo these patterns with full permission to rest in the middle.*

23

Building Our Nest

2005, I'm sitting next to Autumn barely hearing a word she says. My attention always darting to the loudest noise. I miss Autumn, who is now eleven, quiet and sensitive. She presents me with a drawing—a little yellow framed house with an oversized woman in a red dress drawn up to her eyeballs. She is sitting in a rocking chair holding two small girls with bandaged legs, disproportionately large open mouths, and eyes sealed shut by two black lines. Behind the house is a little girl in a red dress with long golden hair skipping rope under an apple blossom tree as big as the house. The little girl is facing the back door—expressionless.

I sit with this drawing, painfully, tenderly aware that Autumn is conveying a vital message to me. She experiences me buried beneath her sisters who have legs that don't work, eyes that don't see, and loud mouths. She is in the background—left out, skipping alone, wondering about the door to the house: *Is there room for me?* Autumn is the soft glow, while Abby and Libby are the flashing neon lights constantly on my skin like mosquitos vociferously biting and itching.

I want to skip rope with Autumn.

But instead, I find myself making preparations for the following day and another day passes without jumping rope with Autumn. It troubles me to know she feels marginalized within our family dynamic. I feel like I am having an affair directly in front of the eyes of my first love. I know she is with us, resilient on the edge. I miss her—immensely, sensing we both long for the connection of our earlier tight, intuitive bond.

A prayer invigorates my mood. I seek guidance for my three children, unsure of how to navigate their needs simultaneously. *Please show me.* I am not asking for things to change, or fighting the reality before me. I want to spread open like an eagle gather soft feathers from Mother Earth and build a nest for Autumn to feel securely held on my lap. As I sit with this intention, I remember that *Nothing is missing inside of us. Earth is our home.* I breathe through tears and an image appears—an owl on a branch without wings; curious: *How do I fly?* Another image follows with Autumn and me sitting side by side on a sturdy branch of an ancient oak tree. We have baskets with leaves and twigs. Together we slowly and carefully build a nest, we learn and grow as we go, guided by the wisdom of Mother Nature, regenerating our relationship. Mother Nature knows how.

Later, on a humid midsummer day, the heavy air cloaks us like a bulky sweater. In our tight farmhouse, without air conditioning, four of us plus a nurse are sweating. It's dinnertime, I'm famished and worn out. I sit down to eat with Autumn by my side, barely touching her food. But before I can take a bite, she complains of a stomachache, clutching her belly and expressing her discomfort.

"It really hurts. Can I go to my room?"

My hunger is fierce, but I follow her. I track closely behind, noticing the bouncy spring in her step is absent.

We retreat to her room. It is small, with minimal furnishings. She sits on the edge of her bed holding her abdomen, I kneel on the hardwood floor beside her bed and swing the door closed. She makes an agonizing face and pulls up her shirt to show her bloated belly.

She rounds her eyes and moans, "Mom, what do you think it is? My belly really hurts!"

"I'm not sure. What do you think it is?" Slowing down.

"I don't know; it hurts," she says sadly. Tears are welling in her eyes.

"Is it okay if I put my hand on your belly?" I ask, leaning in.

"Yeah," she puffs lightly.

"Can you direct my hand to the discomfort and tell me the feeling?" *We're gathering our leaves and twigs.*

She points to a few spots where it kind of hurts, but there is one big hurt right around her navel.

"Tell me about it... What's the sensation?"

"I'll try," she says. "Ever since I came home from my visit with Dad, I'm not the same. I'm just not the same."

This is our third year in Pennsylvania and the only year that Autumn chose to visit her dad in California. She went to visit him for spring break; now it is the beginning of summer.

"Hmmmm, something is not the same?"

"Yeah."

"Something is different since you came back from seeing your dad."

"Yeah, it's strange. I'm not the same."

I listen, aware that she doesn't need my coaxing; she is expressing herself very well. My job is to stay close, go slow, and let her tell me. I feel her slowing down also, staying with her experience. I don't want to interrupt her insights with blabber or fixing. She is quietly receding to her inner world. I wait. *We're building our nest.*

Our exploration continues. Abby and Libby are content downstairs listening to Jack and Annie from *The Tree House Mysteries* on tape. *Do they intuit that we need this moment?*

Autumn pops her eyes open and says, "I can't find me!"

I listen quietly.

"I used to be Autumn. Now I'm not!"

Then she starts to sob, "Whoever I'm with, I become someone different. I'm not me. If I'm with my friend Eve, I become Eve. When I'm with Lorraine [the social worker who comes to our house and often steps outside to have a cigarette], I'm her and I can't breathe. When I'm with Dad, he talks about his dad's heart attack, and I feel like I'm going to have a heart attack."

Without a pause, she continues, "When Libby's nurse [who has intermittent migraines] is here, I have a headache. Whatever I'm around, that is what I become. I can't find me!"

I listen, barely able to withhold my astonishment as she discovers how porous she is. She lucidly expresses the various attributes of the people she comes in close contact with.

"What if I wake up in the night and I can't breathe? What if I have a heart attack?"

Terrified of being overwhelmed by intense sensations, each scenario manifests pronounced symptoms in her body: palpitations, labored breathing, sweating, stomachache, or headache. She speaks about the heart attack as if it happening to her, crying, "My heart might stop right now!"

I continue to sit close, curiously observing her body and attentively listening to every sound. Unsure of what to do, I listen and stay, trusting that Autumn and our instincts will guide us.

She is tender, caring, prone to overstimulation, and in need of a strong safe boundary. *How do I wrap her in safety?*

Autumn's recent visit with her dad marked a pivotal turning point in her healing journey. She no longer suppresses her ache to be with him and expresses her need for a safe nest to process her feelings. Like a sponge, she absorbs the emotions of others, particularly within our family life. She is still developing the ability to differentiate her sensations from others. Establishing healthy boundaries takes time and practice, allowing us to feel without becoming enmeshed, numb, or afraid. Healthy ego mechanisms teach us how to build a boundary around our often fragile sensitivities. Autumn is curious and eager to join and find where she belongs. It is very confusing and harmful when others intrude into a private space without consent. This injures our instincts, fractures our soma, and makes it more challenging to voice our needs. Autumn communicates in various ways, not only words. I want her to feel safe in her body and empowered to protect herself from what doesn't belong to her. I struggle sometimes to create clear boundaries as we frequently have care providers in and out of our homes. I want to learn what is helpful and model the ability to say "no," to create private space, even if it means we go without caregivers at times.

Like birds gathering feathers, Autumn and I nurture our bond, sealing our nest for the days to come. My role is to support her as she navigates transitions, sensitivities, and encounters with strangers in our lives. Like wounded owls, we are growing robust wings that will carry us through the uncertain and scary moments we face. Her healing crisis presents an opportunity to evaluate who and when we will allow others into our home, our private life, and our nest.

Autumn's sensitivity reveals challenging aspects that require crafting guidelines for caregivers to ward off emotional upheavals and projections to establish clear boundaries. We aim to replace Band-Aids with messages that honor our needs and provide ample safety for everyone to breathe easily.

Seeking help and relying on others is not something that comes naturally or comfortably to me. When I need to rely on others to help us, it unsettles me. I realize that I am more sensitive than I care to admit. I listen to people, feel them in the house, and unintentionally absorb their energies. Many have early childhood wounding, *who doesn't?* Some warm up to me like a mother. It's a delicate situation, and boundaries can easily become blurred and messy.

While our family home may be relatively healthy, without beer, blood, or guns, I don't have the capacity to mother more than my own children. And I am fiercely protective of my girls, watching that no one oversteps. There are times when I've missed something like a nurse intruding on Autumn or Abby's private space. I've lost my temper, like a mama bear that roars for her cubs. I'm a mama bear. Our family has boundaries.

In our talk upstairs, after a long breathe out, I ask Autumn, "Can I just hold you?"

"Yes." She lies down in my arms. We are quiet for a long while. Then she says, "I just don't think there's a bunch of me's. I'm me."

"Hmmm. I don't think there are, either. Only you."

Her eyes burst open, "You're here!"

"Yes, and you're here. We're here. Me and you. Both."

"But I have all these things going on. What am I supposed to do?"

I whisper in her ear, "If it's not happening now, it's not you."

Autumn is receptive. I remind her of the hula hoop game that I play with Libby, using a weighted hula hoop to create a personal boundary space and to protect her energies and the integrity of her nervous system. While Libby is sitting tall in her wheelchair, I hold the hula hoop above her head and slowly descend the circumference of her chair to the ground, while singing, "Where is Libby? Where is Libby? Here I am, Here I am. This is Libby's space, her very own space, I am here, I am here," to the tune of Frere Jacques.

I suggest doing the same for Autumn to assure her that the space inside her is for her—only her. She likes the idea as long as she can make up her own song.

She wants to know how to stop her thinking.

"If I say 'don't think of a pink flamingo,' what do you think of?"

"Pink flamingos!"

"Right! As soon as you try to stop thinking about flamingos, a party of flamingos is in your head eating shrimp and snails. You get hungry or have a headache."

She giggles. We talk more about how hard it is to have people in and out of our homes. I share a practice I use in therapy about being soft in the front and strong in the back. My hands shape into mudras, my left hand outstretched at my midline and my right hand bent at the wrist, blocking, as if to say "stop." It signifies a practice to 'do no harm (open in the front) and take no shit (strong in the back)'. I admit it's not always easy for me. I imagine we both will get good at it. She knows I've had plenty of slips and said, "F**K OFF!"

"I like it. Take no shit. Do no harm."

"Thoughts and people will visit us. But we don't have to invite them to live with us all of the time."

Her eyes flash, "Oh no. I like people, but I don't want them to live with us!"

This night Autumn sleeps in my bed like a baby kitten. The next morning, she says, "Mom, if you can't go to camp with me this summer, I don't want to go."

My heart is joy-filled. Mother Nature heard our prayers and responded, and we followed. Autumn has a feather pillow to rest her head. I have my little owl girl back. She is confident that she has a place on a robust branch in our family tree. *With the help of Mother Nature, our nest will forever grow stronger.*

Later, Autumn begins sleeping with her teddy bear at night again, indicating that she isn't ready to be a big kid yet who goes off to camp without her mommy. Our culture pushes our children to grow up quickly and for parents to get busy faster. The sight of Autumn in her pajamas snuggling her favorite teddy, finding room for herself in her mommy bear's bed, is an image that will nourish me in the years to come.

24
Becoming Real

I f you would have told me as we boarded the plane to Pennsylvania that in three years we'd be back in California, I would not have listened. I know things now that I didn't know then. I listen and track differently for when to stay or leave, and what to lean into. A chilling urgency is gone. I can say, "I don't know. Let me think about it. I need more time."

In the morning I wake up happy. It is bright outside, it's late summer 2005, and we're ready to return to California. We will say goodbye to the 200-acre farm that we share with the Camphill villagers; Autumn's friends and teacher, Abby's program specialists and aids, and Libby's special home away from home. The lovely community that we bonded with over the past three years helps us pack through tears and joy as we reminisce about activities, like rolling dough at the bakery, shaping clay pottery, or milking a cow. And the adults with disabilities who boldly knocked on our door to join us for tea and chat with us about their infatuations and bowling events. And there is Scratch, the stray cat who scratched our door daily for food, water, and snuggles.

I imagine Camphill Beaver Run School is one of a kind, and will not be duplicated in a typical special-education classroom. We will carry fond memories and learnings with us, like how Libby's music teacher sings her name each morning. "Libby Ginty, are you here?" Libby's gleeful giggle, *"Yes, I'm here."* Abby's remarkable progress to see, walk, and receive the rose. Autumn's natural emotional intelligence informs our way while she soars as a brilliant student in her class.

I'm proud to complete my fourth year of training in the Hakomi method, which I began in San Francisco before moving to Pennsylvania. It's a body-centered somatic approach to healing that I need both personally and professionally to hone in emotional intelligence, unpack grief, mend fractured parts, resolve trauma, harvest instincts, and fill in missed experiences to feel whole again. I'm hopeful that the tools I've gathered will sustain us with curative care as we journey onward. We will take our family nest with us and remember Libby's song, *I am here.*

Soon we find a lovely one-story, three-bedroom home with an open floor plan on Madrone Forest Drive in Grass Valley—a small town nestled in the foothills of the Sierra Nevada mountains. The house has a deck in the back overlooking the backyard, surrounded by a madrone wood that leads to a bubbling brook and hiking trails. It has an established vegetable garden area, space for our trampoline, and a Mulberry tree to hang our swings. (We came to Grass Valley because the director from the school in Colfax agreed to admit Abby into her program. This was our plan, as Abby is now walking. But when we arrived, we learn that she just closed the school. We did not get the memo and already leased our home in Santa Cruz). *Inconvenient, I know.*

The girls want a dog. I read up on service animals and the benefits for people with disabilities. They provide safety, companionship, and responsibility, the opportunity to care for an animal. Sounds perfect for Abby and Libby. We applied to Guide Dogs for the Blind for a service dog, and six months later a two-year-old longhaired black Labrador with a bulky snout and gentle demeanor arrives at our doorstep. He came with the name Sakima. We nickname him Suki Boy, although Abby calls him *fatso*. We learn his commands; "Sit, do your business, wait, walk on, stay, and okay." He sits calmly until he is given a command. He will bark if he senses a predator or sit by the door if he needs to do his business. On many occasions, one of us will pour his food into his dog dish, tell him to sit, and forget to say "okay." Twenty minutes later he is still waiting, drooling over his bowl with adorable black eyes, eager for his cue to eat. "Such a good fatso boy," Abby will say, cuddling his furry body.

Suki is a career-change dog. He passes all the exams to be a Seeing Eye Dog but the physical aspect, due to hip problems. His hips sway slightly, making it difficult for Abby to walk him. He becomes her official emotional companion dog. I imagine that one day she will stand firmly at his side with his leash strapped around her wrist, confidently saying, "Walk on."

Two weeks after settling into our new house, we are lucky to receive nursing services for Libby in the home. I worry, never knowing if the people assigned to work in our home will appreciate our alternative approach or impose a different agenda. After training Libby's nurse, I look for a sprightly female to coach Abby with her learning tasks. Our new helper delights us with purple hair and surprisingly reveals a plethora of activities for children. She introduces us to a childhood utopia called Camp August. This will become Autumn's playground for high-adventure sports, circus arts, crafts, and amazing friendships. I am fired up to know that there is a place for her to foster her zest for artistic and physical adventures. My body melts like warm honey when I see her face painted with black and green stripes, and watch her swing from rope to rope, flying over mud baths like a chimpanzee and cheering on her mates to climb steep walls—a true team member. She fearlessly tackles obstacle courses in the same way she navigates our family terrain, with resilience and steadfastness like the warrior she is becoming.

Thankfully, with the support of old friends, I manage to resume my yearly silent retreat at Mount Madonna with Adyashanti. At the close of the retreat, a participant approaches me after learning that I led Satsang on the East Coast. "We're neighbors. Will you lead meetings for us?" There are many moments like this. It is subtle, but I pause to connect with myself and look the person in the eyes, as if to say *if you only knew how strange my life is.* I remember Woodstock. *Am I ready? Can I be real?* I'm rejuvenated from the retreat; six nights of uninterrupted sleep, restorative meditations, and inner processing. I feel grounded, ready to explore our new surroundings, *maybe to meet people.*

I remember these words from my friend Adya: "Freedom deepens; it's not final. Just when you think it is time to kick back and coast a little, that's when you get the call to be a retreat leader or to serve another function."

I don't want to play a traditional role. *Can I include motherhood—the full range of human experience—in my teaching?*

The next time I see Rob's face, I say, "I'm happy to offer Satsang. I'll give it my best."

I've come to appreciate that the real retreat happens in our day-to-day life when we step off our meditation cushion and leave the comfort of noble silence. Libby has a night of explosive BMs, which means I immerse her in a full bath, launder her bedding, freshen her room, and rock her to sleep three times. This gives me the perfect theme for my first meeting *When shit gets real.*

Autumn knows Satsang is a sanity check for me. Before I can make a firm commitment, we need a reliable evening helper. She dazzles me with an idea to release me from the house one night a week.

We make a colorful flyer to post all over town, listing the kind of caregiver we are looking for:

"Plays games, sing songs, likes to bake and go on adventures, interested in holistic healing, likes dogs, and communicates well." She adds a drawing of a Mary Poppins figure.

The response to our poster is immediate. A young woman who practices a raw food diet, yoga, nonviolent communication, loves games, and has great references from other families' calls. Our interview is short. Autumn likes her. I ask her if she could commit to at least a year.

"Absolutely. I'm not planning to go anywhere; this is my new home." We hire her on the spot. (She will be with us for three years until she marries the local postal carrier).

I test her stamina: "We just moved across the country; we've already been through a long training sequence with a few people that didn't work out. Do you mind figuring it out as you go along? I'm hammered."

She understands burnout and tells me a slightly comforting story about working with a boy with autism for three years before moving here.

"There was a high turnover with caregivers. It really took its emotional toll on the family."

I'm honest with her. "When helpers don't work out, I crumble. I furiously scrub countertops and floors and forget that I have children to feed. It's frustrating. I lose patience trying to accommodate others in our home."

She seems to understand the vigor and vulnerability involved in teaching strangers about your children and your preferred care for them. She assures me that she resonates with our holistic aspirations and wants to hang in with us. My body relaxes.

"This means so much to us." We easily meld together as a team.

Satsang is my Wednesday night medicine at my new friend's house, but before long, we rent a larger space to hold intensives, six-week embodiment courses, a nine-month women's journey, and three-day silent retreats. *I don't know how this is happening—I'm finding a new way to facilitate meetings.* The participants talk about the hard stuff, they allow feelings, and they cry; they also lighten with laughter after an emotional release. I feel nourished by this— by giving permission to be fully human—by not abandoning myself or pretending to be 'the teacher.'

––––––––––

Abby and Libby are in middle school. I have a sudden surge of energy to use the summer to catch them up—bring them up to speed with their peers. I want to find a way to reactivate my learnings in neurological stimulation and movement to improve function for children with brain injuries. While Autumn has a wonderful summer camp to attend, I thought, *why don't I create a summer program for the twins? I'll contact other parents, rent a space, and build it out.* Ambitious, I know.

At the time, I would have said I did this because I was inspired and I couldn't obtain physical therapy in the traditional classrooms. Special education funding focuses more on autism spectrum disorder and speech therapy, not physical therapy. Honestly, my hunch is that I hadn't digested the *for-life* prognosis. Driven to fix and improve functionality, I began it all over again: therapeutic equipment, educational materials, and added conductive physical movement. I hired a conductive education teacher; we organized a four-week program and gathered a small group of children with physical challenges.

We have three successful summer programs before I come to my senses. In order for any program with children to be successful, you need at least three things: a great design, parent participation, and funding. We were par for the course, specifically on parent involvement. Getting parents to be more involved would have meant they had to sacrifice the sweet joy of 'me time.' Drop-off and pickup, period. I get it, when you are a parent of a special needs child or any child, time for self-care is essential for survival. We didn't have the funding to hire additional team support. Overall, the program flowed along nicely as we were privately owned and our design was sound, but in special education, it is not easy to establish agreements within an institution, as my next story shows.

25
Inclusion – Belonging

People like Libby who sit in a wheelchair for prolonged periods, day in and day out, mold to the form of the chair. The muscles in the body develop contractures from immobilization. The body is more rigid, and stiff at the hips, knees, and elbows unless she has a regular movement program of physical therapy, stretching, or other forms of neurological development out of the chair. It alarms me to see Libby take the shape of her chair.

It is spring 2013. At the end of each school year, we have a meeting that is called an Individualized Education Program (IEP) for the following year. The special education department conducts the IEP and is usually directed by the principal of the school the student is attending. Parents, primary teachers, and service providers are invited to attend. At this time, I have attended IEP meetings to advocate for my daughters for eleven years. I find these meetings necessary, gut-wrenching, and heartbreaking. I sit around a crowded table. Most of the people I do not know, a few may have met Libby once. Libby is unable to speak for herself. I translate her needs. We are the team that will decide an appropriate special education program for Libby, and the services she will receive based on her needs and goals. During this meeting, there is a review of prior services and progress toward goals. The idea is to create an IEP, which is a legally binding contract to best support the needs of the student for educational purposes. The words *legally binding* hang in the air.

For reasons I can't control, I shrink, stranger anxiety kicks in, a power dynamic loops and I feel outnumbered. Libby has a crucial need for physical therapy in order to achieve goals like standing or moving toward a switch to communicate with her teacher or classmates. I don't want to think that the specialists stack the meeting to minimize Libby's need. *Is funding invested elsewhere?*

I'm not at my best, impatient, rude, and defensive, and I can't manage Libby without a school program that fosters functional development. Each person tells us their name and profession. I blank as the credentials build. *I'm just a mom, isn't that worth something?* Well-dressed strangers with official diplomas, intermittently eye me with stacks of papers before them. My mind flashes to traumatic memories. Sign here, "I know what is best for your daughter." I feel my throat close, chest burn, belly clench—an ache to bring my babies back inside. *I can't do this.* When my turn comes, I'm not able to lift my chin, "I'm Libby's mom." *Not resourced enough to advocate.*

They want to eliminate her PT sessions without sound reason, rather than add sessions to advance educational goals. "She enjoys PT," I mutter.

Like medical appointments, these meetings have an untethered accumulative effect on my psychological state. It does not take long for my vision to blur; I'm confused. I might disassociate. I don't like this part of myself; decisions are delayed; papers do not get signed. A stalemate ensues.

I decide to invite Libby's friends from the community to advocate for physical therapy. Libby's PT report states, "Libby, a couple of years ago, was using a stander during school hours, but due to structural alignment of her feet and contractures in her hips and knees, standing is no longer appropriate.... It is very unlikely that Libby's contractures will be resolved; that she will never be able to maintain functional sitting; or integrate her reflexes." The report does not show a required baseline or current measurements, although it does suggest that, in prior years, she was able to accomplish more when she had regular PT sessions. The physical therapist recommends reducing PT to a consultation basis. Consultation means providing advice to the classroom teacher without direct services from a professional skilled in PT. In other words, without having the benefits of therapy sessions. *Baffling, I know.*

At home, Libby has a therapeutic hot sage bath followed by yoga postures, stretching, and a movement routine every day. I decide to photograph her sessions and show all of the positions she moves in and out of, including sitting, head control, and weight bearing on her feet. I post these photos and the comments from the IEP reports on Facebook. Supporting comments for Libby flood in. Ten additional people from the community came with me to her IEP meeting to advocate for physical therapy services for Libby. We want the unsubstantiated PT report removed from her file, as it could prevent her from receiving needed services in the future. We schedule this meeting at a time specified by the principal of special education and the physical therapist. They do not show up. I am advised not to sign the IEP and to request an independent physical therapy assessment. In the meantime, Libby is not receiving PT in school, as I am told they cannot find a provider.

The following day I go to the principal's office. He tells me, "We haven't been able to find physical therapy. The PT who wrote the report left the area."

This sounds closer to the truth—meaning that it isn't that Libby does not need PT, it is that he does not know how to obtain it. A quick Google search in the area brings up seven physical therapy clinics, each with five to ten licensed PTs on staff, not counting independent providers. *I don't think it is a lack of therapists to serve Libby.*

I deal with situations like this all the time. I'm hoodwinked and need to ration my reserves. This may be a losing argument, but I want to be part of the solution. There are countless people working in special education who are constantly going the extra mile on behalf of their students. We have been fortunate to have teachers like this on our team, especially in charter schools.

I reflect inside: *What is the best use of my time and energy to support Libby?* I try to keep in mind what our good friend Judith Bluestone (the founder of HANDLE: Holistic Approaches to Neurological Development and Learning Efficiency) said before she passed away, "If they say it can't be done, it means it has not been documented, or they have not tried." As a child, Judith was unable to speak until she was thirteen. She taught herself to speak by implementing what she learned about neurology from her parents' library books. Her parents were leaders in medicine. She became a nationally recognized speaker on autism, neurology, and learning in many places, including medical schools. We (Abby, Libby, and I) had two evaluations and training with her. She was certain that, if provided gentle tapping and vagus nerve stimulation, which she taught us, both girls would make great strides in their development. We followed her guidance at home as often as possible. Of course, what happens outside of the home is what happens.

Regardless, Libby forms a community around her. She has many friends cheering her on, delighted by her joyous presence. She has an unusual connection to life—to Spirit—and wishes to be included. She tells us so with her smiles and infectious hilarity, which we call 'giggle fits.' Her giggles erupt when we do human stuff like drop canisters, swear abruptly, or get overly serious. She senses tension brewing in the air. Life for her seems comical as if to say, "Lighten up. Life is too short. Let's play." She belts out rip-roaring chortles like fairy dust twinkling in the air, dosing us with ease. Thickness is elevated with captivating glee. This is one of many gifts that Libby brings with her enchanting presence. Her teachers and nurses adore her, and give her oodles of care, better than what I imagined possible. No wonder, her middle name is JOY.

Abby joins the Yuba River Charter School alongside her typically developing peers. Her neurological challenges continue to impact her vision as well as fine and gross motor movement, but not her ability to engage with learning. She is a sprite, bright girl who requires additional time and adaptations. Soon her teacher and the staff will see that Abby is intelligent, and 'mentally retarded' does not apply. Abby receives an educational aide in a class of about twenty-eight students and a teacher that I will call Mrs. Best. An Individualized Educational Program (IEP) is developed to accommodate her needs and bring appropriate support services onboard. I'm happy to find this process entirely different than at the public school. I'm able to make eye contact, listen, and respond. No flashy diplomas, a clear focus on the student's needs. I volunteer to begin as Abby's classroom assistant until they find someone. I love every minute of having a very specific role to play.

Abby is included in every aspect of the day. She immediately adjusts to the routine and is eager to attend school. In the morning, she boasts,

"Let's go, Mom. I have to be at my class on time, or Mrs. Best and the kids will miss me."

In the early grades, most of the curriculum is taught through movement, singing, and stories. For math, the children learn their multiplication tables by standing in a big circle and passing a ball back and forth to count, first by twos and increasing all the way to twelves. This style of learning works very well for Abby. She masters multiplication by the end of grade two. She isn't able to do math on paper, but if math is presented to her verbally with manipulative materials, she viscerally learns through her body, she gets it. For example, adding and subtracting blocks makes sense to her, whereas numbers on paper connected by dots do not. Auditory learning, comprehension, and memory are her strong points. She follows countless stories and is able to cognize and give back correct answers. She needs hand-over-hand assistance for writing and drawing, as her fine motor skills continue to develop.

After I am no longer her aide, Abby comes home from school sad and crying.

"The kids aren't playing with me. They leave me behind."

I know something is wrong when she doesn't want to get out of bed in the morning and throws a tantrum, "I'm not going to school!" I set up a meeting to talk with Mrs. Best and ask if I could quietly observe while I pretend to knit in a corner. Sure enough, when it comes time to go outside, her aide keeps her at her desk or sitting on the sidelines to watch the other children play games. She looks so lonely but doesn't say anything.

Then Mrs. Kim from the special education department presents a stellar idea. We create a sign-up sheet in the classroom. Each day three different kids form a team that rotates Abby in to play games. Abby chooses games like Four Square or H.O.R.S.E. Her favorite is 'Around the World.' She is a star-studded player. This surprises her teacher and the other children. After a while, the kids are eager to see if it is their turn to be on Abby's team. As a result of this, Abby is invited to other events with her classmates, including playdates at our house.

———

Every year we celebrate Abby with a big birthday party; all of her classmates come. When we meet once a year for parent conferences, her teacher says something like, "Prajna, I never thought this was possible. Abby has taught all of us so much. I am proud to have her in my class. Thank you for bringing her to our school." I have equal admiration for Mrs. Best. I will forever be grateful for the care and creative energy the team generated to integrate Abby into this class for five years. At the end of the day, it isn't about how much Abby has learned, although her learning is immense. Most importantly, she is included. *She belongs.*

Belonging is a primal need. The theme of belonging will continue to be a spiritual practice for myself and for each of us as unique individuals, as well as a family unit. As young children, when we are welcomed into this world with full acceptance, we develop self-esteem and inner confidence that allows us to be authentic and vulnerable. As we continue to develop, it seems when parents are more at ease about allowing mistakes to happen, the children have permission to make mistakes as well. We learn that we can be unique and won't be shamed into isolation. True belonging seems to sit side by side with self-acceptance, ripening to the degree we allow our humanness and belong to ourselves without abandon rather than focusing on performance.

As the girls get older, we accumulate silent stares that communicate "What's wrong with you? Or "You poor thing." It's hard not to internalize "staring" and ideas of doubt, shame, and self-judgment. I've heard these referred to as 'microaggressions—tiny paper cuts' that separate us from the mainstream culture that is perceived as "normal.'

For true belonging to happen, we need spaces that empower us to connect while being uniquely different without judgment or shame. This will be a lifetime challenge for us as a family, one I want to wonder about with curiosity and kindness, even when it hurts.

26

When Help Isn't Help

O n a frosty winter day in 2005 when school is closed, Abby is eager to demonstrate the confidence she is gaining in school. Her shrewd curiosity does not let her miss an opportunity to master a task. Earlier in the week I heard a storm was coming and decided to stock up the kitchen with good old standbys for baking projects, like flour, chocolate chips, raisins, and lemons.

When we unload groceries from the car, I ask Autumn to carry in some bags. Abby calls out, "I'll carry them, Mom!" "Okay, Abby; how about you and Autumn carry them together?" She happily agrees. Autumn gives me a cute rolling of the eyes, aware that she will be holding both Abby's hand and the bags while I gather up Libby. In a softer tone, I add, "I'll grab the package with the egg carton in it." Abby hollers, "It's not a package, Mom; it's a grocery bag." I appreciate her ongoing corrections.

We make our way into our cozy home, unpack the goods, and set out for a quick lunch of burritos. After clearing her plate, eleven-year-old Autumn announces, "I'm ready to make my most special smoothie."

Abby, her plate half finished, pushes herself away from the table and says, "Me, too. I'm done. I want to make a smoothie."

Autumn exclaims, "I'm first, Abs. You can be next. You can help me. This is going to be really fun. But there is one thing you cannot know." She has Abby's rapt attention. "That is my secret ingredient."

Abby is game, eager to imitate Autumn's every move.

When they are not engaged in typical sibling rivalry, Abby idolizes her big sister. I'm impressed with Autumn's magical way with her sister, and the clever ways she engages her in both practical and playful activities. They write books, dress up, stage plays, and record karaoke, with Autumn accommodating Abby the entire time. On those days Abby will say, before drifting off to sleep, "Mom, I love Autumn." I smile, feeling the potency of luck that Autumn injects into our family. Her ingenious resourcefulness is a welcome source of inspiration that adds to my cup more often than not.

Autumn assembles the components for her smoothie on the lowest countertop that borders our kitchen: blueberries, bananas, almond milk, maple syrup, and ice. All but the one mystery ingredient that is out of sight. Not knowing the secret ingredient amplifies Abby's intrigue. She is captivated, listening and memorizing Autumn's every move like it's a game of poker. Autumn's charm causes Abby to forget her bid to whip up a concoction of her own. When Autumn is done, they sit at the dining table to slurp down the frothy frozen drinks.

Autumn asks, "Do you like the rooty tooty fruity flavor?"

Abby cracks up and teases, "It's not rooty tooty fruity, it's blueberries and bananas."

"Okay, but do you like it?"

Abby doesn't answer; she is too busy slurping it down. Her taste buds are satisfied, but I sense Abby is upping the ante for a new round with a concoction of her own.

They break away from the table into the living room, grasp the round handles of a yellow and a blue therapy ball, sit upon the top, and bounce across the room. We have one for each girl to hop around, usually without falling off. They frolic back and forth while holding tightly onto each other's hands for balance. Autumn is agile, and quick to offer protective buffers that allow Abby to push and pull without crashing.

The next morning, Abby leaps out of bed bright and early, half-ready for the day. I snatch a peek of her passing the bathroom and waltzing her way into the kitchen. I watch her from the kitchen table, where I am jotting down my dream from the night before. She is wearing loose blue trousers, a bright orange long-sleeve pullover tee shirt, and red socks. Abby is mastering dressing herself, writing her name, and putting together puzzles. She remembers to put on her black socks with a slip-proof grip. Autumn isn't in the kitchen yet and Libby is watching from her adaptive meal chair, all ready for breakfast. I watch Abby breeze into the kitchen, head for the freezer, pull out bags of frozen blueberries and toss them on the counter as if ready to enter a contest.

She exclaims, "It's my turn to make my most delicious smoothie."

Oh boy. I close my journal.

"I need milk, bananas, and maple syrup."

My pulse quickens as I watch her climb on a chair to reach for the maple syrup. I absolutely want her to be able to navigate the kitchen on her own. After all, she's nine years old. At the same time, her limited coordination, blind spots, and brisk movements inject disaster.

"You cannot watch me or know the secret ingredient. I will do it all by myself. I don't want anyone's help."

She has memorized her lines. I sheepishly back away, feeling my body buzz as she pulls out the milk and honey.

"Okay, Abs," I breathe out loud in my best attempt to let her do it herself.

Unloading the dishwasher gives me a reason to hover. She wants to complete this task by herself. *Can I let her?* I feel her urge to yell out, "Look, Mom! Look, Autumn! I did it! I made the best smoothie ever, all by myself!" But anxiousness implodes as I watch her awkwardly standing on one leg, tilting her head, lifting the 16-ounce raw honey jar, and tipping it upside down over the blender. I slip nimbly across the floor, (which I compulsively mopped late in the night) and manage to tip back the honey jar just in time for it to land upright on the counter. Luckily for me, it had been sitting in the refrigerator and was moving like molasses. It isn't so lucky for Abby, though.

She roars, "Get away from me! I can do this!"

Wow! I zip in my tracks.

Abby is absolutely right; if I help her, she will not master this task. She is determined to make the smoothie without help, like Autumn. She is not considering honey or syrup sticking to our feet for days. She needs to work this out on her own, *am I able to let her?*

I stand like a deer caught in the headlights, overtaken by the power of her will. Suddenly the troll in my head falls down into my body and melts into a soup of calm. *Unleash the grip and let her rip!* It's obvious, give her full permission. Learning is messy. I back off.

She does not pour the honey all over the place. She does not dump the entire carton of milk into the mix. She does not overflow the blender, and she does not track blackberries onto the living room carpet. She does exactly as her big sister showed her. She makes her best and most famous smoothie in the world. Someone (me) got out of the way long enough for her to master a gigantic task—and it is delicious.

Autumn comes out of her room just in time to sit down and enjoy Abby's concoction and tell her, "Abs, this is the best smoothie in the world. How did you make it?"

"I can't tell you my secret ingredient right now."

I'm aware that I function better in a clean and orderly environment. We're all wired so differently. This is a challenge for me, but I am imperfectly learning how to relax my urge to give help and to see when my help is not helpful. I'm learning to loosen my reins and appreciate the messes made along the way to learn how to navigate life (and that my room is off-limits).

Autumn goes to the Nevada City School of the Arts, next door to Abby's school. She immediately resonates with the teacher, connects with many of the students, and meets a special friend. After a short time, Autumn and her new friend Jasmine become inseparable. Autumn is invited to outings with Jasmine's family, including to a lake where they go fishing off their boat.

Jasmine became part of our family as well. She learns the ins and outs of our special circumstances and blends in with our flow. On occasion, we take her with us on mini vacations to our favorite places in Santa Cruz like the boardwalk and beaches.

Autumn has a rough-and-tumble playmate to run around with and body surf the waves. Jasmine is also good at holding Abby's hand while I take care of Libby. It's comforting to see little Abby sitting between Autumn and Jasmine on the Ferris wheel or other rides, the older girls getting a kick out of Abby's terror on the rides and choosing to bring her along anyway—true big sisters.

27

What We Know in Our Bones

A couple of months later on November thirteenth, Autumn will turn eleven. Even though she doesn't attend a Waldorf school at this time, Abby does. We still practice a similar philosophy—primarily, limited time for electronics and plenty of play to explore the natural world. Waldorf educators believe that if we put the media in front of a child before they have the intellectual capacity to understand adult culture certain faculties for imagination, creative thinking, and connection to nature may be thwarted. I value these ideas. As a person who has spent most of her adult life cloistered in ashrams or on silent retreats, I have had little exposure to television (or critical thinking). Now, we are living with an onslaught of technological devices for media, with pros and cons that have yet to be accessed.

This year Autumn is introduced to children from families that have radically different home environments and ideas regarding electronics or the media from us. Autumn is perplexed by this new group of friends and isn't sure what kind of birthday party to have. She thinks that the only way to be accepted by this new circle of friends is to have a commercial 'girl' party.

I feel her predicament when she asks me, "Mom, my friends want to dye their hair, paint their nails, dress up like movie stars, and stay up late to watch movies in the living room."

I sense she does not want a tussle. I remind her of her favorite games, like 'Capture the Flag.' She pretends to be snubbed by this idea.

Throughout the party, she is doing her best to mimic pleasure at dressing up like the other girls. I peek in on the dolled-up group from time to time, trying not to hover when the hair dyes set in. At a certain point, uproarious laughter and raucous drama escalate into a full-scale frolic, pots clamoring, water spouting from the sink, bodies hooting and crashing to the floor. I let it peak for a while until Libby begins to shake.

I dart into the kitchen and, in a deliberate commanding voice, say, "Outside energy. Everybody out for twenty minutes to get some air. Go, run around, jump on the trampoline. Outside energy."

Autumn stomps out of the middle of seven girls and flashes a piercing glare. "Not cool, Mom."

I look at her with a smile and a wink, "Everybody out."

The girls ramble outside, hooting and hollering, undaunted by my directive.

The next morning after pancakes, nail polish, and more makeup, the sleepover party is over, and the visitors prepare to go home. When the last girl leaves, Autumn collapses on the sofa in the living room and lets out a huge, "Blah." She looks a bit like a hungover clown after an all-night circus act, her face filled with disappointment, tears in her eyes. I sit down next to her, ready to listen.

In her eleven-year-old voice, she asks, "Mom, are we going to actually celebrate my birthday?"

"We just did."

"I know, but I still want to have a birthday celebration."

"Hmmm, that didn't really feel like the kind of party you like?"

"No. I don't think I can be a commercial girl."

"Oh, is that what you were trying to do?"

"Yeah, I was trying to get them to like me, but I didn't like me like that."

"How do you want to celebrate?"

"I don't know. Maybe just having Jasmine over to play. We can make a cake together."

"Am I invited?"

"You, Abby, and Libby. Nobody else. No helpers. Just us."

As our conversation continues, a sheen of pink returns to her face; she lightens. I am impressed. She realizes an aspect of our culture that does not suit her. She is curious or pressured enough to explore the cultural expectations given to girls, but in the end, she isn't happy. I want to support her exploration by not interfering, so she can make her own discovery. She isn't putting a demand on people or the situation. She doesn't go into a dark hole of despair; she is telling me what she knows and that she does not want to participate in things that make her unhappy. I don't need to coax her for a response, she is learning to honor her powerful inner knowing.

Autumn reminds me that whatever image we have, or try to create, it is not who we are, or the source of our happiness. Images like commercials are manufactured; they come and go. We are entrained to look at images in our external life to make us happy, overlooking a happiness that is inborn—natural—like play. Autumn is tracking an essential element at our core. Happiness doesn't come and go according to our makeup or costumes. It isn't a feeling of constant ecstasy, but does bubble up as joy often when least expected. This feels like serenity, a thread in our nature. I often wonder about the speed at which our culture is hurrying our children to be adults, *will we celebrate our birthright—what we know in our bones?*

Later that evening, Autumn says, "Wow, Mom; that birthday party wasn't me! It was empty! There wasn't any fun. It wasn't really me!"

She is finding her own way. I am content to quietly hold her hand and stand beside her. There is no need to stand in front, telling her the way things are and what I or the culture expects from her.

That night, after I put everyone to bed, I tumble into my rocking chair and sit still for a while, contemplating. *Wow. What an opportunity.* I think about Autumn's twin sisters, the amount of energy and focus that go into their daily therapies, and how capable Autumn is—but reluctantly set to the side more often than I prefer. I sit with this question: *How do we celebrate Autumn's life? How will this transition from age eleven to twelve be meaningful for my young wise owl?*

Memories unfold. I remember Autumn on all of our birthday celebrations since she was in kindergarten, the special gifts and table settings she makes for the twins or me on our birthdays. I see her drawing or painting a landscape on a blank card, printing our names in colored pencil in her best handwriting, and crafting a birthday verse for each of us. I see her gathering flowers for the table setting and making a golden crown for her sister's head. I see her up early with Abby, making eggs, toast, and fruit salad, putting it on a tray, and waltzing into my bedroom at sunrise singing, "Happy Birthday to Mommy." Then I know what to do. I stay up late, make a card with a verse, a silver crown, and a red cape, and set her place at the table with flowers and a candle.

When she wakes up the next morning, I say, "Guess what? You were born at 10:10 p.m. on a Sunday night. Today is still your actual birthday!"

She proudly takes her seat at the table and asks, "What is that tantalizing smell?"

I bring out a pan of hot cinnamon buns (a favorite) from the oven.

"Yummmm," she chimes along with Abby, who joins her at the table.

Autumn doesn't want to wear the cape; "Abs, this is for you."

She's outgrown that, but she sets the golden crown on her head. As I light the candle in front of her, something lights up in her!

She picks up the colorful card I made, clears her throat, and exclaims, "I am going to read my birthday blessing:

> 'I'm happy to be who I am. I can always be me.
> I never need to change who I am to please others.
> Happiness is who I am. I'm happy to be me—what I know in my bones.'"

28
We Can't Unsee

It is an icy autumn Sunday evening, 2008. Friends are leaving our home after a restorative weekend retreat. Autumn (14), Abby, Libby (12), and me are comfortably snuggled together in the living room rummaging through an old box of family videos as if we're on a treasure hunt. Dinner is complete, the kitchen is tidy, and the moon is rising in a cloudless dark sky. Libby is tucked in a side-lying position on our burly sofa, with Abby sitting near her feet flipping through a picture book. Suki's head is nuzzled upon her lap. Autumn and me are sitting side by side in front of the sofa with our legs stretched out under the coffee table that holds our video player and mystery box. We glide in a few family videos from earlier times that ignite roaring chuckles. Next, we find a recording of a yoga training we attended in San Francisco for children with special challenges.

Abby jumps off the couch to see better, "Is that me?"

Autumn watches herself at age five, effortlessly moving in and out of a seated spinal twist. "I liked doing the poses. She called me her assistant. I had so much fun."

We're amused by our quest until we reach the bottom of the box and see, "Sonogram, September 9, 1996," from twelve years ago. I forgot we have this, but here it is, in this box beneath a stack of videos. It was taken six weeks before the twins were born. My hands begin to sweat and my throat tightens as I pull the carriage out of the case. "I don't want to watch this." I put it back.

Autumn says, "Let's watch it, Mommy."

I can't cope. "It's getting late. Why don't we watch it tomorrow?"

"No. Now, Mommy. Now. I want to watch it now," pleads Autumn, with Abby's voice trailing behind her like a parrot, as if on cue.

"Okay," I give in.

The video is only a couple of minutes long, but will hauntingly echo into our lives for many years to come. I put the cartridge into the player. The room is perfectly still, even Suki's breath is inaudible.

The sonogram technician points to the image on the screen and clearly, skillfully, confidently says, "Look! There are two healthy fetuses, with two inner and two outer sacs. There are two of everything. This is the best way to carry twins."

Cheers and sighs of relief fill the room from our midwife, her assistant Kym Ann, and me. This relief is partially due to the fact that I am assumed at the end of the pregnancy window (thirty-eight at the time), and partly because there are multiple formations twins can take in utero—from low-risk to high-risk formations. Sharing one of everything is the highest-risk formation. As shown on the screen, the twins have two of everything. Without a detailed explanation, the doctors at Stanford Hospital framed my condition as twin-to-twin blood transfusion syndrome, meaning one inner and one outer sac without a dividing membrane, that the fetuses shared everything—high-risk. This sonogram shows a different, normal story.

"They're traveling first-class. This is the Cadillac experience. You're doing great."

We sit, like stones in the mud. While my brain toggles and coils, I'm arrested in memory at the hospital—alone, without my midwife, without agency, in disbelief—barely surviving. This memory does not recall persistent contractions or my water breaking, only me clamoring for rest, to go home. I hear the voice of Dr. Kramer, "We're going to the OR." I don't see any faces. I feel impatience, inconvenience, icy stares, "More Pitocin. This pregnancy is failing to progress."

In this shadow of eerie silence, under a dark cloud, a storm of sorrow finds us. I drop my forehead into my sweaty hands, press, and force myself to breathe. Body sensations pulse and race beneath five blue monsters with prominent foreheads and eyes squinting above masks. I want to punch, scream, unstrap myself, and run for our lives. But I'm outnumbered—overpowered—drugged. I'm there again, but my children are here.

Autumn pushes herself away from the table and jumps frantically up and down, screaming loudly, ferociously, "That hospital ruined my life!"

Tears flood my face. Abby crawls onto my lap, her body is tremoring. Libby squeals and kicks herself off the sofa to join Abby and me, sensing gravity. Autumn, who is not prone to outbursts, continues to shatter with agony as if shards of glass are piercing her body. I restrain myself from feeling the torment of a deep cut in my womb—something I have not allowed myself to feel. I'm afraid I'll cause damage and scare the girls. Autumn fumes a good fifty minutes, with a litany of all of the things she hates about her life with disabled sisters: the people that barge into our life and leave unannounced, her dad's emotional aloofness, my endless consumption with matters that concern the twin's care. "Life is unfair!" "I hate people!"

And, "We have to do something!"

All of this time, twelve years, I have been madly driven—initially fueled by survival hormones, then in fix-it mode—forgetting about how much Autumn needs me. None of us remember this sonogram, what it clearly shows, the implications of its significance in relationship to the twins' birth, and our subsequent life of losses. Formations are impossible to change in six weeks (from sonogram to C-section).

Autumn and I fall into an abysmal well; a cloak of grief around our life. We yield to a much-needed cave time, to pull back, to retreat from a world we did not imagine. *How does anyone process injustice?* I don't think we consciously choose to create a cave of our own, but nevertheless, we huddle together.

I want to protect Autumn but it's too late, Pandora's box is open. Injustice is revealed. We can't unsee the sonogram. We can't unhear the technicians' voices, "This is what we want to see. They each have their own compartment. This is the way to carry twins." I can't bring my twins back to my womb, magically birth them over again, create a playful childhood for my three girls, and erase injuries *for life*. Autumn, like us, will carry this, forever being shaped by a decision made by a powerful institution that claims, 'First, do no harm.'

After a good time of isolation, Autumn springs to her feet. The need for aloneness becomes less pronounced for her than it is for me. I am glad she has school and friends to nourish and occupy her, and to partially shield her from absorbing the anguish that erodes me. *How do I calm rage and sedate the monsters?*

A dense ooze beneath my skin flags me. It's not completely alien. It's been here before—shame. The involuntary injection of vials of toxic yuck that impale my body, inhabit my psyche, and insist, "It's your fault. You're a bad person." It adds to the disempowerment and embarrassment I tumble through in the uncalled-for conundrum we find ourselves in. I'm unable to recover what is lost. *How do we come back from this?*

I remember the humiliation of feeling inferior as a woman—for having a womb. The countless trespassers that take, without permission, and leave. Violations that leave ineffaceable marks on the contours of a woman's body. And I remember that quiet stretch of time when Autumn and I gave birth to each other naturally, ecstatically, through the power of my womb—without interruption, just bliss. We centered ourselves on mother and baby as the authorities over birth—our inner intelligence knew what to do. Her birth showered my body clean like a temple adorned with love. She invited me into a magical world that celebrates all life has to offer, the natural reciprocity of listening for when to give—push, and when to relax—receive. She came first, leading the way to possibilities for Abby and Libby to live and celebrate in spite of a very harsh beginning.

This reflection pulls me beneath the bloody edges of these lesions, to feel my way through. I have no idea where this will take me or for how long. I only know that I must, and no one can do this for me. I will journey into the dark gorges of this labyrinth that circles again and again until toxic cuts of shame are devoured. I will refresh our home as a temple, a safe abode for hope to grow. I will grope and learn to navigate these edges in years to come. For now, I obsessively clean house.

———

Sometime later, I heave myself out of seclusion, aware of feeling estranged. I make requests for records from the hospital and our doctors. It isn't a territory I want to visit, nor do I want to spend time, a luxury I don't have, examining stacks of files. But I have unanswered questions. I spoke with several parents who filed malpractice for their medically injured children. One child lived in an oxygen bubble with a horrific story. His parents were consumed by a lawsuit that stretched beyond seven years. By the time they reached a settlement, the child passed way. Everyone I spoke with who exercised their right to justice was bitter, exhausted, and stuck in a frown of sorrow. Their actions did not improve the functionality or well-being of their child. My girls have already exceeded a bleak fate, the medical prognosis of a brief life expectancy.

I don't want my life-force tied up in a legal battle. My children need me. I need me. At the same time, I'm outraged with incompressible grief over a life we will not have.

What can I do? My twins will need support for the rest of their lives. I'm the available parent. I don't want the burden of care to fall upon Autumn and I'm sure she thinks about it. In the years to come, I unravel myself on the inside, alone or with a skilled guide, and in my women's group. I continue to research themes around trauma, birth, C-sections, and practicalities for moving forward. I imagine my three girls happy and able to adequately attend to their needs without this grief. *Is compensation possible?*

Blame is a nasty affliction; one I grapple with. I don't drop our case all at once; it percolates in the back of my mind—wondering: *What could I have done differently?* Torrents of audacious negativity toward myself and people I usually hold in high regard pluck my consciousness unabated. I blame myself for agreeing to a hospital backup plan, the doctor who swept me onto a helicopter, earlier traumas for numbing me down, and people for not catching this earlier.

Other times, when I'm taking better care of myself, *'what could I have done differently?'* lands and paints a wide-ranging picture. I realize that regardless of my inner strength, knowing, or years of recovery and healing to trust and empower myself as a woman, our most well-intentioned institutions are permeated with patriarchy and disconnected from nature. *How does inner healing transform the outer structures of our institutions in society and culture? How do we create safe and equitable places for everyone?*

I've come to understand that our situation is not insolated—it's endemic. Honestly, I do not trust high-powered medical institutions and despise the hurdles I navigate regularly to advocate for services for my daughters. I feel like I am pleading for equipment and assistance in error—for something imposed upon us. Often, I feel like an unseen bystander watching my friends plan vacations and colleagues advance in their careers while I puree food, track schedules, and push wheelchairs. I sob at missed experiences but involuntarily withdraw from opportunities to connect with people I love and love me, like my yearly silent retreat or my women's embodiment circles; spaces and people I need. Books that I love sit on my shelf collecting dust. At times my mood is so intensely lugubrious that I think nothing can change it. But it does, because Autumn, my owl, is an ingenious mood shifter and lightheartedly tugs me along.

29
Enlightenment is Backward

In the midst of treating myself to an aroma-steamed Epson salt bath, Autumn probes: "Mom, you haven't been to Satsang in a while; when are you going to go?"

Autumn senses my need to surrender to grief and, hopefully, be brave and wise. To self-assuredly join life again. In fact, she makes a cover for a book I was writing and she names it: *A Continuum of Light, Thresholds of Surrender*. She is concerned when I tell her I am putting my Satsang and dharma practices on pause—that I want to rest and focus on family.

She sits down next to me on the living room sofa like a true fan. "But, Mom, you're so close to finishing your enlightenment book."

I smile at my owl teacher; sparked by her instincts.

"I have a Satsang tonight in town."

"Are you going to give an enlightenment talk?" She rings the meditation bell.

"I don't know, because there isn't enlightenment," I say, barely interested.

She jumps up. "What? You can't tell them that!"

"But I tell them that all of the time. That's why they keep coming back. I think, inside, everyone must know there isn't a final destination or perfect state of bliss called enlightenment."

"Really? Well, if there is no enlightenment, what will they do?"

I laugh. "Maybe they'll stop striving for something outside of themselves, a mystical destination to hoist a flag and say, I've arrived."

"I think the people come to your Satsang to become like a Buddha," she beams while shifting into a picture-perfect lotus posture, hands in an elegant mudra.

"Hmmm." Transfixed, I probe, "Do you remember what Buddha said some thousand years ago?"

"What?" She grins.

"Be a light unto yourself."

"Huh?"

"Stepping back into yourself, getting comfortable in your own skin. Being yourself. Feeling that no one else can give you permission to be you. You get to be you—a light unto yourself."

"Oh," she says, and scurries off to the kitchen to make brownies.

She peeks around the corner and charmingly perks, "Remember to tell them that the path to enlightenment is backward."

I savor for a bit. "Thank you. That's it. We go back to us, to the inside, to find out that nothing is missing. You are the light. I am the light. We are what we're seeking... We have everything we need within us."

"Oh, Mom; that is way too relaxing. People don't want to relax and do nothing. People want goals."

I want to stay with my Autumn owl tonight, take her in, and rest together. She is holding a flag: *'Enlightenment means to occupy yourself.'*

I am satisfied sitting here on the sofa listening to Autumn, the scent of brownies in the air. But I go because Autumn gave me a dharma talk that is so simple, and truly profound.

As I am walking out the door, "Mom, remember. You have everything you need inside."

I drive off feeling luckier than I have in some time. "Everything you need inside." Somehow, I am given full permission to meet myself—all of myself. All that I turned away through seeking and reading spiritual books, attending retreats or workshops, and all of the external adornments I collected. All at once, a well of wonder emerges—to be in relationship with life, as it is, from the inside out. My job is to harvest ways to stay in my body—and not leave home. I can dial in practices that calm my nervous system, like a warm bath, tapping, a walk in the muddy woods, or playing with my children. I can drink in pleasure.

Autumn can spot when I'm descending down a rabbit hole and is offering me brownies. She's a circus performer throwing me a rope, "It's time to be Mom." I realize I enjoy descending; *transcendence is seriously overrated.* I'm pulled within, down, to cultivate an aspect of my soul left unexplored in traditional models. I begin to awkwardly talk about how patriarchal systems divide us, separate us to believe this, do that, follow him, look like him, behave like him, accomplish like him, go after him, pray to him, retreat to him, meditate like him, wait for the approving gaze of him, then superior 'Enlightenment' will be earned. Always a duality of separation: higher, lower; above, below; worthy, unworthy; pure, sinful; subject, object; glutton, deny; and so on. It doesn't matter which end of the seesaw you are on—extremes enslave us as perpetrators or victims and hijack our lives. Once again, I'm crawling to find the middle ground in life, to hold what we have, to have what we hold, to soften dualities, lighten, harmonize, and rest in some kind of sustainable balance.

My body is finally getting this, only unity consciousness—feminine love and care—that does not power over but births fresh creative ways of being. Maybe for the first time I truly 'look within' and see myself unable to match what has been held up around me. I shiver with readiness to make the invisible visible, *will we join together in sisterhood to unveil silenced voices and unleash ourselves, without apology? We must.*

My little teacher shines. "In the totality of life—nothing is missing."

By the end of this meeting, I chuckle inside. *I don't have a special teaching to offer. My dharma is my life as Mother. More than enough. Special beyond measure.* "Go home—back to yourself. Your life—as it is—is the doorway, the playing field for the most sacred offering to unfold, to celebrate life. "Enlightenment is backward."

Maybe the most important and enlivening part of awakening is re-parenting, re-birthing yourself, being yourself—becoming real. Allowing for our messiness, for soft edges, for loving off the armor that we thought was protecting us—keeping us safe. I realize this is what fortifies my personhood and my family with integrity, wholeness, and connective tissue that cannot be broken, a way to step away from institutionalized constructs and unnatural conduct for personhood—for becoming real. I also know that re-birthing, becoming real doesn't happen all at once, and parenting is not a project of perfection. In my girlhood, I was taught to believe there is a man-god that I must please to avoid harm and receive praise like, "well done;" in other words, *well tamed*. Now that my womb has been cut open by 'man-gods' I see the dehumanization and disproportionate damage this assigned power has brought upon women's bodies and their children for ages. I own the feeling of 'well done,' without apology for the shame I will no longer carry. This is my sovereignty as a woman, intrinsic to my body, not separate from the women who have gone before me, walk beside me, and are yet to come. We will not be invisible, silent, or neatly kept.

30
Love in a Body

S oon, on a mid-summer morning before sunrise, Abby tugs me awake, "Mom, get up!"

She stands at my side like a gazelle, reminding me of her steadfast decision to complete a forty-five-day hot yoga challenge before school begins in the fall.

"What time is it?"

"It's time to go. Come on. I don't want to be late. Amy and Sally are waiting for me."

"Come on, it's dark out. It's too early. Let me sleep." I peek out from under my covers and notice she is wearing red high-top Converse sneakers, skimpy yoga shorts, and a black sleeveless tank top with "GRATEFUL" printed in bold white letters across her chest.

"You need to drive me now." Her yellow mat is rolled up under one arm, and a rucksack with a water bottle over her shoulder.

"Give me a chance to wake up. It's five in the morning. Class doesn't begin until nine."

"No, Mom. We have to go now," she says with bulldog determination.

Abby's emotional connection to an adult leader boosts her commitment to learning and growth like a spring chicken. She is eager to gain mastery over her body by imitating her teachers.

Her mind is made up, the challenge is on. She is engaged with purpose. I'm the designated driver, reluctantly slogging along at her side.

Abby's high tone in her muscles makes stretching difficult. The heat brings elasticity to her fascia tissue. Movement brings additional oxygen to her brain; her body softens a bit. She walks less on her right toe when her tendons stretch. Her mood and energy are markedly elevated.

Abby takes classes, each led by Sally or Amy, the owners of the studio. Both inject joyous creativity into their instructions if you can imagine having fun in suffocating heat. Abby has a private session to modify the postures in an effort to adjust the poses to accommodate her physical limitations. That's when she designed the forty-five-day challenge for herself and enlisted my full participation, whether I liked it or not. I'm stunned. No way. This was the feisty girl I usually cajoled to yoga with bribes like iTunes gift cards, cookies, or smoothies. But now, she is firm; she seals an emotional deal with the teachers and is amped to emulate them.

Abby has a knack for drawing attention to herself in extra-curricular activities. She has placed herself front and center. I'm in awe at her uncensored exuberance. Her rising stardom tends to annoy her older sister, especially when she encroaches on the circus art platforms where Autumn shines. Yoga is Abby's territory, an interest not shared by her sister yet honed by me. She has found a place that doesn't compete with her able-bodied sister. An indisputable relief for Autumn.

On the ride home after finishing a morning class, the meaning of the boldly printed slogan GRATITUDE seeps into my heart.

"I forgot how much love and gratitude I have," Abby tells me.

I listen quietly. She proudly speaks about the different poses she likes. "Mom, did you hear what Sally said during Shavasana at the end of class?"

"What did she say?"

"She said, 'I'm love in a beautiful body.'"

"Hmmm…. That's right," I agree.

She is quiet as we drive along in the car.

After a long pause, as if an alarm dings in her pocket, she says, "I am Love in a body. I forgot. I am Love in a body. And I'm tall."

As we approach the end of the challenge, Abby decides to double up on classes to ensure she reaches her goal. It doesn't matter when I do the math; she is not going to risk falling short of tallied stars. This means I also attend two grueling ninety-minute classes in a 105-degree room each day, crowded with thirty-plus hot bodies training barefoot in puddles of sweat.

I will never forget the last day of the challenge. Abby nicknames her teacher Amy, Giraffe. She is standing tall side by side with Giraffe, balancing on one leg in tree pose, knees facing out, holding the completed chart of her forty-five-day challenge, with a beaming smile and her head held high.

This is the summer I stop chasing Abby.

Abby reminds me of a story I once heard about chasing the Goddess (feminine spirit). It goes something like this: Early in our search for love, healing, or freedom, we chase Spirit hoping she will give us what we think we need to feel worthy of love, happiness, and connection. At a certain threshold on our journey, the table turns and Spirit is chasing us. She is calling us home and showing us, in a multiplicity of ways, the capacity for beauty, power, and love to blossom within us. She shows us that love is within, in our bodies. That we are love in a body. Abby caught me.

31

Laughter is Contagious

S eptember 2005. Libby is vividly demonstrating happiness in her new classroom in Nevada City. Her teacher, Bobbie, is remarkably supportive and receptive. She enthusiastically incorporates methods of communication, equipment, and props that we use at home with Libby. We have a daily communication log that goes back and forth between home to school. In the beginning, Bobbie reports that Libby giggles hysterically through the main lesson. They need to wheel her out of the classroom so the other students can focus on the task at hand. Or she cracks up when it is time to eat lunch. This entices other students to do the same and mishandle their food. Her outright silliness throws off the routine of the day. That's my Libby, a natural troublemaker. We're pressed to modulate her behavior by teaching her when it is time to listen to the teacher, do her work, or eat, and when it is time to play, socialize, or engage others with her merriment. The plan is to roll her out of the class when she is disrupting the routine, and to give her consistent positive feedback when she is on course. After several weeks, she figures it out, internalizes the routine and understands what is expected of her.

I have three predictable questions that I ask Libby each day when she arrives home on the bus from school. In an even tone, I ask, "Libby, did you listen to your teacher?" She replies with a similar even tone, "eeeaaahhh." "Libby, did you do all of your schoolwork?" Again, she replies, "eeeaaahhh." Then I say, "Libby, did you talk to the boys?" I hit the jackpot. Each time without fail, her reply is loaded with exuberant squeals, kicks, and giggles. This tells me she had a good day, was socially engaged, and probably did not have to be wheeled out of the room. On a rare occasion, her response is solemn and quiet. When I look into the matter, I find out there was a substitute teacher, or Lucy or Tommy was absent. On these days she feels an emotional thread in her classroom circle is missing.

Libby's intelligence continues to blossom—not with words, but in the way she engages with people and the environment. I discover through trial and error that she has a need (like all of us) to belong. When she knows that she is missing an outing, her kick is fierce, as if to say, "I'm coming! You can't leave me here!" *She knows. I don't know how she knows, but she knows.* When she has not been on an outing with Autumn, Abby, and me for a while, mostly because we live in a world designed for abled bodies, she is upset. It is not always easy to navigate an outing with a sensitive body in a wheelchair. When we bring her with us, her behavior is rambunctious. This is especially difficult in a movie theater. Libby rollicks and kicks her legs with gusto, showing us her excitement. She interprets the silent pauses as if it is her cue to take the stage. The "get a grip on your child" stares of impatient viewers sting us. Many people assume that Libby is distressed, hurt, and perhaps having a traumatic episode. I wheel her out and implement the classroom routine until she is ready to listen like a good moviegoer.

In the early days, I felt embarrassed or protective by suddenly becoming the focal point in a crowd of strangers. Instead, now I talk to Libby. "Libby, you're excited to be here, to hear new sounds, to feel all of these people, aren't you?" She squeals with positive delight. Sometimes I hear a few conscious parents whisper to their children, "Don't stare," while other curious children will charge over to us and ask, "What's wrong with her?" I say something like, "This is Libby. She's laughing and having fun. Do you want to say 'hi'?" At this point, the child either shies away or touches her hand. For example, one day we are strolling around at a local park. A little girl comes over to us from the sandbox and gently holds Libby's hand. She moves her eyes from Libby to me.

"What's her name?"

"This is Libby. You can talk to her if you like."

"Hi, Libby. I'm Angie. Do you want to play with me?"

Libby sits quietly, feeling the texture of Angie's hand in hers, listening to this new voice, welcoming her into a magical moment that they share together.

Something is nourished between them. Libby relaxes with her new friend as if to say, *I belong.*

32
Returning the Favor

B efore the end of July 2013, my mother is swimming laps and pulling weeds from her garden, unaware this will be the last day she walks. I received a phone call from one of my sisters. She tells me, "Mom has been admitted to the hospital." I pace and immediately book a flight to New York to find out what is happening.

My brother-in-law picks me up at the airport and explains the situation. For years my mother had quietly dealt with colon issues, opting for natural remedies instead of pharmaceuticals and doctor's visits, much like me. But this time, she is forced to encounter medical care. She has lost thirty pounds, grown weak, and struggles to eat. Now she is strapped to a hospital bed with an IV dripping medication into her veins, flushed skin, nostrils flaring, and seemingly disconnected from reality. After she attempted to leave the hospital, the doctors increased her medications, and declared her "unsafe." The details of what transpired are unpleasant and unclear.

It is agonizing to see my mother reduced to this fragile state, a sturdy woman who raised eight children with limited resources. She was a source of boundless compassion, now unable to recognize her family. A few weeks prior, she told me, "I'm not eating much. I'm not interested in food anymore." She dismissed my suggestion to have a checkup. I mailed her a care package, unaware of the extent of her trouble.

In a few days, a doctor administers an exploratory exam that reveals a blockage in her colon the size of a softball. He requires a signature from my sister to perform surgery. I question the delay in addressing the blockage, as the staff intervenes with more tests and medications. Three days later she undergoes surgery, with the warning that she might not make it because she is eighty-three years old and has already been through a lot. *You're telling me!* I anxiously await the results.

In the waiting room, I fidget alongside six of my siblings. The surgeon arrives clad in his blue scrubs: "I have good news and bad news. We successfully removed the blockage but her colon perforated and we had to remove all of it. She has a colostomy bag and will require to be fed by a tube. She isn't the same woman who swam a mile every day."

My mouth falls open; my eyes twitch. My heart is pounding fast as I swallow hard to clear my throat to ask questions. "Is there anything else we need to be concerned about?"

The middle-aged surgeon responds to me as if I'm a first-grader. He sketches a diagram of the intestines and points out my mother's missing colon. My siblings stare at me in disbelief, shocked that I dare to question a doctor.

Fuck you, I mumble to myself, clenching my jaw. *Entitled asshole.*

During my two-week stay, I find myself sighing heavily and frequently, interrupting people when they speak. Eventually, I return to my daughters on the other side of the country.

Soon my mother is released from the hospital Autumn, Abby, and I fly back to New York, sad that we are unable to bring Libby to see Grandma. She still doesn't recognize us. She spends most of her time sleeping, her body limp, mouth ajar. The first thing I do is read her medical report—a list of unidentifiable medications. The doctor attached a twenty-four-hour pain patch to her leg loaded with six potent drugs. I researched each medication and discovered that each is as lethal as morphine, with countless side effects including: drowsiness, lack of memory, weakness, appetite suppression, amnesia, and potential loss of vision. Each drug comes with a warning: If any of these symptoms occur, contact your physician immediately. My mother has every symptom. I call her doctor, but I can only speak to the receptionist. The doctor insists that the surgery was a success, he removed all of the infection and her entire colon. I want to know why she has been endangered by highly toxic drugs for weeks.

I'm told, "For pain."

I ask, "Is she in pain?"

No one knows for sure. I take off the pain patch, cancel her prescriptions, and announce, "No more pain medication unless she asks for it. If she is in pain, we will give her something mild, if she wants it."

Everyone agrees.

I can't tell if it is the haunting memory from sixteen years ago when I was at the mercy of Western medicine's disrespect, or if it is the unbearable sight of my recently resilient mother fading before my eyes. I can't sit still. I squirm, tap, and stomp. I refuse to stand by idly and witness my mother's unconscious descent into death. Her treatment plan does not anticipate her recovery. The feeding tube they insert is permanent and unchangeable. I confront the surgeon, my voice trembling with anger. "Why doesn't she have a tube that can be replaced when it gets dirty?"

The surgeon is surprised by my knowledge of interchangeable gastrointestinal tubes. He doesn't realize that my daughter who was not able to come with us has a replaceable feeding tube.

"This is sewn to her stomach lining. It can't be changed." I howl, standing firm with clenched fists, withholding a punch.

He patronizes me again with facts that I must accept. "She is no longer the vibrant determined woman who swam across the lake." With an air of certainty, he transfers her to hospice care, destined to fade away in a state of unconsciousness, without knowing who she or anyone around her is. She is entrapped by what some call a 'goodbye plan' — an abandonment of elders deemed hopeless, lacking societal worth. This cruel act denies her the opportunity to die well and bid farewell to the cherished ones she loves and who love her.

On the second day without the pain patch, a rosy hue graces her face. I am by her side, holding her hand, when she opens her eyes. "Hello, Nancy—Prajna. When did you arrive?"

"Two days ago. How do you feel, Mom?"

"I'm not sure. Do I have weights on my legs? What happened to me?"

"Are you in any pain?"

"No. I don't think so. What happened to me? Oh. Who else is here? Oh, I see, Autumn and Abby." She leans forward, "Hello, girls."

The girls approach Grandma. Autumn gazes into her eyes, squeezing her hand. Abby angles away, initially avoiding eye contact, likely unsettled by the scent of medications in the air.

"How long will you stay?"

"For as long as we can. We want to help you get better," Autumn smiles, her eyebrows lifting. Her gentle features and high cheekbones resemble my mother's girlhood photos. We engage in a lively conversation, ensuring comfort, and soon realize she does not have any pain. The suffering she endures is a consequence of senseless medication.

Her words rush forth, "I'm getting up to see you girls!"

"What's the matter with my legs?" she asks repeatedly. "I was walking last week."

We all know she was walking before she was admitted to the hospital. It continues like this; she wakes up in the morning, I massage her legs, we administer a superfood meal supplement through her tube, and continue with her care.

And each day she asks, "What happened to me?"

We cautiously inform her. She struggles to comprehend a period of time that doesn't register in her memory. As we continue recounting the events, she shows some recognition, but she is unable to understand how the removal of her colon affects her legs. After a week, my sisters (Barb and Tracy) and I manage to lift her out of bed to a chair at the kitchen table. One of her legs is more anesthetized than the other; she manages a few steps before she falls back into her wheelchair. She longs to enjoy books with her reading glasses, but the pages are blurry. Autumn, Abby, and I discover a new bakery café nearby and decide to tantalize her taste buds as her interest in food returns.

"I'll have some of that!" perks Grandma the moment she sets her eyes on sweets.

"We got it for you, Grandma. It's vanilla ice cream covered with chocolate."

"Yep!" Abby joins Autumn, grinning with glee.

"Don't tell your mom, I turned her into a health nut!"

"We won't! But she'll probably want some, she loves chocolate!"

"Okay, but hide that awful green drink. I want ice cream every day."

Autumn signals me to stay upstairs, whispering. "We're making a plan."

Like three carefree children, they relish the moment.

After three weeks, my mom has made significant progress. She is stronger, enjoying massages, spending time out of bed, engaging in conversations, and watching movies with us. Her numerous grandchildren and great-grandchildren visit regularly. Autumn, Abby, and I need to return to California soon for Abby and Libby's birthday. While we're impressed with Grandma's improvement, I sense that she needs support to adapt to the profound changes in her body. She lost her colon, the use of her legs, and her ability to read.

As she naps in bed, I gently wake her. She peeks out from under the covers, "Are you going now?"

"Yes, Mom; we need to be with Libby for her birthday."

"Oh. I see. Are you coming back?"

"Yes, Mama. We'll be back, and I'll call you every day."

With tears in her eyes, she cries, "Who will take care of me when you're gone?"

I reassure her, naming my siblings who live nearby, and contribute enormously to her care.

I recall how she overcame her fear of flying to come and support me when my twins were in the NICU.

"Mom, if you need me, please ask Tracy or Barb to call me, I'll come. I promise."

With a mix of sadness and longing, she weeps and embraces me tightly, making it harder to leave.

Abby dives in with a big hug, "Grandma, I love you."

Autumn adds, "I love you too, Grandma. It's been wonderful spending time with you and watching you grow stronger. You're so fun."

Earlier in our visit we openly conversed about dying. It's inevitable for all of us. "Maybe you'll come back as one of Autumn's children." I say this not knowing if such things happen.

"That would be nice." She grins, with a tint of light glowing from her blue eyes.

We celebrate Abby's and Libby's seventeenth birthdays on the twenty-first of October (2013) with our traditional dance and game party. It's a blast, with musical chairs as a highlight, second only to Abby ripping open the gifts for herself and her twin (in that order).

I'm at a Satsang meeting in Sacramento when I hear my mother calling me. The host wants to book me for another meeting.

"I can't. I'll be with my mother in New York." I know I will fly out the next day.

I arrive late at night. I find my mother, Camille, in bed, her face radiant, luminosity saturates the room. She smiles when she sees me. I hold one of her hands as she drifts in and out of sleep. Each time she opens her eyes, she asks about specific people and moments. I imagine she is finding closure, bringing life to rest.

"Where is Harry? Is he OK now?" Referring to my father, who died a tragic alcoholic death.

"He is at rest," I assure her.

"Good," she glows as if under a light. "And my brother and sister, where are they?"

"Tommy is here, looking after you. Mary Ann is resting in peace."

"Oh. They always called me baby sis, and I never liked that."

"I know."

"But that's OK. I love them just the same."

For two days, she drifts between sleep and wakefulness, each moment lighter than the last. Our relatives, young and old, gather by her side, offering their own tributes and honoring her as the guiding light of our family. It is an emotional process, filled with exquisite love and sorrow. She is deeply loved by all.

At my sister's request, the local priest arrives. All eight of her children encircle her bed, holding hands. Father Michael leads her final rite of passage, his booming voice shakes her slumber. Her eyes shine open wide, fully present and aware of all of us. Together, we recite the Our Father and the Hail Mary, a lively Irish family setting aside our slings and arrows, transcending conflicts that kept us apart. Holding hands, we make a promise to preserve the peace that our mother bestowed upon us—unconditionally.

I keep vigil at my mother's side throughout the night, tracking as others come and go. My brother and sister weep nearby. I don't want to leave her side. It is my birthday, October twenty-ninth. She is my precious mother, that birthed me into this life. I am blessed to be here now, returning the favor.

My mind drifts to the memory of my tenth birthday, my godmother, also my aunt and my mother's closest friend, lay in a hospital bed. Unafraid, at her side, curiosity burned within me.

Alone with her, in a quiet moment, I ventured. "Aunt Joanie, are you awake?"

No response, yet her delicate features captivated me, exuding an ethereal lightness that permeated the room. Boundaries dissolved; time stood still. A nurse returned to check her vital signs. With three solemn sighs, she closed my aunt's eyes and departed. I remained, transfixed with wonder—a completion and a continuation, as if a portal to another dimension opened, where bodies don't go. My fingers rest loosely on my lap, my head nods in acknowledgment of this mysterious phenomenon of dying to greet life.

By my mother's side, time fades as tearful words spill from my lips: "Beautiful mother returning to beautiful peace." Christian mystics guide us through the night. My brother and I are with her as she takes her last breath. Sunlight glistens through her window.

"Peace I give to you. Peace I leave you."

33

As Good as it Gets

B efore we move from our rental home in Nevada City to a bigger city with more resources, we have the task of painting Autumn's room to the bright yellow it was when we moved in. It was odd for her to request that her walls be dark blue, almost black. Nothing else appealed to her at the time. She is eager to help me prepare the room for painting while Abby and Libby are off with a caregiver to their chiropractic appointment. It is a rare opportunity for us to be together through a project. We listen to Jack Johnson in the car on the way to gather snacks from the market.

We begin immediately before I am sidetracked by other packing projects. Clearing Autumn's room is more difficult than I thought. Being with her in the intimacy of her room—her space. As we sort through collections of creative projects from grade school and summer camps, it feels like I am seeing some of her things for the first time. I lift a homemade book bound with lace, decorated with musical scales, from a bundle in her bottom dresser drawer.

"I remember when you made this in first grade. It tells the story of the notes to sing on a music scale. Let's keep it."

Her lips tilt upward as she holds up a birthday book from Mr. Lehman's class in fourth grade. "Remember my friend Rebecca and the drawing she made for me?"

"Oh yes. I love that. Let's keep it." I declare often.

"Mom, we have too many things to pack if we keep everything."

I smile through tears about sadness of moments that passed by quickly without taking the time to savor them. Autumn is making space for new things to come into her life while I struggle to move on. I'm absorbed in memories that I want to recapture and celebrate. I want to say all the things I didn't say earlier, all the things that were impossible to express, now, while alone with her in her room and not attending to her younger siblings. Autumn is weeding through drawers of clothing she has outgrown, tossing them into a plastic bin. I retrieve some, imagining us sitting together cutting and sewing old jeans into shoulder bags or pencil holders. After sorting through the clothing, we turn to the unfinished bookcase, which I'd been meaning to paint ever since I found it at a thrift store. She removes all the books and art supplies to a pile on the floor. Soon, we have three designated bins; one for hand-me-downs or donations, one for recycling, and one for trash.

As these piles grow, I worry. "What are you keeping to pack for yourself?"

I realize my quandary. *Am I willing to let go of my ideas for Autumn and let her decide what is important to take into the next chapter of her life?*

Rather swiftly, the room is emptied by Autumn, with four boxes outside her door ready for the move. If it were up to me, I would still be sitting on her floor rummaging through stages of her childhood. We have taped the edges of the windows, doors, and baseboards. We take turns rolling the walls with two coats of yellow. I sigh at the murky yellow paint job, aware it will need a third coat, maybe four.

"I'm done. This looks good," Autumn says, shuffling off to the living room where Abby and Libby are with a different caregiver who just arrived. Autumn easily joins them, content to play. Jane is familiar to Autumn and enjoyed by the girls.

It is 11 a.m.; an unusual noise brings me out of the bedroom to see what is going on. Jane is sitting at the dining room table, eyes closed, with her hands spread over an elaborate meal, spouting prayers of thanksgiving out loud. I rant to myself. This is unexpected; she arrived an hour ago covered in sweat from the bike ride up the hill, took a shower, and casually announced, "Oh, hi. I need to eat. My blood sugar is low."

While Jane lounges over her lunch, Autumn and Abby make quesadillas. I feed Libby her morning snack of a thick smoothie that she slurps down in less than fifteen minutes (it usually takes twenty). *Is Libby more eager than our helper to help me get back to painting?*

While I begin to settle Libby into Jane's care, she stares at me with a panic-stricken face, "What's that smell?"

"Paint."

"I feel a massive headache coming on. I must be having an allergic reaction!"

"It's nontoxic low-fume paint. It's supposed to be safe." I accelerate around the house, opening more windows.

"I'm sorry. I can't stay. I'm going to be very ill."

Crap! I break eye contact, take a sharp deep breath, and moan, "Huh?" I waited for her to shower and luxuriate over lunch. My mouth is opening and closing, unsure what to say.

"How am I going to finish this job? You knew we had to paint today. This is why I hired you for today."

She lowers her eyes, her voice apologetic. "I know. I forgot what paint does to me."

My self-reliant character enters center stage with a huff. *Get ready for a plow-through-it day!*

Jane leaves on her bike. Autumn is in the kitchen, humming the tune to "Sk8er Boi" while she chops tomatoes. Abby is shredding a chunk of white cheese, dropping shreds alternately in the bowl or her mouth, while a voice in my head torments: *This is too fucking hard; I can't do this—alone. Caregivers never work out. Who will watch the girls?*

Somehow, these thoughts dart by as I turn my attention to my girls. A different possibility emerges and relief comes. Suddenly the entire situation is comical. I join the tune Autumn is humming in the kitchen. My body relaxes as if a reserve tank of energy is tapped, ready to forge ahead without a cacophony of rubbish in my head. *Today the caregiver did not work out. She took care of herself. That is all. I don't have to dehumanize her with blame.* I consider how our moods can positively or negatively impact each other and morph into a collective impulse to attend to or detract from the task at hand. In this not-uncommon predicament, each of us seems to know the part we have to play.

Autumn announces in a humorous, high-pitched voice, "Hello. I am the babysitter for today. My name is Mrs. Froutenlimer. I expect full cooperation and obedience." (This is the name of a silly character from a book on tape.)

Straight away, Abby chimes in with guffaws of agreement. Libby adds howling squeals.

"You're on, Mrs. Froutenlimer," I applaud.

"I am taking over from here. You go and paint. I will take the children out for a walk. Now let us finish our lunch and gather our rucksacks."

Abby and Libby collapse in giggle fits at the lively character on the scene.

Autumn straps Libby into her stroller.

Abby imitates Mrs. Froutenlimer. "I'm getting my baby twins for my stroller."

"You do that, young lady, and make sure you stop in the bathroom to pee, so you don't spring a leak on our stroll."

"OK, Mrs. Froutenlimer," screeches Abby as she crawls to the bathroom, aware that her bladder might burst at any moment.

I'm delighted to watch Autumn push Libby out the front door and down the ramp with Abby at her side, humming as they stroll. Suki boy trails along wagging his tail, sniffing the bushes for a spot to do his business.

For the first time I realize, they can do what siblings do with the oldest child in the lead. They go outside to play while their parents attend to chores and projects—the minutiae of life. I'm grateful to lie down on the couch and not able to quickly return to painting—savoring how good this feels. A euphoric sense of goodness swells through my body. I don't feel the push to work faster, better, or perfectly. Together, without speaking about it, all of us are allowing the situation to be what it is, inform itself, with Autumn guiding like a magic fairy posing as Mrs. Froutenlimer. I recall a former recognition from Autumn's classroom teachers, who see, value, and acknowledge her contributions to the class. Her eighth-grade teacher told me she has untapped potential for intellectual growth and would do well in a private progressive school.

On one occasion, the class took a poll for a future presidential candidate with the students as the nominees. The vote was unanimous—"Autumn." When they were asked why, they answered, "Autumn is honest and fair." This teacher, along with her previous teachers, highlights her creativity, kindness, and capacities as important qualities to nurture. Like me, today they experience the sheer pleasure of having her nearby.

An epiphany happens: *This is as good as it gets.* This is our story: hard, beautiful, and spilling over with mysterious magic.

My girls once again opened my eyes to see that there is nothing wrong, missing, or a perfect way to do life. Autumn's sprightly resourcefulness is contagious, we all join in. A creative solution springs forth that revitalizes the situation and releases the worry, blame, resentment, or anger that could have been our story. I see how when I clamp down and insist something needs to be different, my creative juice is blocked, and my body contracts and dampens our parade. A potential doom day initiates an opportunity to pause and receive the intelligence woven through life, ready to offer a shared creative possibility.

I rise up from the couch, rejuvenated, with a focus that steers me to the bedroom to finish painting. It is an effortless endeavor that probably takes half the time it normally would have. Tears spring to my eyes and drip into the paint. I don't feel sad. My gratitude is uncontained. I am without shame, yet messy and able to be with discomfort—happy for this one precious life. As the bright yellow paint rolls over the final remnants of dark blue, I hope to remember the sunshine yellow that brightened these four walls, this day, our life. Working through dark contours, the ones that don't cover quickly, don't disappear all at once but hold treasures of memory to grow us and illuminate our capacities. Like all good stories, light and dark play off each other until the curtain closes and presents a new story. Without this story, our story would lack the powerful momentum of mystery, meaning, and satisfaction.

While at the kitchen sink to wash out my roller and brush, looking at our back garden, listening to the warm breeze work its way through the treetops, a grander vision of *as good as it gets* fills me with hope and contentment.

Mrs. Froutenlimer has a firm hold on Abby's hands; they are counting by twos as they bounce rhythmically on the trampoline while Libby rolls around in an enthralling frolic, safe at the boundary edges. Leaves flicker and still my urge to run for my camera to seize this moment. But I stop to etch this scene to my soul. Autumn and Abby are confidently trusting each other's bodies bouncing together without apprehension that they'll land on Libby, who rolls freely from side to side. My three daughters—in a bubble of joy and safety. A conversation disentangled from harm's way is happening between the bodies birthed through my womb, nourished with my milk—happy at home. I stand, embodied in myself as mother, gazing at my girls with wonder.

Autumn catches me at the window and beckons in her Mrs. Froutenlimer German accent, "Are you quite finished yet?"

"I'm just cleaning up. I'm hungry, are you?"

"Yeah. We didn't eat all of our lunch. Let's make a new one."

The girls come in and we make a lunch of steaming Thai noodle soup, stir-fry broccoli, sliced pineapple, and chocolate pudding. This is a special ritual, all of us sitting down together enjoying a meal without a helper. Libby has her special spoon; we have our cloth napkins. I light a candle; Autumn and Abby lead a song, "Blessings on the blossoms, blessings on the root, blessings on the leaf and stem, and blessings on my tooth." All of us burst out laughing. I help Libby ring her it's-time-to-eat bell. Suki patiently waits for his command, "Okay."

I feel abundantly blessed to sit at this table with my three little women, aware that the journey ahead will be hard and beautiful, and grow us in unimaginable ways. And I can't imagine who I would be without knowing and having all three of these precious children to love and to hold.

Because I knew you… I have been changed—for good.

Epilogue

Readers wonder and ask how each of us are faring since these stories unfolded. My short response: as well as can be expected given the circumstances.

Libby continues to bless our lives with her contagious giggles and unspoken language of love. Abby is unstoppable; she bravely enters able-bodied circles of peers with curiosity and eagerness to belong. She has become more self-conscious of her differences which is sometimes hard for me to watch. But I trust in time she will have a tight circle of friends who see her, accept her, and engage with her for who she is, as so many of her teachers and mentors do. Both Abby and Libby graduated from high school with special education services; Libby with a certificate of completion and Abby with a graduation diploma. Abby attends our local community College and continues with circus arts and dance classes. A variety of services and assistive technologies from agencies like the San Andreas Regional Center (SARC) and the Talking Book Library allow my twins to receive support, adaptive equipment, knowledge, and the enjoyment of books that foster engagement and function in our complicated and diverse world.

Autumn is a shining star but has not been spared challenge. She graduated with honors, traveled abroad for a year, and made her way to Reed College and the New England Center for Circus Arts (NECCA). She has mastered several apparatuses including the Chinese pole. She currently attends Smith College School of Social Work. She has left her home nest to discover more of who she is with the certainty that I have her back. I and her sisters miss her tremendously and keep in close contact.

I, like all parents continue to care for my children to the best of my ability with the resources that I have. I continue to grieve loss and missed experiences and struggle at times with the reality of living on the margins. This has led me to in-depth training with three indigenous mentors in the Amazon jungle. I am privileged and passionate about learning from these mentors who have introduced me to the wealth of knowledge and healing of master plant teachers, their culture, and their ancient health care system. I will share more stories about our adventures in my upcoming book. This book will feature stories that capture fresh perspectives on birth, trauma resolution, and the challenges faced by marginalized families. It will be a resource that celebrates our unique differences, fortifies our innate wholeness, and teaches skills to care for our bodies and each other in ways that foster belonging, connection, and sacred reciprocity.

We will explore the history of women that trace the origins of our current birth practices, the roles of women in medicine and midwifery, the impact of interventions like birth monitoring and c-sections, reestablish our roots in ecstatic birth, and reexamine 'informed consent.' No system, medical facility, or professional can ever give us the ecstatic joy and tremendous benefits that come with having completed the journey of birth ourselves. We will relearn respect for birth, babies, bodies, and mothers in sustainable ways for all of us and Earth Mother to thrive.

We will explore plant medicine healing as an ancient healthcare system to understand our nervous systems and heal injured instincts in our animal and plant bodies. The indigenous people of Columbia's Sierra Nevada revere women's bodies as the earth—our source of connection to all beings—a vital social network crucial for healthy communication, connection, and weaving community. My hope is that as we embody the wisdom within the culture of women, motherhood, and our connections—the earth to transform and survive.

I value many aspects of modern medicine, but it must be used to serve the whole person and respect the crucial bond between mother and baby, and the diversity within our families and communities. When we fail to administer drugs, technology, and surgery in this way, human beings are born yet disconnected from their bodies and the earth. Strikingly, modern childbirth is a rising ecological disaster area. The overreliance on technology erodes what human beings need to grow healthy and robust as evident in immunity breakdowns, degenerative diseases, emotional disorders, and all forms of neglect. We are amidst a mental health epidemic and environmental crisis that underscores the urgency to address this profound disconnect.

If you would like to share your birth story whether it be ecstatic, tragic, or both, and everything in between, I want to hear from you. Many seeds have already been planted through sharing our stories throughout time. Let us continue to attend to our individual, community, and collective gardens, to reap a bountiful harvest together, in balance and sacred reciprocity with nature. Let us write a new and beautiful story for all of life.

Acknowledgments

To my daughters Autumn, Abby, and Libby, I owe the greatest debt for making this book possible, first for being born to me, living it with me, then in the writing of it. Our invaluable care providers, who Autumn tracked at eighty-one by the time she graduated from high school; Alice, Carolyn, Tina, Karen, Liz, Mary, Lesli, Lara, Linda, Amy, Rachel, Emily, Randi, Shelly, Vanessa, Aruna, Steve, Simon, Joe, Sophie, Beverly, Colleen, Lori, Joel, Anisa, Jeanette, Cheyanne, Shannon, and many more.

I am grateful to Flowing River Publishing Team: Henry Hansen, Larren Merriman, Coy Cross, Louise Renehan, Ivan Lourie, and Catherine Weiss Boucher for patient and diligent editing and proofing to bring edition one to a beautiful completion. More recently to Sarah Tavner, Jessica Carew Kraft, Autumn Wheeler, and Shelley Mann for being tireless champions of this revised edition.

I am especially grateful to the many people and teachers that came into my life at crucial moments, for offering generous support, believing in me, and standing strong to create a more beautiful and connected world for all people.

Thank you!

Thank You for Reading My Book

I greatly appreciate your review.

Please take a few minutes for an honest review on <u>Amazon</u> or <u>Goodreads</u>.

Your words are greatly appreciated and help ensure that more readers, like yourself, parents and/or women will benefit from our story. I would personally love to hear more stories that empower women to reclaim and celebrate the ecstasy of natural birth and to leave coercive medical technologies in their proper place.

You are invited to stay in touch for my next book and to share your story with us. Together we are stronger!

Thank you!

Connect @ PrajnaOhara.com

Made in the USA
Monee, IL
09 September 2023

42330626R00142